Ideology and Power
in Soviet Politics

IDEOLOGY
AND
POWER
IN
SOVIET POLITICS

Revised Edition

Zbigniew K. Brzezinski

FREDERICK A. PRAEGER, *Publishers*

New York • Washington • London

FREDERICK A. PRAEGER, *Publishers*
111 Fourth Avenue, New York, N.Y. 10003, U.S.A.
77-79 Charlotte Street, London, W.1, England

This is a revised and enlarged edition of the book
first published in 1962
by Frederick A. Praeger, Inc., Publishers

Library of Congress Catalog Card Number: 66-18893

This book is Number 103 in the series
*Praeger Publications in Russian History and
World Communism*

Printed in the United States of America

Contents

Part II
FOREIGN AFFAIRS

Ideology and Power
in Soviet Politics

Introduction

The purpose of this short volume is not to convince, but, hopefully, to stimulate. Each of the eight essays presents a thesis of its own; the first four are devoted to Soviet domestic politics, and the remaining four to Soviet international politics. The essays were written at different times during the last decade, and the reader may find it useful to note not only the persistence of certain themes but also some major changes in the author's approach, emphasis, and judgment. I have not tampered with my past views, in the belief that my "learning process" may perhaps prove to be of some value to others.

The first essay examines the problem of continuity and change between the Czarist and Soviet political executives. The second is a discussion of the general character of totalitarianism and its relationship to a modern, "rationally operated" industrial society. The third attempts an over-all examination of the salient features of the Soviet political system. The fourth, departing from some of the assumptions underlying the second essay, discusses the developing strains in that system and suggests some possible remedies.

3

The remaining essays focus on foreign affairs. The fifth attempts to weigh the role of ideology in the Soviet world outlook, with special attention to the prospects of ideological relativization and erosion. The sixth reviews Papal control of doctrinal conflicts between organized units of the Catholic Church some centuries ago, and compares that experience to the Soviet handling of the Sino-Soviet relationship. The seventh outlines some of the causes of the failure of "deviation control" in the Sino-Soviet conflict and assesses the implications of that conflict for the West. The final essay analyzes the Russian attitude toward European integration and develops some general guidelines for Western policy.

The close interaction of ideology and power in both internal and external Communist politics is the theme that links all the essays. The distinction between ideological and power considerations, often made when Soviet conduct is analyzed, appears to this author to be, first of all, an artificial abstraction and, secondly, a rather misleading issue. Soviet political leaders, being politicians, naturally are preoccupied with the maintenance of power and with its maximization. But political power in every circumstance involves purpose, assessment, communication, action, and legitimization. It is impossible to wield power, to exercise it effectively, and especially to use it actively unless there is a sharing of certain values, implicitly or overtly, among the leaders, the ruling elite, and (particularly in our age) the masses. This is particularly so in the case of a movement with a history of acute ideological ferment, somewhat like the intense religious debates of earlier times. There is a natural tendency in

4

this movement to elevate major issues into matters of principle and to try to fit actions into a general framework. Furthermore, when the movement is built around an ideology that combines both an overt statement of normative ends and a set of intellectual categories for analyzing changes in the existing reality with specific guides to action, then considerations of ideology and power become so enmeshed in the performance of a particular political act that to isolate one from the other is to deny that which is precisely most characteristic of the movement—the blending of ideology with power.

Although it is dangerous to attempt to reduce the meaning of ideology to a one-sentence statement, the following might be suggested as a working definition: It is essentially an action program suitable for mass consumption, derived from certain doctrinal assumptions about the general nature of the dynamics of social reality, and combining some assertions about the inadequacies of the past and/or present with some explicit guides to action for improving the situation and some notions of the desired eventual state of affairs. Ideology thus combines action— and since its object is society, it must be political action—with a consciousness both of purpose and of the general thrust of history. It gives its adherents a sense of consistency and certainty that is very often absent among those who have been brought up in the tradition of short-range pragmatism and empiricism. Commitment to the ideology establishes a standard for discrimination between the important and the unimportant. It encourages the ideologically oriented politician to engage in programmatic thinking, to ask himself repeatedly these questions:

What is the real meaning of my historical epoch? What are the essential forces changing reality in our lifetime? How can I best relate myself to those changes so that both my power and my ends are well served?

Few Western statesmen do this. Some, like De Gaulle, do because of their personal, instinctive sense of history. But most, especially those who operate in the Anglo-Saxon tradition, do not—reflecting the spontaneous and organic development of their societies—and, for many decades, they have not paused and examined consciously their social organization, their purposes, their direction. Their policies naturally tend to be both more pragmatic and more reactive than those of ideologically oriented leaders. But it does not follow, as often assumed, that the nonideological Western leaders are therefore more "rational" than the Communists. The matter of political rationality depends very much on the actual content of the ideology itself. The Nazi leaders, for instance, adhered to an ideology that so obscured their vision as to make them repeatedly engage in actions that were irrational even in terms of their own purposes. The Communist leaders, however, subscribe to an ideology that, whatever the rationality of their ultimate ends and basic assumptions may be, has given them some insight into the contemporary anticolonial and industrial revolutions. While, as some of the essays show, it has often led them into dogmatic stands, their ideology has also given them a keen appreciation of contemporary social and political dynamics, an appreciation often lacking among their *dogmatically* undogmatic Western opponents.

Indeed, one could even argue that the Communist

6

ideology involves such a conscious emphasis on the development of skillful political strategies and tactics, and on always relating the latter to the former, that the chances of "irrational" conduct on the part of the Communists are not greater than those of their more pragmatic Western opponents (particularly Anglo-Saxon ones). For example, Suez in 1956 and Cuba in 1961 provide good illustrations of desperation and impatience leading us into what might be appropriately described as irrational conduct. In both cases, the chief Western errors were failures of theoretical and ideological omission, and from them followed the military and logistical inadequacies. The theoretical error involved the failure to perceive that in Nasser and in Castro one was dealing no longer with a traditional-type system that could be overthrown from within by the application of merely limited external force. Both leaders have successfully eliminated intermediary social groups and skillfully mobilized the masses. What is the political nature of our opponent? That question was either not raised or inadequately answered. Ideologically, both cases involved failures to assess the long-range and more basic forces at work—in one the intensifying wave of awakened Arab nationalism, in the other a left-wing revolution that could only be effectively countered through the mobilization of the democratic left rather than of the center and the right. In both, the "case method" and the common-law tradition of viewing each issue in isolation resulted in the loss of the broader perspective and led to actions that history may judge disdainfully.

The Communists, however, have frequently tended to

the other extreme—namely toward the elevation of their social, economic, and political system of analysis into a semireligious, absolute dogma. The reason for this lies primarily in their political history: in the linkage of the ideology with a one-party dictatorship, usually led by a personal dictator. This condition eliminated creative dialogue and disagreement. It equated the decision of the dictator with infallible ideological insight. And it has often resulted in grievous errors. The Sino-Soviet dispute might not have taken such a disastrous course if both parties had not insisted on elevating tactical issues to matters of principle. Perhaps the somewhat more diversified situation prevailing today in the Communist bloc may lead to more regular discussions within the Communist movement, and thus gradually overcome the inherent tendency toward dogmatism and arrogant self-righteousness so characteristic of contemporary Communism. However, this would eventually require a major change in the nature of the movement itself (see Chapters 3 and 5).

That change, however, as both the Twenty-third Congress of the CPSU and Khrushchev's fall have shown, is bound to be firmly opposed by the increasingly bureaucratized Party elite. To the members of that elite, the ideology has become a ritualized dogma which reinforces and justifies their power. Brezhnev and Kosygin, products and beneficiaries of the Stalinist system, represent a professional Party elite that is determined not to release its hold on the reigns of power. This has led to a situation in which the country's economic system is being reformed in keeping with the needs of the times, while the political system remains static and unresponsive to new societal

8

forces. Implicit in this condition is a social-political contradiction with ominous implications for the political stability of the country. It would be supreme irony, indeed, if in the years to come the ideology of the Soviet political system, by blocking badly needed governmental reforms, became the source of a major threat to the effective exercise of political power.

The issues raised in this introduction are the outgrowth of the essays. They certainly need much more elaboration and thought. Perhaps some readers will be provoked into doing just that. If they are, the republication of these essays, which have previously appeared separately, will have been justified.

"Patterns of Autocracy" appeared as a chapter in a col lective volume edited by C. E. Black, *The Transformation of Russian Society* (Cambridge, Mass.: Harvard University Press, 1960). "Totalitarianism and Rationality" was first published in *The American Political Science Review* (September, 1956). "The Nature of the Soviet System" appeared in the *Slavic Review* (October, 1961). "Transformation or Degeneration" was published by *Problems of Communism* (January-February, 1966). "Communist Ideology and International Affairs" is reprinted from the *Journal of Conflict Resolution* (September, 1960). "Deviation Control: The Dynamics of Doctrinal Conflict" first appeared in *The American Political Science Review* (March, 1962). "Threat and Opportunity in the Communist Schism" and "Russia and Europe" are republished from *Foreign Affairs* (April, 1963, and April, 1964, respectively; copyright © 1963 and 1964 by the Council on Foreign Relations, Inc., New York).

To the editors and publishers of the above go my thanks for allowing the essays to be collected in this volume. For purposes of consistency and to take into account recent events, a number of minor editorial changes have been made and some repetitions eliminated. I am also grateful to the Research Institute on Communist Affairs and the Russian Institute of Columbia University for their support.

ZBIGNIEW K. BRZEZINSKI

May, 1966
Englewood, N.J.

Part I

INTERNAL POLITICS

1. Patterns of Autocracy

Executive power combines policy-making with the direction of policy execution. It is this combination that endows the executive organ in the governmental structure with its crucial functional importance and vests it, or rather the persons who symbolize or control it, with the mystique normally surrounding a head of state or a monarch. In the minds of most people, a president, a king, or even a premier—and today, in one third of the globe, a First Secretary of the Party—plays the role of leader, much in the tradition of the family head, the village elder, or the tribal chief.

Through the ages, society has depended on the chief executives for a sense of direction, and they have stood at the apex of the social and political hierarchy whenever necessity has forced men to band together. Executive power may, in fact, be the oldest and the most necessary social institution in the world. It has taken many forms, has been established through diverse channels ranging from birth to purposely perpetrated death, and has been invested with different ranges of authority at various places and times and in response to varying requirements. Nonetheless, for our purposes it might be useful to distinguish in broad terms between the two types of executive power usually found since the rise of the modern state: the constitutional and the autocratic.

Constitutional executive power, of somewhat more recent vintage and normally a product of a more sophisticated stage of social, cultural, and political development, generally involves an executive organ operating within confines delimited by an institutional structure in which the executive power is both shared with other governmental organs and restricted, even within its own sphere, by a series of formal and informal restraints. The most classical sharing of power is, of course, that involving its division into the executive, legislative, and judicial branches, each relatively free from the domination of the other. There are legal restraints on the arbitrary exercise of power, as well as those inherent in the pluralistic character of modern society which produce their own shifting patterns of social alliances, pressure groups, and veto groups. In such a context, the executive power, while not deprived of its functional significance, is prevented from becoming the dominant and relatively unrestrained source of political leadership.

The autocratic executive, by way of contrast, is relatively unhindered in the exercise of its power and does not share it with other organs, such as the judiciary or the legislature, since they are either absent or subordinate to the executive. Formal restraints, such as legal injunctions, also are either absent or circumvented, while informal restraints—for example, those involving the church as a major institution—are somewhat more elastic in the assertion of their claims against the executive. In brief, the autocratic executive is the central, dominant, and leading governmental organ.

It should further be noted that the autocratic form of executive power is in many ways the older and more basic of the two types. The much more complex constitutional form has arisen only under certain favorable conditions of social stability and economic well-being, and under the guidance of an enlightened elite. Such conditions have not been as frequent as might be desired. A mere glance at the political history of mankind reveals that most people have lived under some sort of autocratic (that is to say, nonresponsible and nonrepresentative) form of government.

The above observation is pertinent to the problem of continuity and discontinuity in the Russian executive in the years since 1861. Throughout the century (with one brief interlude, measured not in years but in mere months), the Russian executive has been an essentially autocratic one.* As we shall see, however, within this dominant autocratic pattern, varying degrees of intensity and directions of change have been discernible.

AUTOCRATIC TRADITION

The autocratic character of the Russian executive during most of the last century, with the consequently important element of continuity, can be brought out in sharper

* More will be said later about the implications and nature of the Duma period just prior to World War I. It is not possible, in this brief space, to present both a detailed institutional account of the roles played by the Czarist and Soviet executives and a meaningful analysis of their continuities and discontinuities. I will concentrate on the latter and merely point to certain relevant institutional aspects.

focus if we attempt to examine more closely some of the salient features of the Czarist and Soviet executives to see how they show a definite perpetuation in autocratic pattern. What have been some of the important political characteristics of the Russian executive during this period?

To a political observer, the concentration of power in the executive organ to the detriment of the judicial or legislative bodies might well be the crucial criterion. The supreme authority of the Russian emperor as the autocrat was acknowledged by basic law and cemented by tradition. This supreme power was exercised on the emperor's behalf and at his will by ministers selected, appointed, and dismissed by him. These ministers were sometimes headed by an informal chairman of the ministerial council who, at least nominally, was the emperor's closest adviser.

However, unlike Western practice, it was always the emperor, and not the chairman (a post not regularized until the twentieth century), who personally selected and nominated the members of the ministerial committee. Thus, even the element of indirect restraint on the emperor—inherent in the cabinet system, in which the ministers developed a measure of institutional authority of their own—was absent in this case. As a result, cabinet ministers did not feel compelled to coordinate their operations with the chairman of their council, and they rarely met in a body. The normal practice was for the emperor to closet himself with especially trusted ministers and to decide in this small group what the policy on an issue ought to be.

In the case of the more important policy posts, such as foreign affairs or defense, the ministers dealt directly with the emperor, even as late as the twentieth century, when the practice of appointing a premier became institutionalized.* Count Kokovtsov, Premier under Nicholas II, recalled with a touch of bitterness how the Minister of Internal Affairs neglected to keep him abreast of developments and how the Minister of War obtained funds for the ministry without even consulting with the Prime Minister.[1] Of course, a particularly strong-willed chairman such as Stolypin could resist these tendencies. However, it was not the general pattern. As a result of this poor bureaucratic coordination at the top governmental levels, matters of high policy involving the executive power were resolved through the direct intervention of the emperor, to whom the central governmental organs— the Ministerial Committee, the Council of the Empire,

---

* In the late nineteenth century, the Committee of Ministers was composed of the following: War and Navy, Finance, Interior, Communications, State Domains, Education, Justice, Foreign Affairs, and Control. The Ministry of the Interior was probably the most important ministry for domestic matters, not only directing the state bureaucracy but, in a sense, setting the broad patterns of domestic policy. It frequently competed for power and prestige with the Finance Ministry, which shaped fiscal policy. Budgetary provisions for the respective ministries suggest their relative weights (except for the Foreign Ministry, the importance of which was less dependent on the vastness of its bureaucratic apparatus). Thus, for instance, in 1887, the expenditures of the Ministry of War and Navy were 251 million rubles; Finance, 109 million; Interior, 73 million; Communications, 26 million; State Domains, 23 million; Education, 21 million; Justice, 20 million; Foreign Affairs, 5 million; Control, 3 million. (See C. Skalkovsky, *Les Ministres des Finances de la Russie* [Paris, 1891], p. 292.) In the case of the War Ministry, many of the expenditures were for the construction of strategically important railroads that were otherwise nonprofitable.

the Senate, and the Holy Synod*—were directly subordinate.

The personal power of the emperor also was enhanced by the monarch's practice of relying on a coterie of personal favorites who often were appointed to fill chief governmental posts. These appointments did not necessarily involve men distinguished by a specialized knowledge of a particular aspect of government, but instead went to persons considered as personally loyal to the emperor and to the general orientation he held at the time, whether liberal or conservative. As a result, the emperor became the focal point for competing groups: Those in favor of reforms and those against change felt that their objectives could be achieved only if the emperor could be induced to make his appointments accordingly. Growing political conflict thus advanced the political influence of the emperor, since reform, of whatever kind, could be achieved only with him and through him.

An additional factor in the autocratic pattern was the device of parallel informal and formal channels of executive power. Apart from his chosen ministers—whom the emperor would begin to suspect after a while of harboring views alien to him (views that, in fact, the ministers

* The Council of the Empire, which in the mid-1880's had sixty-four members, was a consultative body for legislative matters. Its members, appointed by the Czar, were usually members of the Imperial family, former and present ministers, and distinguished servants of the Czar. The Senate, likewise composed of appointed dignitaries, was to be the highest judicial body, a court of cassation, and the supreme body for adjudicating administrative conflicts. One of its seven departments also handled governmental auditing. The Holy Synod, headed by a lay procurator general and composed of the metropolitans and bishops, dealt with religious matters as well as general problems of state morality.

frequently acquired by being brought into contact with the realities of Russia once they were appointed to cope with them)—the emperor would consult special advisers not burdened with executive posts. These would most frequently be drawn from among his personal courtiers, many of whom held high military ranks and were his devoted and disciplined servants, jealously protecting his power but often suffering from a lack of native intelligence.[2]

The most notable exceptions in this period to the pattern of courtier-advisers were Pobedonostsev and Rasputin, though the latter was influential through the empress.[3] Pobedonostsev's relationship with Alexander III is particularly illustrative of the role played by *éminences grises* in autocratic regimes. His influence had a far wider range than was justified by his post of Procurator General of the Holy Synod. He was Alexander's adviser on important matters of policy and a vigorous defender of the Czar's power against real and imagined encroachments on the part of those allegedly favoring constitutionalism. He effectively torpedoed Loris-Melikov's cautious reforms and successfully urged the Czar to replace Loris-Melikov with a more rigid minister. Pobedonostsev's correspondence with the emperor, in which he skillfully exploited the prejudices of this intellectually limited monarch— who was fearful of further reforms and mindful of the assassination of his father—and his personal intrigues, his little coups, his distrust of intellectuals, and his general philosophical position [4] immediately bring to mind an analogy with Stalin. Pobedonostsev combined in one person Stalin's Poskrebyshev (whom Khrushchev sarcastically dubbed Stalin's "loyal shield-bearer" in his 1956 "secret speech") and Zhdanov, but without the latter's political role and position as erstwhile heir-apparent. He provided the monarch with informal sources of information and served as his ideologue, his chief defender and rationalizer of the status quo.*

Soviet political practices have not, on the whole, deviated significantly from the pattern sketched above. Throughout most of the political history of the Soviet Union, one-man rule has been the norm, and recent events do not augur an imminent departure from long-established practice. Indeed, it has been argued cogently that a system such as the Soviet one cannot operate without producing overwhelming internal pressures toward the elevation of some individual to the top of the political structure. Furthermore, Soviet political leaders have come not from the ranks of the administrators but from the Party, which endows them with a certain aura of "scientific" insight into history, analogous to the personal charisma of the anointed emperor.

---

* It is interesting to reflect that Pobedonostsev's insistence on a rigid system based on law strongly suggests that his ideal would have been the Platonic society, with its reliance on state religion, family training, indoctrination of the intellectual—all within a firm legal framework. These were precisely the things that Pobedonostsev was advocating and, in some measure, implementing. However, judging by his criticisms of the idea of a search for truth, one might speculate that the *Laws*, rather than the *Republic*, would have been more to his liking. For some discussions of his views, see A. A. Kornilov, *Kurs istorii Rossii XIX veka* (Moscow, 1918), III, 269; and R. F. Byrnes, "Pobedonostsev on the Instruments of Russian Government," in Ernest J. Simmons (ed.), *Continuity and Change in Russian and Soviet Thought* (Cambridge, Mass.: Harvard University Press, 1955).

The Party secretaries, while not ignoring the significant role played by the bureaucrats, have maintained the tradition of keeping the administrators tied to administrative procedures and have retained policy-making as their own domain, to be shared with those of their own choosing. It was only following Stalin's assumption of the Premiership that the Party and the administration came to be closely linked at the top. But even throughout the Stalinist period, which was marked by a growing ascendancy of the administrative structure, little doubt remained as to which post was politically the more important. Khrushchev's career is mute testimony to this point.

While coordination of decision-making has probably improved since the Czarist days, there is no doubt that problems of policy are still resolved by informal cabals of "politicians" and not by administrators: Stalin with Poskrebyshev and Malenkov for administrative-personnel matters, Zhdanov for ideological issues, and his more trusted Politburo members (depending on the dictator's whims) for broader consultation; and Khrushchev with his reliable *apparatchiki* as the source of necessary support and counsel and sometimes as the manpower for important administrative appointments. Given the voluminous literature on Soviet politics, these brief observations may suffice to suggest some strong parallels with the previously outlined pattern of Czarist executive power.

Another important area of political relationships pertinent to this investigation involves the related questions of political centralization and political coercion. While the latter does not necessarily follow from the former (as with France), there is a strong tendency in regimes that are not constitutionally based for the two to merge. This was the case under the Czars, and it is the case today in Soviet Russia.

In Czarist Russia, centralization and coercion took the form of strict subordination of local authority (such as the *Gubernator,* the *Gradonachal'nik,* or, since 1889, the *Zemskii nachal'nik,* as well as the *Stanovoi,* the *Ispravnik,* and the *Uriadnik*) to the Minister of the Interior,[5] and the employment of centrally controlled police power for political ends. Of course, a particularly dynamic governor could achieve a certain amount of autonomy, especially in an outlying region, but usually by virtue of his ability to anticipate the desiderata of St. Petersburg and to execute them even more efficiently than anticipated.* In this sense, there is a strong resemblance to the able and energetic Stalinist satraps in the republics—people like Bagirov, for instance, who held his post for some fifteen years without interruption. However, centralization normally breeds overbureaucratization, and the Russian local officials were frequently swamped with dreary paperwork and red tape —again much like their Soviet counterparts.[6] A measure of internal decay is a corollary of autocratic bureaucracies.

Political coercion was also a major preoccupation of the

---

* The check, supposedly provided by the local procurator, subordinated to the Ministry of Justice, unfortunately often proved illusory since the governor normally wielded more influence back in St. Petersburg. Cf. N. Flerovsky, *Tri politicheskiia sistemy* (1897), pp. 54–55. Another check involved the periodic inspections by delegated senators. In a sense, they performed the functions of control somewhat like the Party control commissions or RKI. But again, personal factors were of critical importance.

22

Russian executive organ, a preoccupation lasting to this day. The police were under the administrative supervision of the Ministry of the Interior, and the chief of police was appointed by the minister, was personally responsible to him, and retired whenever the minister retired. Following the reorganizations of 1880 and 1882, the Assistant Minister of the Interior became the commander of the Special Gendarme Corps, a security formation. The Okhrana, part of the police department of the Ministry of the Interior, provided the intelligence and counter-revolutionary operations. This was the political branch.[7] With the increasing ferment, there was a growing tendency to exempt political cases from judicial "interference" by placing them under the jurisdiction of military courts. Between 1891 and 1901, all political cases were handled by military tribunals, and the extraordinary procedures provided in the decree of August 14, 1881, "Measures for the Preservation of State Order and Tranquillity," were renewed every three years until the fall of Czardom.[8] Death sentences, which (as in Soviet Russia until very recently) were applied only in political cases, for acts undermining the executive power, were imposed with sufficient frequency to underscore the autocratic character of the regime.[9]

A common characteristic of autocratic regimes is the effort on the part of the executive branch to subvert judicial independence for the sake of political ends. In Czarist Russia, this took the form of direct and indirect pressure on judges trying political cases, removal of such cases from the jurisdiction of established tribunals (as indicated above), promulgation of emergency punitive measures (as in 1905), and administrative dispensation of justice.[10]

In the words of the last chief of the Okhrana: "There was only one form of extra-judicial punishment, and that was administrative banishment; sentences of up to five years could be pronounced." He adds that this was "frequently but leniently applied."[11] The absence of a strong legal tradition in Russia facilitated these deviations from the rule of law, which, when firmly rooted, inherently serves as a check on executive power.[12]

The Soviet parallels are self-evident. Political centralization in the U.S.S.R. is achieved, despite constitutional provisions, by the subordination of republican (and lower) organs to the central political administration in Moscow. Beyond that, the Party acts as the chief coordinating instrument and has lately acquired an even more important coordinating capacity as a result of the economic reorganization. Soviet archives, such as the Smolensk *Obkom* and *Oblispolkom*,[13] leave little doubt that, underneath fictitious lip service to federalism and the importance of local initiative, central executive control is indisputable and has been so during the entire Soviet period, despite some modest efforts during the NEP to give meaning to republican autonomy. Organized violence, to protect the Soviet form of government and hence to destroy all real and potential opponents, has been associated from the very beginning with central executive power and has not been impeded by excessive judicial sensitivity on the part of the Soviet leaders. Vishinsky's statement that "the contents and form of judicial activities cannot avoid being subordinated to political class aims and strivings"[14] still holds today, even though its author may have been at least partially repudiated. Death penalties for political crimes have been applied more generously than under the Czars, and administrative organs have freely imposed severe penalties on those accused of political offenses. Centralization and coercion continue to be important attributes of the executive in Russia.

One final similarity between the executive organs of Russia before and after the 1917 Revolution lies in an area that is not necessarily characteristic of autocratic regimes, but has been important to the maintenance in power of the Russian regimes. This is the relation of the executive to the military. In many autocratic regimes, political power becomes so dependent on the military establishment that power ultimately passes to the military, or the military, as a group, are continually involved in attempts to "salvage" the national interest. This was not so in Czarist Russia (except for the short and untypical period after 1916) or in Soviet Russia. Apparently, the Russian military leadership—somewhat like the Russian Orthodox Church leaders—has developed a sense of political noninvolvement that makes it difficult for any would-be Bonapartist leader to use the army as a cohesive unit for political purposes. In the case of the Czar, there were the elements of personal loyalty and wise personnel policy: For instance, many high officers occupied influential and lucrative administrative posts. In the U.S.S.R., there may be ideological loyalty, and there is certainly a complex network of police and Party controls and purges. Whatever the technique or causes, the political effect is similar.*

Russian history indicates that a crucial element of continuity in the Russian executive since 1861 has been the almost uninterrupted maintenance of an autocratic pattern of executive power, with the resultant minimization of restraints on the arbitrary exercise of that power. In this sense, the Soviet Union merely follows a trail blazed by centuries of earlier Russian political tradition. But this establishes only the broad outlines of continuity and hardly exhausts our problem. Are historical parallels enough to posit historical continuity?

TOTALITARIAN INNOVATION

Within the framework of an essentially autocratic pattern, there are significant differences between the Czarist and Soviet executives, both in degree and kind, which demand investigation and theoretical evaluation.

As noted in Chapter 2, there are basically three broad types of restraints on political power: the direct, the indirect, and the natural. Of these three, the Czarist executive, in the final analysis, effectively subverted only the first,

---

* Of course, there have been plots among younger officers, impatient with the Czarist policy of status quo, such as the Voennaia Organizatsiia Partii Narodnoi Volii. The officers, however, were all of junior rank, and this made it quite impossible to use the Army as a unit for political purposes. These traditional considerations, apart from the more immediately significant factor of highly institutionalized controls and intense indoctrination, might also have been taken into account by those who for the last few years have made a profession out of predicting an imminent takeover of political power in the U.S.S.R. by the military.

sometimes came into conflict with the second, and never challenged the third. Its relationship with the church or the *zemstvos* was one of control, especially in the case of the former; with the growing industrial and middle class, it was, broadly speaking, one of adjustment. As far as the family is concerned, it never went beyond the point reached by most modern states—insistence on education and a degree of patriotic conformity. The Soviets have continued this subversion of the direct restraints, but have gone beyond that in destroying the second kind and effectively challenging, if not entirely overcoming, the third. Thus, we have a broad area in which important differences appear in sharp focus and demand closer scrutiny.

The following question arises: If both executives can be considered autocratic, why is there such variation in the relation between political power and political restraint? The answer is to be found in the nature of the basic attitude of these executives toward the existing society. A traditional regime, with its paternalistic sense of authority, recognizes a transcendent system of values that inherently limits its otherwise institutionally wide scope of action. The Czarist executive was motivated by just such a curious mixture of autocratic paternalism and a strong belief in the immaturity of the people. This frequently made it resort to violence, but never allowed it to seek the logical conclusion of that violence—the complete extermination of its enemies—because of the conscious and unconscious assumptions inherent in the paternalistic attitude. Conflicts that did arise, such as the challenge to the economic interests of the gentry by state-encouraged industrialization or, subsequently, by the

Stolypin reform, were still the result of an attempted response to changes in society and not a matter of pre-conceived policy of subordinating or destroying rural interest groups for the sake of eliminating restraints on the power of the regime. The powers-to-be in the Czarist executive, ranging from Pobedonostsev or Rasputin to Loris-Melikov or Stolypin, and including the Czars, all shared in the desire to defend the broad outlines of the status quo, although obviously differing on such specific measures as the need for reform or the desirability of reaction. But commitment to the status quo involves a limitation of power by that status quo and a measure of acceptance of its inherent values. If one takes society and the political system as they are, then one's power is fitted into the existing framework of that society, even if such things as law and constitution (direct restraints) are not too vital. The other types of restraints compensate somewhat for this absence of the direct restraints.

The Soviet attitude, motivated by an ideology that puts a premium on *conscious* political action based on a rela-tively defined and dogmatic action program (qualities lacking in the more general and traditional viewpoints of the Czarist reforms), aims at the transformation of existing society, which it initially rejects. This act of rejection liberates the Soviet leadership from the limitations of the status quo, and the conviction of the Soviet leaders that they possess an insight into the inevitabilities of history justifies all their acts. The reliance on a revolutionary movement, for which there was no parallel in Czarist Russia, gives the Soviet leadership an independent tool for the removal of restraints on its power, even if some bureaucrats (because of their professional interest in a measure of stability) are wary of excessive change. As a result, the power of the executive pervades the entire society, maintaining its grip even as the impetus of the initial blows fades, as the new society begins to take shape and its rulers develop a vested interest in the new status quo. By then, the society has become both molded and penetrated by political organs that parallel the purely administrative structure and give the top executive a significantly greater scope of action. It could even be argued that, at this stage, the distinction that could be made in the case of Czarist Russia between the political system and society becomes meaningless. At the same time, because of the dynamic and ideological quality of the struggle undertaken, the executive is much more conscious of the need to keep its movement vital, especially since the elimination of pluralistic groups tends to give the movement a monopoly of power without the invigorating effect of continuing competition. Purges thus become the inherent device for coping with this situation and maintaining the revolutionary dynamics.

The process of pulverizing society effectively eliminates all political opposition and leads to the mobilization of all social energy for the achievement of the politically defined goals. The result is a far greater pattern of compliance to political power than under the Czarist executive. While many examples could be cited involving such fields as the arts, sciences, or the press (despite censorship, the Czarist press was an example of diversity compared to the Soviet),[15] it may help to review the handling of political cases and the general problem of political opposition to the regime in power. The summary treatment of political opponents by Czarist military tribunals and the relative absence of inhibition with respect to the execution of such opponents has been noted. However, there were also spectacular cases of judicial independence, even in the more violent days of Russian political history. In the trial of Vera Zasulich, the presiding judge, at the risk of prejudicing his future career, effectively resisted political pressure from the executive; the defense made impassioned appeals on behalf of the defendant, and the jury, acting with an overriding sense of justice, acquitted her to the accompaniment of thunderous applause. What a contrast with the behavior of the spectators and the judges in the Hall of Crystals exactly sixty years later! At the nonjury trial of the Czar's assassins (the government had become more cautious), the chief defendant, Zheliabov, unflinchingly defended his position and forcefully demanded that a jury trial be held—behavior not noted in Soviet political cases. Until the collapse of the empire, many defense lawyers courageously and devotedly defended, in many cases successfully, political prisoners accused of subversion or revolutionary activity. Soviet judicial history is not marked by such episodes.

The executive in Russia under the Czars was committed to a defense of a political status quo in which the autocratic power was traditional while the society itself was changing with increasing tempo under the impact of slowly expanding literacy, economic reforms often initiated by the regime itself, growing urban centers, and a spreading consciousness of the need for change. This meant that the regime's security was more and more frequently challenged by revolutionary groups desiring drastic reforms. The executive could not take measures violent enough to uproot and wipe out all opposition without shattering much of the status quo. The absence of technology, while important, was not crucial; certainly, revolutionary regimes in the past (Cromwell or Napoleon) have been able, because of their revolutionary liberation from existing societal limitations, to cope effectively with domestic opposition. As a result, much of the political history of the last few decades of the empire could be written in terms of political plots, conspiracies, assassinations of countless important officials (not to mention the Czar), and intensive revolutionary propaganda.[16] While their political significance should not be exaggerated, they did contribute to the political atmosphere of the time. Pobedonostsev's letter of advice to Alexander III, shortly after Alexander's accession to the throne, catches the atmosphere of internal fear, bred by conspiracy, terror, and ineffectual counterterror:

(1) When you are retiring, Your Majesty, do shut the doors behind you, not only in the bedroom but in all adjoining rooms, the hall included. A trusted person should carefully check the locks and make certain that inside door bars be slid shut. (2) Definitely check every evening before retiring whether bell wires are intact. They can be cut easily. (3) Check every evening underneath the furniture to see whether everything is all right. (4) One of the aides-

31

de-camp ought to sleep near Your Majesty in the same apartments. (5) Are all persons around Your Majesty trustworthy?[17]

The revolutionaries whom Pobedonostsev feared so—even though they were frequently tracked down, arrested, and executed—combined their revolutionary zeal with a mixture of romanticism and fanaticism that somehow would seem out of place among the current Soviet generation of *tekhnikum* students.[18]

Thus far, the Soviet executive has avoided such a situation by stamping out the opposition while constructing a new society. This revolutionary procedure freed it from traditional limits on power. By the time a new generation grew up, matured, and prepared to take stock (a development delayed by World War II and the Cold War until the mid-1950's), a situation had been created in which opponents of the policies of the present Soviet executive face what might be called "the dilemma of the one alternative." Even if rejecting the system in a personal sense, any critic is forced to admit that by now no meaningful alternatives to it exist. That seems to have been the position of many Soviet students whom I met in the U.S.S.R. in the fall of 1956.

Although a broad pattern of continuity in the autocratic character of the Russian executive is obvious, there is a sharp distinction between the roles played by the Czarist and the Soviet executives. This distinction is inherent in the apparent difference between an autocratic regime based on certain traditional values and generally committed to the status quo, and an autocratic regime revolutionary in its policy and committed ideologically to a radical destruction of the past and long-range programs of utopian reconstruction. Regimes such as the latter have been called totalitarian, and it is this totalitarian development *within* the broad autocratic pattern that reveals a sharp discontinuity in the role and character of the Russian executive since 1861.

CONTINUITY AND CHANGE

A further question now arises. A comparison between the present British Government and that of 1861 would show certain very important differences within the constitutional pattern, leading to the conclusion that a sharp discontinuity is involved. The change from a parliamentary form of government to one that is fundamentally a centralized party form of government might be considered a sharp discontinuity, despite its occurrence within the constitutional pattern. However, continuity and change are in constant interaction, and the present British form of government evolved out of its predecessor. Although the change was gradual, today's government is quite different from what it was in 1861. The question this poses is whether the totalitarian pattern of the present Russian executive was implicit in the gradual changes occurring in the autocratic Czarist executive. If so, then the totalitarian role of the Soviet executive, though different in many respects from the role of the Czarist executive, is nevertheless the natural child of trends implicit in the past.

To examine this position, a review of the confusing

and multidirectional courses pursued by the antecedent regime in Russia might give some indication of a general trend toward patterns of fundamental continuity or proofs of an essential discontinuity. That the record of the Czarist executive was mixed as far as liberalizing and reactionary policies are concerned is clear from a cursory glance at Russian political history. Yet, it also becomes evident that the second half of the nineteenth and the beginning of the twentieth centuries were periods of great changes—changes that might be called spontaneous—in the social and economic life of Russia.

Heavy industry, railroads, and coal and iron complexes were beginning, and the cities reflected the growing opulence and power of a new class of bankers, merchants, and industrialists. These changes, even though they were occurring under the cloak of a political power dusty with antiquated traditions of autocracy, were beginning to make themselves felt. Violent radical conspiracies were their extreme expression. But much more important than these conspiracies was the growing desire of many citizens for reform, for a constitution, for a liberal monarchy.[19] This desire penetrated even the cold walls of the Winter Palace, and the emperors gradually found themselves surrounded by whispered, and sometimes loud, warnings that something must be done.

To reform an old autocracy from within is not an easy task. Many vested interests are always against any change other than the natural, imperceptible one. This proved to be so in Russia. Yet, the executive power, which, given the system, was the only effective source of reform, did initiate a number of significant changes. These changes involved not only important areas of the social and economic life of the community, such as the liberation of the peasants or the later Stolypin agricultural reforms, but also political changes that had direct bearing on the power of the executive. The law reform and the organization of jury trial (1864), while still subject to severe limitations in statute and practice,[20] meant that the judicial branch was gradually becoming institutionalized. The law on assemblies, passed in the same year, similarly implied a modest development in the direction of regularized patterns of self-government, albeit on a very limited scale. The press reforms of 1865, the growing vocal activity of the *zemstvos*, and Loris-Melikov's projects were all efforts to bring the autocracy in line with the requirements of the changing society, to bridge the gap between political institutions designed to fight off the Tatar yoke, and to build a society that was now beginning to feel more strongly the impact of growing pains in an age of economic and social revolution.

The dilemma of power in such a context—to liberalize or to contain—meant frequent oscillations and reversals. And yet, even though the executive would shrink back into apparently the only safe refuge of reaction (as in 1882), parts of the society would continue their pressures for change, and the executive would finally respond. But the ambivalence would persist: The Duma period, the desire for a buffer between society and the executive (as explicitly stated by Witte), the electoral reforms would be followed by a relapse, by electoral amendments designed

35

to limit representation by a re-emphasis of Czarist autocracy and by a reassertion of violence, all often welcomed by those who feared change.[21]

Nevertheless, a residue of change would remain and would serve as a springboard for further intensification in the pressures for reform. The development of the prime ministership* and the embryonic growth of a multiparty system were part of institutional changes that even subsequent relapse into reaction could not undo in their entirety. That the change was slow—too slow—seems to have been the final verdict of history, and the regime did not surmount the accumulated pressures when they came to be combined with external blows. However, these considerations still lead one to suggest that the role played by the Soviet executive, given its policies and power, involves a reversal in an admittedly timid and regrettably blurred trend.

In the process of carrying out the Communist revolution, the successor government expanded its powers to a degree unprecedented in modern political history: It reversed the trends toward an independent judiciary, a freer peasantry, and a modest system of political representation based on a pluralistic society. Much of the violence used to build the new Communist society was a product of the need to overcome the inertia that is the usual social response to rapid, purposeful, and ideologically motivated change pushed forward by an organized minority. Much of it was a product of brutal zeal and a lust for power. But one must remember also that the

---

* The October, 1905, reform formally set up a Council of Ministers, with a prime minister, both modeled on the Western pattern.

terror used by the empire against the revolutionaries in itself contributed to the sharpening of their dogmatic convictions and strengthened their belief in the necessity of violence for the sake of "morally" good ends. This psychological legacy of the empire makes the rulers of the past share responsibility with the rulers of the present for the continued reliance on violence, despite the deep existential and normative differences between the Soviet and Czarist executives.

Recently, there have been some indications that, with a decline in the momentum of internal transformation, voices might be raised inside Russia to dispute the unlimited claim of the executive to rule over the destinies of the Russian people. But the occasional voices of nonconformity are still timid when compared to the literary outcries of the disaffected intellectuals or the heroic declarations of the revolutionary brethren of less than a century ago. The Czarist executive was very gradually, indeed haltingly, moving in the direction of closing the gap between the political regime and society at large by adjusting to the requirements of the society. But it moved too slowly. The Soviet leadership changed society in the image of its own doctrines so that no such gap should exist. The 1957 reforms in the Soviet administrative structure, allegedly granting a greater voice to component federal and economic units, could have been significant in altering the role of the executive and its relation to society. But an element lacking in the empire is now present—the parallel and pervading structure of the Party —and all indications point to the fact that the Party is as powerful as ever. Having surmounted domestic obstacles and being rather optimistic about current world trends, it is not likely to atrophy in the foreseeable future.

Success in itself breeds conservatism and vested interest in the status quo. These, in turn, gradually involve restraints on power, especially as an industrializing society becomes more complex and literate. But neither industrialism nor education is incompatible with totalitarian autocracy. The former breeds pressures for central control and direction; the latter, popular slogans to the contrary, is *divisible* and subject to manipulative controls that stress only those aspects compatible with totalitarian demands and de-emphasize those that are not. Scientific training unaccompanied by the humanities does not inevitably come into conflict with a totalitarian regime that puts a premium on scientific achievement and gives it every opportunity for development. Furthermore, modern scientific education, by being dependent on specialization instead of fostering a true spirit of inquiry, can also be used to promote the acceptance of certain purposes and to instill a peculiar perspective that increases the power of the regime, by making it accepted. A commitment to science or to industrial technology and management, especially if accompanied by a system of high rewards, can be used as effective blinders to social dilemmas and political questions.

Beyond this, given the situation in the U.S.S.R. as well as in the Communist camp in general, a myriad of decisions which are essentially political will have to be made and will require an elite with political skill and a sense of purpose. Since a screening process for promoting such an elite has been developed over the long period dominated by Stalinism, we can expect that for many years to come only dedicated "politicians," or those who successfully pretend that they are, will rise in the hierarchy and ultimately shape decisions. Even if partially due to mere inertia, motivation for such decisions is thus likely to continue stressing common ideologically defined purposes. Considering their revolutionary character and fundamental commitment to struggle, such purposes are bound to cultivate a profound hostility toward even incipient manifestations of social pluralism, without which effective restraints on political power cannot develop.

2. Totalitarianism and Rationality

The crux of any attempted definition of totalitarianism is the perplexing issue of its uniqueness: What is distinctively new about it? Certainly, autocratic systems in the past displayed many of the features developed and accentuated by modern totalitarianism. Diocletian's tyranny or the Shogunate in Japan, for instance, stressed to a high degree the acquiescence of the population in centralized control. Both systems also institutionalized an atmosphere of fear through a system of secret-police informers not unlike the totalitarian societies of the twentieth century. Similarly, we find among many of the nineteenth-century European reformers a readiness to use violence for the sake of postulated improvements and reforms much like the ideological intolerance and consequent brutality of the Rosenbergs or Zhdanovs of our own age.[1] Cromwell's regime also displayed some analogies. The examples could easily be multiplied to include many other cases involving features similar to some of the characteristics of totalitarianism. Spain is a contemporary example.

A DEFINITION OF TOTALITARIANISM

Totalitarianism, being a dictatorship, characteristically includes the coercive qualities noted in such varied dictatorial systems. But unlike most dictatorships of the past and present, the totalitarian movements wielding power do not aim to freeze society in the status quo; on the contrary, their aim is to institutionalize a revolution that mounts in scope, and frequently in intensity, as the regime stabilizes itself in power. The purpose of this revolution is to pulverize all existing social units in order to replace the old pluralism with a homogeneous unanimity patterned on the blueprints of the totalitarian ideology. The power of the totalitarian regime is derived not from a precarious balance of existing forces (e.g., church, landed gentry, officer corps), but from the revolutionary dynamism of its zealous supporters, who disarm opposition and mobilize the masses both by force and by an appeal to a better future. This appeal is normally framed in the official ideology, or action program, of the movement. In time, of course, the dynamism decreases, but by then the system is buttressed by complex networks of control that pervade the entire society and mobilize its energies through sheer penetration. An institutionalized revolution, patterned on the totalitarian ideology, thus makes totalitarianism essentially a forward-oriented phenomenon. Most dictatorships, on the other hand, have as their object the prevention of history from keeping in step with time. Their survival depends on maintaining the status quo. When they fail, they become history.*

This proposition can be further developed by examining the fate of restraints on political power—which are present in varying degrees in all societies, once the totalitarian movement seizes power. These restraints can be broadly listed in three categories: 1) the direct restraints, expressed through *pacta conventa* such as the English Magna Charta or the Polish *Nihil novi* . . . , the Bill of Rights, constitutional guarantees, a rule of law, or even the broad consensus of tradition that rules out certain types of conduct, such as the use of violence; 2) the indirect restraints that stem from the pluralistic character of all large-scale societies, necessitating adjustment and compromise as the basis for political power—e.g., the churches, the economic interests, professional, cultural, or regional pressure groups, all of which impede the exercise of unrestrained power; and 3) the natural restraints, such as national character and tradition, climatic and geographical considerations, kinship structure, and particularly the primary social unit, the family. These also act to restrain the scope of political power.†

In constitutional societies, all three categories of restraint are operative on political power. In practice, of course, various violations occur, but these generally con-

---

* This is the political tragedy of such leaders as Chiang Kai-shek and Nagib, who came to power to effect a revolution, but became dependent in their control of power on conservative elements.

† One might also consider a supernatural restraint in the sense of a transcendent moral order to which many governments pay lip service. In fact, however, its *political* significance is probably covered fully by the three outlined above, and particularly by the first two.

43

stitute a deviation from the norm rather than the norm itself. Dictatorial or ancient autocratic societies are characterized by the absence of the direct restraints, since these are incompatible with the nature of arbitrary, and frequently personal, leadership. Suspension of civil rights, open or masked subversion of established constitutional practices, and negation of popular sovereignty have been characteristic of all nonconstitutional states, whether totalitarian or not.

The indirect restraints, however, have usually escaped the dictatorial scythe except when a significant social grouping chooses to resist directly the dictates of those in power. If, for instance, the church or the nobility, for one reason or another, clashes with the ruler, it is then subjected to the dictatorial pattern of coercion. Generally, however, the broad outlines of social life are not disturbed by the dictator even though an individual objector, even in a high place, is struck down. An average Hungarian under Horthy or a Frenchman under Louis XIV was not directly drawn into the operations of the regime and could continue in his traditional associations much as before the advent of the ruler. The ruler himself based his power to a great extent on the varying alliances reached among combinations of social-political forces and maintained himself in power as long as such alliances endured. Revolutionary changes were hence anathema to a dictatorship of this kind.

It is only totalitarianism of our own age that rejects all

three kinds of restraints.* It not only subverts the direct restraints immediately after the seizure of power but, unlike traditional dictatorships, it proceeds, once entrenched, to destroy all existing associations in society in order to remake that society and, subsequently, even man himself, according to certain "ideal" conceptions. In time, it even attempts, not always successfully, to overcome the natural restraints on political power. Without doing so, totalitarianism can never achieve the isolation of the individual and the mass monolithic homogeneity that are its aim. Only with both of them (the paradox between them is more apparent than real) can the existing pluralism be changed to an active unanimity of the entire population that will make the transformation of society, and ultimately of man, possible. Only through them can man be conditioned to the totalitarian image, for the totalitarian hope is that action patterns will lead to thought patterns. This process, however, even if purposely gradual (as, for instance, in Poland under the Communists), inevitably involves the regime in increasing applications of coercion. Some of the "unredeemable social misfits" have to be removed, and it is difficult for the regime to single out for extinction particular social groups without soon involving itself in large-scale terror. Society is composed, after all, of largely overlapping associations and loyalties.

---

* Democracies do so, to a limited extent, in time of recognized danger; this is the concept of constitutional dictatorship. However, it always has some time limit.

Terror thus becomes an inevitable consequence, as well as instrument, of the revolutionary program. But the totalitarian revolution would be meaningless without a justification to induce the active unanimity of the population. Hence, ideology is not merely a historical guide. It becomes a daily dose of perpetual indoctrination. The total social impact of the totalitarian efforts to make reality conform to totalitarian thought, involving terror and indoctrination as well as institutional and social reorganization, makes for a quantitative difference from old dictatorships that is sufficiently great to become a qualitative difference.

In order to define totalitarianism, one may also attempt to isolate its objective attributes, some of which have already been implied. Carl J. Friedrich suggests that these may include, in a syndrome, the following: an official ideology, a single mass party, a technologically conditioned near-complete monopoly of all means of effective armed combat and of effective mass communication, and a system of terroristic police control.[2] The combination of these by no means exclusively totalitarian characteristics with the total social impact stemming from the inherently dynamic revolutionary spirit of totalitarianism makes it, in terms of the accepted categorizations of political systems, historically distinct. Totalitarianism, therefore, has to be considered as a new form of government falling into the general classification of dictatorship, which includes the ancient autocracies, tyrannies, despotisms, absolute monarchies, and traditional dictatorships. Totalitarianism is a system in which technologically advanced instruments of political power are wielded without restraint by centralized leadership of an elite movement, for the purpose of effecting a total social revolution, including the conditioning of man, on the basis of certain arbitrary ideological assumptions proclaimed by the leadership, in an atmosphere of coerced unanimity of the entire population.[3] This definition thus goes beyond Friedrich's descriptive syndrome of discernible characteristics of totalitarianism and attempts to point also to its essence—i.e., its institutionalized revolutionary zeal.

DYNAMICS

Existing political situations in a number of countries provide useful illustrations of the stages of totalitarian development. Admittedly, these overlap. In France and Italy, the totalitarian movements operate today, competing electorally and plotting conspiratorially, in a nontotalitarian environment. Their task is to overthrow, at an opportune moment, the existing political systems and to seize power as a prerequisite to the implementation of their programmatic goals. Their situation, broadly speaking, is analogous to the position of the NSDAP in the Weimar Republic prior to 1933 or of the Bolsheviks in Russia prior to 1917, although the latter had to rely much more on conspiratorial action. This is the pre-revolutionary stage, which may range through varying phases of maturity and ripening before the actual moment of seizure of power.

The next stage follows the seizure of power, with the totalitarian movement solidifying its hold on the instruments of power. This is the period of entrenchment, of

47

occasional compromise, of preparation. Active opposition elements are removed, and comprehensive plans for future operations drafted. Gradual efforts to penetrate and neutralize hitherto abstaining groups, which could become potential sources of resistance, are made in anticipation of their total absorption. This was the situation prevailing in Italy during almost the entire Fascist period,* in Germany roughly until the war, in the U.S.S.R. until the early 1930's, and in Argentina until the actual collapse of the Perónist regime when it was about to embark on its revolutionary program. It is thus a stage of consolidation and anticipation, of tactical appeasements masking strategic planning.

The totalitarian system begins to materialize with the launching of the internal revolution and the attempted destruction of existing social units. At this stage, not only the indirect restraints but even the so-called natural ones are assaulted. As the image and the structure of the totalitarian movement come to be reflected in the new institutions, organizations, and factories built on the ashes of the old society, the system takes shape. In all walks of life, the operational principles of the movement become the standards for conduct, and the race into the future starts. All the energies of the population are mobilized through force, rewards, opportunities, and propaganda. Ideology, reduced to the level of the daily exhortation, is used to justify the existing sacrifices and to give meaning to the

* Fascist inability to cope decisively with the old officer corps, the monarchy, and the Vatican probably also explains the relative swiftness of the collapse of Fascist power as compared with the Nazi capacity to control the situation until the final annihilation.

unending search for the ideal tomorrow. This is the situation initiated in the U.S.S.R. by the First Five-Year Plan, and in the satellites since about 1948.

Inevitably, however, stabilizing factors begin to intervene even before the full impetus of the internal revolution is felt. Power, like wealth, has an inherent tendency to attract strong attachments in those who enjoy it. Consequently, the triumphant elite, while not officially abandoning its ultimate ends, tends to stress immediate power considerations. An ideological rationalization for such a tendency is ever ready: Power must be consolidated if further advances are to be made. The sincerity or insincerity of such reasoning notwithstanding, the consolidation of power becomes a conservative tendency. In an ideologically motivated, zealous organization, this breeds its own antithesis among those anxious to push ahead. Those who toiled and risked to seize power accordingly become all the more fearful of the rising young stars and new constellations in the movement, into which many late arrivals have flocked. Some therefore urge that revolutionary changes be pushed immediately lest new elements come to the fore. Others urge greater restraint and even compromise with the former dominant groups, now suppressed but still not liquidated. Purges provide a partial solution for this dissension. The history of the right- and left-wing deviations in the U.S.S.R., and of the SA-SS clash in Germany, is instructive in this respect. The intervention of such stabilizing factors, in the initial stages at least, thus tends merely to accentuate the tension. Its longer-run consequence, however, so far as available experience indicates, is to generate even greater violence and unpredictability.

But in time, other pressures toward gradualism and stability develop. As the ruling elite ages, it becomes more and more concerned with succession, with status, and also with the transmission of its privileges to its children. Revolutionary considerations begin to be obscured by a desire to assure one's own offspring better education, advancement opportunities, etc. Such processes develop unconsciously as an inevitable consequence of privilege. Distinct class differentiation thus develops, producing another element impeding the totalitarian revolution, which tends to emphasize social mobility, arbitrariness, and uncertainty.

This process in Communist totalitarian systems has been specifically linked with the rapid development of an industrial economic order. Communist dictatorships have made industrialization and (to a lesser degree) collectivization the central theme of their internal revolution, partially to prove ex post facto the correctness of Marxist assumptions, partially because, in a technological age, industry is the backbone of national power, and especially because they seized power in backward areas where industrial development had been seriously retarded but had become the focal point of aspirations. Industrialization, imposed politically and without regard to cost, not only necessitates great sacrifices from the people, but also involves the application of tremendous coercive force on those who, because of tradition, self-interest, or apathy, resist it. In that sense, Soviet terror in the 1930's was functionally rational, although its aberrations and excesses were frequently irrational. Some theorists have tended, however, to overemphasize the latter aspects. The oppression and terror of the Soviet system was significantly linked with this ruthless attempt, at all costs, to destroy the existing way of life. It involved the commitment of all the energies of the regime to push the program and mobilize the entire population to carry it through.

The first repercussions of this program were therefore in the direction of accentuating the totalitarian character of the system. As industrialization and collectivization through coercion grew in scope, an increasing number of people were affected. Traditional allegiances and alliances were shattered, and those suspected of opposing the Party program were arrested, deported, or shot. Terror and fear grew rapidly. Not even the Party was immune, and countless members were purged for alleged inefficiency, often translated into accusations of sabotage and wrecking.[4] The first consequences of industrialization, to repeat, were thus to maximize existing fear, arbitrariness, caprice, and terror—in other words, to stress the irrational elements. At the same time, a tremendous social upheaval was created, and literally millions of people were torn from their traditional occupations or surroundings. While this meant misery or death for many, it also opened up unprecedented opportunities for rapid advancement. The totalitarian revolution, therefore, not only stimulated negative reactions; it appealed to the imaginations and self-interest of many others. The presence in this upheaval of a disciplined, and the only organized, body, the Communist Party, gave its leaders almost unlimited power to channel the revolution, to direct it, to head it. A society in this stage of destruction and construction could not produce any restraints on the totalitarian leadership. A society subjected to so total a revolution, socially and economically, offers only two political alternatives: anarchy or totalitarian control. The disciplined and militant totalitarian movement ensured the latter alternative.

We do not know what forms the totalitarian revolution, unhindered externally, would have taken in the more advanced societies where totalitarian movements came to power before World War II. Those, like Poland and Czechoslovakia, that have come under Communist dictatorships since the war have in a broad sense been subjected to the same pattern, although with significant variations pointing in the direction of greater gradualism. Nonetheless, collectivization, nationalization of trade, and expansion of heavy industry all have tended to reproduce this total social impact that dissolves the traditional society. Very specific circumstantial factors prevented the Fascist and Nazi regimes from launching similar large-scale schemes of social reconstruction. Nonetheless, it is sufficient to read Starace's plans to change the Italian national character or Mussolini's remarks on the need to eradicate the Italian "softness," as well as some of the Party regulations on daily behavior of the citizen issued in 1938, to realize that such a revolution was being seriously contemplated in Italy. In the case of the Nazis, there is even more ample evidence that the New Order in Europe would have resulted in revolutionary changes in Germany proper, changes highly inimical to the established order. Hitler's wartime conversations and Himmler's plans for the SS are full of projects that would have involved radical changes in German society and economy.

The question arises, however, as to what happens when the initial impetus of purposefully induced change has spent itself. What happens when the initial economic drive is more or less achieved, and further efforts are merely the accentuation of something already existing?

A RATIONALIST TOTALITARIANISM?

It could be argued, and some have, that Soviet totalitarianism, the most advanced totalitarian society of our age, is now entering upon a new stage of development, the character of which will be determined by the industrialized nature of the Soviet economy. This analysis, partaking somewhat of a material determinism, stresses the incompatibilities between totalitarianism and the requirements of a modern, industrial, and hence also bureaucratic order. Noting that totalitarianism in the past has seemed largely irrational, it argues that the rationalistic routines of the indispensable managers of the industrial society will necessarily transmit themselves to the totalitarian leadership and gradually effect a fundamental transformation of the system itself. This transmission will be aided by the fact that the totalitarian movement has become highly bureaucratized and therefore shares in many of the operational patterns associated with running the industrial machine. Furthermore, it is argued, the totalitarian movement itself has increasingly become staffed by the managerial-bureaucratic elements to whom Party membership

means no more than an important club association necessary to satisfy career ambitions. The revolutionary torch
and the unending quest are accordingly displaced by the
swivel chair and the time clock.

Totalitarianism, in the extreme form of this argument,
is thus to disappear imperceptibly and unintentionally. As
stability, predictability, and over-all rationality set in,
fear, terror, and arbitrariness will fade. Mass enthusiasm
and passionate unanimity will give way to disagreements
on matters of expertise, and hence also on policy. Policy
discussion will then become genuine arguments on alter-
nate courses of action; selection will be made on the basis
of rational (technical, objective assessments of the implications of perceived reality) considerations without
violent (hence arbitrary and fear-inspiring) consequences
for those whose arguments did not prevail. This, together
with the growing stability of various privilege groups.
will in turn lead to a form of pluralism, suggestive of the
existing democratic systems. Democracy, even though
likely a curtailed one, will enter by the back door.

One example of this type of reasoning is the argument
advanced by Deutscher. He stresses the point that "the
economic progress made during the Stalin era has at last
brought within the reach of the people a measure of well-
being which should make possible an orderly winding up
of Stalinism and a gradual democratic evolution." [5] This
argument leaves considerable room for dissent. Democracy involves more than what Deutscher suggests. It
requires, in the view of some, a certain philosophical
tradition, a basic recognition of some sort of higher law,
a fundamental attitude of toleration, an absence of doc-

trinal fanaticism—all of which are, at most, only indirectly linked to a state of "well-being," and none of which seem to be even remotely present in the existing Soviet scene. One may also wonder what is actually meant by "a measure of well-being," especially since wants are relative. Furthermore, there is little of substance in what is known today of totalitarian institutions to indicate the likelihood of such a democratic development. It is difficult to assume that the Party, having such a vested interest, will be willing to resign its absolute control of the instruments of power. The argument also assumes a short-range quality to the goals of the Party, and it ignores the impact of international developments on domestic policies. Deutscher's analysis thus falls down on two counts: Its highly monistic interpretation of democracy fails to see democratic development in its complex and pluralistic perspective, the economic aspects of which are merely one component part of a diversified whole; and its interpretation of Soviet totalitarianism fails to perceive the self-generating power of the system of controls and the resulting vested interests in the maintenance of these controls.

The question remains, however, whether in the long run totalitarianism is compatible with a rationalistic orientation prevailing in its extensive bureaucracy and in the managerial classes of its industrial order. To some extent, this issue, like the one discussed above, is made more complex by the general problem of the range of predictability in political science. It is doubtful that any "scientific" prediction can be made in matters not clearly connected with institutional, legal, stable processes—such as, for instance, one that Presidential elections will occur in the United States in 1964 and 1968, and that, barring some drastic denouement, the contenders will be the Democratic and Republican parties. Predictability becomes more difficult, and its range much shorter, in matters involving general problems of political-social development in a system where little is known of the processes of decision-making at the top, of the motivations and considerations involved, of the nature of the various power alignments, and, last but not least, of the morale of the leaders. There are also few biographical data, beyond the barest essentials, about most of the leaders. In such cases, one must rely to a considerable degree on the projection of past experience, and estimate the future implications of current commitments of the system.

The experience of Germany with Nazi totalitarianism, albeit brief, may therefore not be irrelevant. The Nazi system was imposed with all the earmarks of revolutionary totalitarianism on a society with a highly developed industrial order, with an established and conservative managerial class, with the most efficient and routinized bureaucracy in all Europe. Yet there is no indication in all the available evidence that the fanatical, often irrational, and usually brutal Nazi leadership was in any way deterred from its purposes by the influence or orientations of the German technocrats and bureaucrats. With few exceptions, the bureaucrats and technocrats adjusted meekly to the requirements of the totalitarian movement and were happy to reap any material benefits that Nazi successes produced. It was not until the Nazi regime began to crumble that the bureaucratic and technocratic elements (e.g., Speer) showed any initiative or purposeful action of their own. Until then, it was more a matter of the bureaucrats absorbing Nazi values (e.g., in the treatment of slave laborers) than of the Nazis absorbing a bureaucratic orientation. It seems, therefore, that a violent, arbitrary totalitarianism can, at least, arise and maintain itself in an industrially advanced area without loss of its revolutionary zeal and fanatic brutality. It did so in Germany, Italy, and Czechoslovakia.* The crucial factor throughout was the presence of a movement with a revolutionary morale able to wield effectively the instruments of power.

A rebuttal might point, however, to the facts that both the German and Italian systems were of brief duration and that the experience of Czechoslovakia is too recent for confident evaluation. Furthermore, the emergence of a new and imposing industrial and bureaucratic order under the totalitarian regime itself in the U.S.S.R. is obviously of the greatest importance for the domestic political development of the Soviet society. It is a development not paralleled in any of the other countries mentioned, where the totalitarian movements were superimposed on already existing industrial systems.

One must acknowledge, therefore, that conceivably totalitarianism may become, because of the factors suggested and in spite of the Nazi experience, rationalistic and hence less unpredictable, arbitrary and openly terror-

---

* There is also the case of Japan, where industrialization advanced rapidly under a form of government increasingly marked by totalitarian tendencies. All indications prior to ·1945 suggested that a "democratic evolution" was not to be expected.

istic. But there is no evidence to suggest that this in itself is incompatible with totalitarianism, which need not be interpreted in terms of irrational terror almost for the sake of terror. Such a rationalist system, arising in the context of one-party domination (not to mention international pressures), could be nothing less than a rationalist dictatorship, just as total in control as its less predictable and more violent antecedent of the 1930's. The institutionalized revolution that still characterizes the existing totalitarianisms will inevitably slow down in the future, but by then it will be involved in an economic commitment that also has its own political logic. The totalitarian economy, as many have observed, has been developed in the U.S.S.R. over the last thirty-five years in keeping with plans oriented to a final (if not yet precisely defined) goal. It is thus a goal-oriented economy, the goal being Communism. That this goal needs more definite formulation is, for our purposes, irrelevant. The important thing is that those in charge of the Soviet society have assumed that economic and social development in all its aspects can be purposefully steered by man in the direction of an ideal solution. This produces consequences that are not only economic but also political, quite different from those induced by other equally technologically advanced economic systems where, to a large extent, economic life is self-directive and ultimate goals, such as plenty and progress, are purposely vague. These goals have less bearing on current decisions than such factors as past experience, demand, prices, competition, and opportunity. In the latter case, a measure of freedom of interplay is inherent. In the former, all decisions and plans are made, or are rationalized, in terms of the ultimate goal.

Consequently, it makes little *political* difference whether the range of man's alternatives is limited by uneducated revolutionaries or by scientific Ph.D.'s, once the entire economy is subjected to a process of human engineering oriented on a goal that cannot be questioned. Admittedly, operations conducted by trained bureaucrats and technocrats may be more rational and less directly oppressive (insofar as extreme oppression may be uneconomical, which is not entirely certain). But to be less totalitarian, such operations would have to involve some degree of withdrawal on the part of those in charge from their commitment to total social and economic engineering, thus granting to those living under the system the opportunity to make important choices *not* in keeping with the goal. But such a politically meaningful development would, in turn, involve a further condition, which at present appears highly unlikely—namely, the decline of ideology and a basic reconsideration of the firmly instituted schemes of economic development. Barring that, the totalitarian economic system would continue to exert pressures for the maintenance of a dictatorship capable of enforcing the kind of discipline that such total plans demand. It is doubtful that, as long as the Party remains in power, the tendency of the regime to stress unattainable goals will vanish. Indeed, it is these goals, inherent in the current ideology, that justify to the population the sacrifices the Party's domination involves. Thus, as long as the Party continues to hold its successful grip on the instruments of power, we can expect it to continue stressing, first, the long-range goals of an ultimate utopia, and then the consequent sacrifices to achieve them, even though possibly at a diminishing rate of effort.*

The rationalist tomorrow, if it ever comes, will therefore not be an introduction to a democratic form of government, but rather a stage in further totalitarian evolution, accentuating rationalist features present from the start and minimizing some of the irrational outbursts already noted. The prototypes of such a rationalist totalitarianism need not be sought only in Orwell's *1984*. They exist, in an embryonic stage, in our own industrial organizations and bureaucracies. If one could imagine the entire United States run like some executive department, with its myriad of minute, and often incomprehensible, regulations, routinized procedures, even sometimes arbitrariness of officials, one would be all the more inclined to be thankful that the rule of law (rooted in a traditional regard for the individual) and legislative fears of administrative expansion (a democratic "irrationalist" feature) act as a check.[6]

Totalitarianism and rationality, therefore, when viewed in a developmental perspective and not merely from a standpoint of a static definition pinpointing certain characteristics of a given epoch, are not necessarily incompatible. Rationality alone is hardly a sufficient condition for the inevitable growth of a democratic order. At different stages, totalitarianism can be characterized by a minimiza-

---

* The most recent illustration of this is the extensive program adopted by the Twenty-second CPSU Congress in 1961.

tion of rationalist considerations (as in the 1930's in the U.S.S.R. and in China more recently) or by an increased emphasis on them. But it is as unlikely that totalitarianism can become fully rational as it is incorrect to claim that it has been essentially irrational in the past. Today, for instance, in the U.S.S.R. the totalitarian system is operating in an environment where the need (as seen by the leadership) for unbridled violence, terror in its most open form, and unpredictability based on dictatorial whims seems no longer to be present or desirable. The population appears to be relatively pliant, the younger generation has absorbed a great deal of the indoctrination, and resistance of an active kind is almost entirely absent. The domination of the Party in the country, and of the leadership in the Party, appears to be firmly established. If only the Party could be satisfied with the status quo, a rationalist totalitarianism could possibly become reality.

But even then the problem of power would not disappear. Governmental rationality cannot go far beyond the realm of function and account for all human action. Basic drives for power are not likely to wane. And given the nature of the system, even if the Party declines and is supplanted ultimately by the bureaucracy (or merges with it), the total control of the system over those under it will not disappear even though its exercise will become more functionally rational. In such a system, it is likely that the institutional controls will be utilized to maintain the existing interests of the ruling class, and social stratification will become even more marked as position, education, and even wealth become inheritable. The abyss between those wielding power and the masses will create a real ruling caste, which itself will be highly stratified in terms of the proximity of its members to the center of power. It will create, too, an entire nonpolitical stratum of those who will be given a vested interest in the status quo by virtue of their utility to the system, such as the specialists, artists, military scientists, etc. In many respects, such a system will more nearly resemble the Nazi-Fascist dictatorship than the earlier Stalinist model. This curiously dialectical consequence might deprive Soviet totalitarianism of its revolutionary essence while maintaining its institutional forms. The lesson of history, however, is that this does not necessarily spell the end of the system.

But at best, that appears to be only a distant prospect. The tasks that face the totalitarians today in the captive nations in Europe, among the long dormant masses of China, in the rice paddies of North Vietnam, or in the Malayan jungles—not to speak of the virgin lands, overgrown urban centers, and ever-struggling collective farms in the U.S.S.R.—are very difficult and likely to command all their energies for many years to come. Indeed, the commitments currently made by the present Soviet leaders indicate that the Party is not satisfied with the status quo; hence the abandonment of large-scale drives, which involve in turn the maintenance of discipline, does not seem imminent even in the U.S.S.R., the most developed totalitarian system. These commitments are both domestic and international. Domestically, they suggest a three-pronged attack on the following goals: an increased emphasis on Party zeal, especially in terms of a reassertion of Leninism as defined by the present leadership; continued expansion of industry with major goals set for 1970; further drives in the agricultural sector, including both reclamation projects and the diminution of private plots. On the international plane, briefly, the commitments made to China and the satellites, coupled with those now being made to the underdeveloped countries, will continue to be felt on the domestic scene through scarcities and insistence on maximum effort. At the same time, with Stalin dead and Stalinism impracticable without him, the new leadership is searching for a new basis for power in the realm of both ideological justification and practical measures. This already has meant the rejection of some of the vicious attributes of Stalinism as well as an attack on Stalin himself. It involved in turn some unsettling consequences, as an accepted frame of reference was destroyed and old slogans and operational procedures fell by the wayside. Finally, the problem of succession, given the ages of the present leaders, cannot be dismissed as having been resolved entirely. From all this, it might appear therefore that both internally and externally the likelihood of a status quo situation in the foreseeable future is doubtful. If so, the era of revolutionary totalitarianism may not yet be over.

3. *The Nature of the Soviet System*

> If the mind is obligated to obey the word of command,
> it can at any rate feel that it is not free. But if it has
> been so manipulated beforehand that it obeys without
> even waiting for the word of command, it loses even the
> consciousness of enslavement—André Gide.

All modern societies involve mass manipulation, especially since the masses have now become economically and
politically important. Whether it is an election or merely
a matter of consumption, the crucial factor is the behavior
of the activated mass. Motivational research and public-
opinion polls are ways of gauging the anticipated reactions
of the consumer and the voter. The asymmetry in decision-
making between the masses and the businessman or the
politician is thus diminished.

But Gide (in the above quotation) had something far
more ominous in mind. He was pointing to the possibility
of a society's maintaining total political-social conformity,
not just with the leadership anticipating the mass reactions, but with the masses, in effect, almost anticipating
the desires of the leadership. A self-enforcing unanimity

and conformity would be the consequence. But for such a condition to arise, there would have to be some overt, systematized framework of socially instilled values that could guide—almost without command—the behavior of the masses. And if that were to come to pass, perhaps one would be safer not to raise the baffling question of whether such a society were, in fact, free or enslaved. By comparison, Nazi Germany and Soviet Russia of the 1930's and China of today would be examples of admirably simple tyrannies, with the continuous use of force leaving little doubt as to the internal essence of their systems.

ORGANIZATIONAL COMPULSION FOR IDEOLOGY-ACTION

The most prevalent political system has always been some form of authoritarianism, although the scope of arbitrary power has often varied, depending on circumstances, local traditions, the nature of social-political alliances supporting a given regime, and the vitality of institutional and legal customs. Furthermore, with very few exceptions, such regimes have tended to be conservative, usually adopting major reforms only in response to social-economic pressures or political unrest, but rarely actually initiating them. In the event of occasional reform drives, the usual pattern has been one of temporary bursts of initiative, followed by lengthier relapses into conservative passivity.

Regimes of this sort could endure as long as the majority of the population remained politically neutral and passive. A variety of well-known factors undermined this neutrality and passivity. Rapid social-economic changes brought about by the machine age, increased literacy, and the rise of nationalism have contributed to the politicizing of the masses and have made the politics of mass consciousness a feature of our age. Practically all contemporary leaders have to appeal to popular sentiments and organize various forms of mass action in order to wield power effectively.

The extent of the appeal and the manipulation depends on the nature of the objective for which power is wielded and on the susceptibility of the given society to a more or less extensive domination of the masses by an elite. When widespread social disintegration because of war or social-economic crises occurs, the opportunities for the emergence of extremist elites and for the direct domination of the masses are greatest. The weakening (and/or disappearance) of intermediary pluralistic forms of social organization allows for the consolidation of centralized power and for the eventual use of that power to effect large-scale societal reconstruction. To do the latter, both the ruling elite (organized into a revolutionary movement) and the masses must share certain general notions of what was wrong with the past society, as well as an action program for the building of a better one.

The political systems established by such revolutionary movements differ profoundly from old-fashioned dictatorships. Instead of using societal pluralism to manipulate various interests in order to maintain power, these movements take advantage of the occasional weakness of such pluralist groups to seize power and use it first to eliminate all intermediary groups, and then to construct a new society, reflecting the movement's ideology. Such elimination can take place with particular thoroughness and intensity if the given society happens to have lagged behind in the process of modernization. In that case, the construction of a new order can be linked to rapid social-economic and technical development. Today, force and progress make a formidable combination.

Because of the unprecedented total social impact of these regimes, they have been labeled "totalitarian." The word is used to suggest that at some point the scope of arbitrary power and the domination of society by a political elite, especially one that tolerates no barriers between itself and the population, becomes so extensive that differences of degree become differences of kind. Although it is often difficult to define that point with great precision (as is also true in defining "democracies"; for example, is Mexico or France a democracy?), it may be suggested that the totalitarian systems differ in kind from other forms of authoritarian regimes—traditional dictatorships, what has been called the "totalitarian elements in pre-industrial societies,"[1] or the contemporary nationalist single-party regimes—because: (1) their ideology provides a total critique of the antecedent form of societal organization and a prescription for a complete reconstruction of society and man; (2) the absolutist character of their ideology frees the movements of any moral or traditional-legal restraints on their power, and they consider themselves justified in undertaking even the most ruthless steps to consolidate their power and execute their ideology; (3) the combination of these two factors, linked with the urgent belief of the committed members, produces within the movement an *organizational compulsion* for ideologically focused and compatible action (ideology-action) to absorb and/or destroy all social groups that might even constitute passive obstructions to the movement's dynamic need to subordinate society totally to its power. This organizational compulsion absorbs both the leadership and the membership. A good negative example is the difficulty encountered by Lenin in trying to effect a temporary truce between his ruling party and Russian society; the built-in pressure toward action that was felt so acutely within the Soviet Communist Party in the mid-1920's may be seen as a positive example.

The Soviet system has now existed for over forty-four years, and its political history has been closely identified with three major Communist leaders, each symbolizing a distinct but related, stage of development of that system. Broadly speaking, the phase of Leninism after 1917 can be said to have involved primarily the consolidation of the Communist Party's rule over society and the internal transformation of the Party from a revolutionary vanguard into a more disciplined ruling elite. While some small measure of internal diversity remained within the Party, especially at the top, perhaps the most enduring achievement of Leninism was the dogmatization of the Party, which in effect both prepared and caused the next stage, Stalinism.

The Stalinist phase, particularly during the years 1928–41, was the time of what might be called the totalitarian "break-through"—that is, the all-out effort to destroy the basic institutions of the old order and to construct at least the framework for the new. The postwar period, 1945–53, was in some respects a repetition and extension

of the preceding period. The process of postwar reconstruction once again meant a conflict with society, destruction of established ways, and an extension of earlier efforts
to build "socialism" in agriculture, through industrialization, in the arts and sciences, etc. The political consequence of these efforts, as well as of Stalin's own personality, was a decline in the importance of the Party, the
personalization of leadership, the growth of the secret
police, and the dominating role of terror as the crucial,
most characteristic feature of the system. Indeed, Stalin's
totalitarian edifice could be said to have rested on three
supporting columns: the secret police, the state bureaucracy, and the Party, with all three coordinated by the
old dictator's personal secretariat. This was perhaps the
low point in the Party's career since the seizure of power.
Weakened and demoralized by the purges, it became less
and less the instrument of social revolution. Decline in
zeal, dogmatic stagnation, and bureaucratization were the
familiar consequences.

During the fourth phase, which began with several
years of instability within the Kremlin, but can still be
associated with the name of Khrushchev, there occurred
a gradual lessening of the conflict between society and the
regime coupled with a certain maturation—and social
acceptance—of the new order. This phase was made possible by the Stalinist liquidation of all nonpolitically
directed social groups, so that the regime could afford the
luxury of diminished violence. Thus, Stalinism paved the
way for the relative leniency of the post-Stalinist phase. In
the political domain, it has been characterized by the
re-emergence of the Party apparatus as the dominant

political force and by Khrushchev's increasing emphasis on linking technical-economic achievement with broad and intensive ideological indoctrination. The revitalization of the Party and the renewed emphasis on ideology marked an effort to make the system "move again" (to borrow a phrase made popular during an American election), and the personal success of Khrushchev is in large part due to his instinctive perception of the organizational compulsion of the Party toward ideology-action. Stagnant in Stalin's later days, the Party almost naturally responded to a man whose appeal involved a reactivation of the Party's historical role.

THE PARTY AND THE IDEOLOGY

Obviously, Khrushchev's political system is not the same as Stalin's, even though both may be generally described as totalitarian. Therefore, the next step in examining the nature of the Soviet system in 1961 is to find clues to important continuities and changes by looking more closely at certain key dynamic aspects of its political regime. The most revealing seem to be the role of the Party, the role of ideology, and the role of violence. Each of these will be considered briefly, and certain issues involved will be highlighted.

Perhaps the most important single development of the last few years in Soviet politics has been the revitalization of the Party and the reassertion of its dominant position in Soviet life. One by one, the secret police, the state administration, and the army, as well as the planners, the intelligentsia, and the youth learned this lesson—sometimes painfully. A direct relationship between the leadership and the masses has thus been reasserted—the relationship of access and mobilization.[2]

But the implications of this may be even broader. The recent assertion of the Party's role suggests that certain conclusions reached by sociologists concerning the comparative roles of specialized experts and managers in large-scale American enterprises may be highly relevant to the Soviet totalitarian system. These studies have implied that experts are unable to provide the "integration" that a large-scale, diversified organization requires, since such integration is often incompatible with the narrower, highly specialized focus of the expert and requires a high degree of skill in human relations, which an expert rarely possesses. Studies of the two groups have further suggested the following important differences between them: personality types, background and promotion procedures, orientations and goals.[3]

It would not be far-fetched to suggest that the role of manager in the Soviet system, if that system as a whole is viewed as a goal-oriented large enterprise, is performed by the *apparatchiki* of the Party. They are the ones who are skilled in human relations or in social organization, who have a sufficiently wide perspective to provide broad integration, and who rise from the bottom with their minds and skills focused on the over-all objective of the organization—the fulfillment of its historical purpose. Thus, they enjoy an inherent advantage over the expert, whether he is a technocrat or a professional bureaucrat. This picture is confirmed by the valuable studies of Soviet political and managerial elites carried out in recent years by Armstrong and Granick.

A certain amount of technical expertise does not handicap a manager. In fact, it makes him more able to cope with his sometimes recalcitrant experts. The same holds true with the Party. The growing penetration of its ranks with technically and professionally trained individuals need not mean a transformation of its organizational values or a decline in its vitality. A local Party secretary who can now deal with a recalcitrant expert by both cajoling and arguing with him may be far more effective in asserting his goals than his predecessor of twenty-five years ago, who probably approached the problem with loud swearing and ignorant threats. What is essential, however, is that this political goal-orientation of the Party be maintained. The recent intensification of indoctrination within the Party suggests that the leadership intends to maintain it. The vital importance of *agitprop* activity and the size of its staffs on all levels are good indications of the importance attached to this task by the regime. Technical know-how and doctrinal sophistication was the secret of the Jesuits' success. It is important and revealing to note the CPSU's efforts in this direction.

In a consideration of the changing role of the Party, it is also revealing to examine the problem of leadership conflicts within it. The character of the contestants, the issues over which they fought, and the methods used to resolve the struggles cast light on both continuities and changes within the Party and the system. In this connection, it is instructive to ask who, what about, and how? For example, take the difference between some of the major Party opponents of Stalin and Khrushchev. Trotsky symbolized the revolutionary, almost anarchistic traditions

of Communism. To defeat him, Stalin skillfully exploited
the instinct of self-preservation of the Party, not ready
to sacrifice itself on the altar of world revolution. No
contrast could be sharper than between that flaming and
flamboyant revolutionary and the quiet dullness of Malenkov, a Party *apparatchik* who, perhaps in spite of himself,
became the symbol and maybe even the spokesman of
the managerial technocracy. Similarly, when the time
came for Stalin to move forward with domestic reforms,
he was opposed by the brilliant and articulate Bukharin.
Is it just a coincidence that his counterpart thirty years
later was the hulking, sullen, and anything but efferves-
cent Kaganovich? The change that has taken place within
the top elite is well symbolized by the individuals who
failed in the struggle for power—and this change is as
important for the future as any of the similarities that
one may wish to draw between the victors.

The issues of the conflicts are also revealing. They no
longer involve basic questions of the very survival of the
Communist regime. The problem now is how to promote
a venture that has been eminently successful but cannot
stand still (much like a prospering business in a competitive environment). Domestically, the major challenge
to the ruler's power does not come from the visionaries
and revolutionaries. To succeed, a challenger must be
able to work within the ruling organization, and this
successful organization, even while compulsively requiring
ideology-action, does not wish to undertake reckless initiatives. The greater threat comes from the dogmatic con-
servatives and the undogmatic managerial and technical
intelligentsia. To the former, all the necessary wisdom of

theory and practice is to be found in the experience of the years 1928–53. To the latter, the construction of socialism tends to be equated with the process of building a technically advanced industrial society—and once the process is completed, the wherewithal for the further operation of society can come from within the technical cadres of experts and specialists.

But to each group, the other is a greater threat than Khrushchev's leadership, and hence the two neutralize each other, much the way the Left and Right did in Stalin's early days. At the same time, they both illustrate the fact that the ruling party is no longer faced by fundamental questions of life and death, that the revolutionary phase of the great dilemmas of principle and practice is finished.

The "how" of the conflicts, however, serves as a timely warning against premature conclusions concerning any fundamental change in the internal political practices of the Party. In both cases, the victorious contestants were individuals who skillfully combined their perception of the innate collective interest of the ruling elite with effective manipulation of the Party's *apparat,* particularly through the secretariat. It would be difficult to explain Khrushchev's success merely in terms of his control of the secretariat. After all, his opponents were strong in it as well. The case was similar, as Deutscher shows in his *Prophet Unarmed,* with respect to Stalin versus Trotsky. Both involved muted appeals for support and perceptive appreciation of the dominant aspirations of the ruling elite. And in both cases, there were inherent pressures toward centralization of power in the hands of a single individual, pressures that he could exploit but which he alone could not have generated. Considering Khrushchev's age, one is well justified in analyzing clues to a new—or at least potential—struggle for succession, and in doing so one can learn a great deal not only about the power struggle itself but also about the *Gestalt* of the ruling party.

A discussion of the role of the Party as a dynamic factor in Soviet politics leads directly to a consideration of the political function of ideology. (See Chapter 5 for a discussion of how ideology affects the external conduct of Soviet leaders.) One of the most distinctive features of the Soviet system, and particularly of its ruling regime, is its conscious purposefulness. Everything it does—in fact, its very existence—is related to a conscious striving toward an announced but not exactly defined goal. Since this action is necessarily focused on the immediate tasks facing the Party—be it collectivization and class struggle at one time or the further limitation of the individual's opportunity for personal ownership at another—varying emphases of the ideology are involved in such actions. These provide clues to the changing preoccupations of the regime. As already noted, much of the ideological emphasis today is centered on making Russia a highly advanced, technically skilled nation, and the Party a rational, efficiency-oriented organization. But it is one thing for the Party to be rational in its operations and another matter if this rationality begins to impinge on the utopian ends of political action and instead makes the efficient functioning of the system an end in itself. It is the Party and the ideology together that provide the system with its built-in momentum. The decline of either would force the regime to rely almost exclusively on terror, as did Stalin, or face the prospect of far-reaching transformation of the system.

Therefore, internal indoctrination within the Party is of prime necessity. It is important that power within the Party should not gravitate into the hands of "experts," but that broad, purposeful "generalizers" remain at the helm, assisted on the one hand by loyal Party experts (Gosplanners, or managers) and on the other by the watchdogs of ideological purity. The split between these extremes is more objective than subjective. Both are subjectively loyal and dedicated, but with the modernization and development of Soviet society the Party, as noted, has necessarily absorbed the new, highly trained elite, with the concomitant danger of gradual change of orientation within its ranks.

Partly as a balance, and partly almost by a process of reaction, there has developed within the Party a professional cadre of "ideologues," a group of specialists in doctrinal matters, who bear little resemblance to the creative revolutionaries of the 1920's. Yet, the growth of the *agitprop*, and its professionalization, is in itself an indication of the process of change that, in this case, involves strenuous efforts to maintain the commitment of the Party membership to the Party ideology and to express that commitment in action.

At the risk of excessively speculative generalization, one may perhaps suggest the following scheme as far as the present relationship between the Party members and the ideology is concerned: The very top of the Party hierarchy is generally staffed by "ideology-action generalizers," individuals like Khrushchev, Aristov, and Kozlov, with the extremes of technical experts (who may be said to specialize in aspects of action alone) and of ideologues (who specialize in ideology) both represented. It would appear that among the probable successors to Khrushchev the ideology-action generalizers still predominate. (Of the various individuals one may mention—Kozlov, Polyansky, Brezhnev, Aristov, or Suslov—only the last one is an ideologue, and none is a narrow expert of the Kosygin type.)* On the intermediary level, there are two broad categories: the professional Party bureaucrats, the *apparatchiki,* from among whom the top level generalizers eventually emerge, but to whom, on the whole, the ideology has become internalized and is not a matter of continuous preoccupation; and secondly, the large staffs of the *agitprop,* containing the often dogmatic, doctrinaire, and conservative professional ideologues. They are the ones who most often view any new departure as a betrayal. In the lower echelons, it is more a matter of simple stereotypes and formulas than fanatical commitment, although some cases of the latter can be observed even by a casual visitor to the U.S.S.R.

* It may be tentatively posited that the ideology-action generalizers at the apex are usually in a closer relationship to the ideologues than to the more subordinate experts. On lower levels, the Party *apparatchiki* are usually in a closer relationship to *agitprop* than to the experts. (By closer relationship is meant less direct subordination of the latter by the former). In revolutionary times (in early post-1917 Russia or even in China today), there tends to be a relative fusion between the ideology-action generalizers and the ideologues (symbolized by Lenin or Mao Tse-tung). With stability, a process of differentiation has taken place, and in some respects the *apparatchiki* come closer to the experts. In recent years, Khrushchev has been trying to counteract this process by stimulating increased activity by the *agitprop* and by assigning greater responsibility to the *apparat,* thus compensating for the necessarily greater importance of the experts, given Soviet industrial-technical development.

However, it should be remembered that all three levels operate within a system that already reflects institutionally the basic notions of the ideology and that a more assured mood thus prevails than in the period of struggle against the old order.

Another aspect of the role of ideology involves the almost frenetic efforts of the regime to indoctrinate the masses. It is not an exaggeration to say that indoctrination has replaced terror as the most distinctive feature of the relationship of the regime to society, and perhaps even of the system itself as compared to others. With the completion of the destruction of organized intermediary groups between the regime and the people, with the basic outlines of the new society erected, the emphasis on class struggle has given way to a massively organized effort to instill in the Soviet people the values of the ruling party. The closer one studies the Soviet political system, the more one becomes impressed by the totality of the effort and the energy and resources committed to it. There is just no comparable example elsewhere to this total effort (in the words of *Pravda,* September 14, 1960) "to rear the new man." While the Party often meets with major difficulties because of boredom, hostility toward uniformity, absence of free contacts with the West, and disbelief and/or just formal acquiescence, it is able to exploit a very major advantage—that it is in a position to link the process of ideological indoctrination with technical modernization of society, which has become the universally accepted good in our age. It is not an accident that, in all recent discussions of propaganda, the Party has been stressing the need to link the two, and because of its monopoly of power the Party can make modernization seem like the consequence of its ideologically inspired action. The organizational compulsion of the Party for ideology-action thus becomes the source and the means of modernization, thereby strengthening the Party's social legitimization.

Thus, ideology has the important effect of transforming the Party's power into authority and of replacing terror as the chief buttress for the Party's power. This is a major change from Stalin's days. It is now clear that terror has to be seen as a manifestation of a particular stage in the development of the system. In its most intense form, terror manifests itself during the break-through stage of totalitarianism, when the old order is being destroyed and the new erected. At that stage, the secret police emerge as the crucial organ of the regime, dominating the political scene. Given the objective of total reconstruction, terror quickly pervades the entire society, and the police become supreme. To the extent that the dictator is inclined toward a personal appreciation of violence, in some respects such terror can be even more extreme and sadistic. However, it is doubtful that the social impact of Soviet terror in the 1930's would have been much less even if Stalin had not enjoyed (as it is alleged he did) the physical liquidation of his enemies and friends. As terror mounts, the apparatus of violence becomes institutionalized and develops a vested interest in the continuation of the operation. Therefore, it is difficult to halt it rapidly, while the ruling elite is naturally aware of the storehouse of social hostility accumulated by terror and becomes fearful that abandoning terror might bring about a violent upheaval.

Terror thus tends to perpetuate itself even after the regime's need for it recedes.

The abandonment of terror was facilitated by the involvement of the terror machine in the struggle for succession after Stalin's death. While it is likely that terror would have declined anyway, the desperate need to decapitate the secret police, lest it decapitate the various heirs-apparent, precipitated a more rapid decline of the secret police than perhaps would have been the case. It is quite conceivable that Stalin's successors were pleasantly surprised to find that their system could work and work quite well, or even better, without terror and that the social response was not one of a revolution but of gratitude. Thus, they pushed the process forward, and today one may justifiedly say that terror is no longer a dominant feature of the system. To be sure, the potential is there, and it acts as a restraining force. But it no longer pervades society, and it is certainly no longer one of the central means for effecting social change.

Instead, organized coercion performs the function of enforcing societal conformity. The acceptance of the new forms of society by a large part of at least the urban population permits the regime to utilize social orthodoxy for the purpose of enforcing ideologically desirable behavior. The Comrades' Courts and the Citizens' Militia, staffed by narrow-minded and intolerant low-level activists, are forms of organized mass coercion designed to stifle politically dangerous individualism that might threaten the pattern of positive indoctrination. For that purpose, the potential of political terror in the background and organized social intolerance in the forefront is sufficient. A voluntarist totalitarianism can be far more effective than a terrorist one.

The theme running through the three aspects previously discussed is the organizational compulsion of the Party toward enforcing social integration around its overt, stated, dogmatic beliefs. To abandon these efforts to ideologize society, even if this process is already highly ritualized and may no longer involve general individual commitment, would signal the first real step in the direction of the transformation of the system. The regime has shown that it can rule with far less violent means than was the case with Stalinism, but the kind of power it needs to continue changing society, even if at a decreasing pace, demands a degree of social integration that can be achieved only if a sense of purpose, organizationally expressed, is energetically maintained.* Only then can the emergence of alternative values be avoided; only then can the appearance of groups showing alternative goals be prevented; and only then can the individual be faced with the politically paralyzing dilemma of the one alternative—that to be against the regime is to be *against* everything and *for* nothing.

POLITICS AND SOCIAL DEVELOPMENT

In recent years, a great deal has been said about the social-economic development of Soviet society. It has been argued that the achievement of the highly literate and eco-

* One might add that an older example of the expression of the survival instinct of a goal-oriented movement through such organizational compulsion toward indoctrination and social integration is provided by church history.

nomically mature society would necessarily cause a profound transformation of the political order, and in this connection the words "liberalization" or "democratization" have often been used. The burden of the preceding pages suggests that politics is still supreme within the Soviet system, although such political supremacy cannot be viewed as existing in a vacuum, independent of the social-economic context. The role of the dynamic factors in shaping Soviet politics clearly must be seen within a framework relating them to the significant changes that have taken place in the U.S.S.R. over the last few decades, and this has been taken into consideration in the preceding discussion.

There can be no doubt that several aspects of Soviet society have particular relevance to a discussion of the Soviet political system and pose special problems for it. The relationship between the regime and four such sectors—agriculture, the industrial organization, the intelligentsia, and the evolving public organizations—deserves special note.

For the past few years, agriculture has been in the forefront of domestic policy dilemmas. The failure of Stalinist policies to improve agricultural production appreciably forced the succession leadership to re-examine some hitherto sacred tenets concerning the untouchability of the Machine Tractor Stations and to adopt urgent measures to expand the acreage of arable land, to improve productivity, to increase individual incentives for the deplorably underpaid *kolkhozniks,* and (last but not least) to strengthen the direct control of the countryside by the Party. The extremity of the crisis, as well as the fluid

83

situation in the leadership, quickly led to the emergence of alternative positions, and the Central Committee plenums that attempted to deal with the situation (starting with the September, 1953, plenum and including both the 1958 and the 1959 meetings) also became arenas of bitter political conflict, with consequent political casualties at the very top. However, what is particularly interesting in terms of a political system that is ideology-action–oriented is that, although ample evidence has been cited even by the Soviet leaders (as well as by the recent statistical yearbook) showing that productivity on private plots far outdistances the "socialist sector," all the solutions offered, both the conservative and neo-Stalinist as well as the innovating Khrushchevist ones, specifically excluded any alternative that could increase agricultural production at the cost of the ideology. Furthermore, the least controversial measures have been those resulting in highly successful steps to politicize fully for the first time the agricultural sector. The present trend, involving the amalgamation of collective farms, their increasing formation into state farms, and the liquidation of private plots and livestock, suggests that efforts to improve production and the lot of the collective farmer by making him, in essence, similar to an industrial one, involve conscious political direction based on ideological considerations. In effect, the way of life of roughly 50 per cent of the Soviet population is still being actively and profoundly changed by political action.

The situation in the industrial sector is somewhat different. Here, too, the question of reforms was linked with serious political conflict, as was openly admitted after the

July, 1957, plenum, particularly at the December, 1958, plenum. However, neither the policy issues nor the measures actually taken involved, to the same extent at least, the problem of ideology versus efficiency or further politically directed changes in the way of life of the urban proletariat. Instead, the issues centered on the problem of planning and managerial organization and on their relationship to effective Party control. The solution adopted—namely, the system of *sovnarkhozy*—is familiar. In many individual cases, it certainly involved important changes in the accustomed mode of life. A bureaucrat's family, moving from Moscow to Irkutsk, may perhaps have reflected, in the course of the long train ride on the Siberian railway, on the relationship of political decisions to their way of life. However, a more significant consequence of the reforms was that increased efficiency of operations (achieved, it is claimed, by de-bureaucratization and decentralization) was linked to a consolidation of direct Party control over the industrial sector. The Party remained as the only vertical and horizontal source of social and political cohesion in Soviet society, and on all levels of the industrial organization direct Party participation in the decision-making process was assured. A Party secretary, Brezhnev, personally supervised the reorganization, and it is the responsibility of republican and regional Party secretaries to make certain that increasingly frequent manifestations of *mestnich-estvo** are subordinated to over-all national objectives as set by the top leadership.

The relationship with the intelligentsia is more difficult

* Overemphasis of local considerations; literally "localism."

to define. As a group, it enjoys special privileges, and many of its members have direct access to the leadership circles. As a result, it can make its influence felt perhaps even to a disproportionate degree. Furthermore, the experience of recent years, particularly of 1956–57, shows that there is restlessness and even dissatisfaction among a great many Soviet students, writers, and poets. The intellectuals in particular have always been the carriers and the disseminators of new ideas, either indigenously conceived or adopted from abroad. However, in order to do this on a politically significant scale, they must live in an environment that is at least passively receptive.* By and large, one is forced to conclude that those intellectuals who are inclined to question the existing taboos have not found the Soviet Union to be either actively or passively receptive. With the possible exception of the small artistic communities in Moscow and Leningrad (within which a novel like *The Trial Begins* could be created), the regime has so far been able to prevent the development of anything like the intellectuals' clubs of Warsaw or Budapest, and it has successfully maintained its general monopoly on all means of communication.† Furthermore, the first generation of urban dwellers of the U.S.S.R. is

* An actively receptive community is one that, because of a continuous and often competitive interplay of groups, is necessarily responsive to the impact of new ideas; New York and Paris are good metropolitan examples. By a passively receptive society is meant one that does not set up purposeful impediments to the inflow of new ideas.

† The political experience of intellectual unrest in Hungary and Poland on the one hand and in China on the other might be relevant here. In the former, it was closely associated with demoralization in the Party and led to an eruption. In the latter, it did not penetrate the Party, and the regime was able to suppress it quickly.

86

not the epitome of intellectual tolerance, and the regime successfully appealed in 1956–57 to the anti-intellectual bias of the masses when it needed to intimidate the intellectuals. Beyond that, Party control over *nomenklatura,* publications, rewards, and awards has served to contain occasional individual violations of the politically determined limits.

As far as the intelligentsia as a whole is concerned, the prevalent tendency seems to be toward professionalization and a compartmentalization of interests. An engineer or doctor is given relatively unlimited opportunities for advancement on the basis of merit, provided he meets certain minimum political criteria. Party membership, but not necessarily an active one, is often a necessary condition for a position of major professional responsibility, but as long as formal behavior lives up to the political norm and the expected degree of ideological know-how is demonstrated, the regime does not impose heavy and objectionable demands. To the extent that such a relationship can be appraised, it would appear that there is at present mutual satisfaction with this arrangement.

A relatively new phenomenon in the regime-society relationship is the emphasis placed on the public organizations that are to absorb certain state functions in view of the latter's gradual "withering away" in the course of the transition to Communism. Although as yet little of major significance has passed into the hands of such organizations, there appear to be three major objectives for stressing them: to revitalize public zeal and stimulate interest in the transition to Communism; to develop through popular participation a form of citizens' control over bureaucratic operations; and to enforce societal conformity over wayward behavior. All three suggest that the regime is increasingly confident that it enjoys some measure of popular support and that, if it is to increase the scope of social initiative, it will do so at the bottom, where ideological intolerance and social conformity are probably the strongest. At the same time, the regime will be in a better position to appraise popular moods (recent Soviet interest in public opinion polls is revealing) and will therefore be better informed for the difficult task of both running and changing a large and an at least semi-modern society.

The Soviet political system thus involves one-party dictatorship, with its outstanding characteristic being the active indoctrination of the society in the Party's ideology and the shaping of all social relations according to that ideology. For this reason, words such as "liberalization" and "democratization" are somewhat misleading. They are, after all, terms used to describe a process of political, social, and economic change that took place in Western societies under entirely different conditions— essentially organically, often spontaneously, and usually pluralistically.

The process of change within a totalitarian society has to be seen in a perspective that considers the means used to modernize the existing society, since the means that have been used tend to affect the longer-range patterns of development. In the Soviet Union, a primitive society was industrialized and relatively modernized through total social mobilization effected by violent, terroristic means wielded by a highly disciplined and motivated political elite. The very nature of this process is inimical to the emergence of a separate managerial class (not to speak of the even more amorphous concept of "a middle class"), which would be a first step in the direction of a limitation of the Party's power. Furthermore, a society developed under total political direction has a need for continued political integration on a national scale, since the liquidation of both the private economic sector and all informal leadership groups creates a vacuum that must be filled. In such conditions, the Party—its discipline, morale, and zeal—remains the determinant of change.

To the extent that this ruling party desires to maintain continued mobilization of society, it may even be argued that a modern industrial society provides that party with more sophisticated tools of social control and permits it to maintain that mobilization. Indeed, one may further state that the more modern and developed the society, the more malleable it is. Terror and violence may be necessary to change a primitive, uneducated, and traditional society rapidly. Persuasion, indoctrination, and social control can work more effectively in relatively developed societies. Czechoslovakia, in contrast with Poland and Hungary, would be a good example. Close students of Soviet scientific development have already noted that there are ominous indications that even more sophisticated techniques of psychological and social manipulation are in the offing. Gide's observation has not yet reached its stage of obsolescence.

The present Soviet discussions of what the future Communist society will be like offers us a revealing picture that should not be ignored (if past experience is a guide). Professor S. G. Strumilin, the Soviet expert on the transition to Communism, assures us (in *Novy Mir*, July, 1960) that: "Any Soviet citizen who enters the world will automatically be enrolled in a nursery, transferring to an established children's home and then, according to age, placed in a boarding school. His transition to productive life or to further special studies will also be arranged." The Professor adds: "Too much parental love often has catastrophic results for the children, hindering the development of the children. We are absolutely opposed to the old tradition that regarded children as the 'property' of the parents." People will live together in large communes, eating together; their children will play only with communal toys: "personal property, such as toys, ice skates, bicycles, will not be recognized in the commune. All gifts received by the children will go into the 'common pot' and be there for everybody." Everyone will be dedicated, behavior will be enforced by the sheer weight of communal orthodoxy, which necessarily excludes individual self-assertion. Dachas and automobiles will no longer be the objects to be desired by an individual, and public servants will toil with a dedication deeply rooted in the Communist ideology.

It may be comforting to dismiss all this as sheer fantasy, but to the extent that the stability of the present regime depends on the continuous, even if gradual, implementation of the ideology into practice, such descriptions are a good guide to an understanding of the goals of a party ruling an increasingly mature and voluntarist totalitarian system. They suggest that the CPSU has not yet resigned itself to playing merely the role of a Soviet chamber of commerce. Indeed, every indication points to the conclusion that Soviet society is again on the eve of momentous changes whose process of execution is not likely to weaken the Party's power.

THE IMPACT OF EXTERNAL AFFAIRS

It is at this point that a consideration of the interaction between external and domestic affairs becomes particularly relevant. Many past cases of such interaction can be cited. For example: in 1926, the China policy and the domestic struggle for power; in 1936, the mounting war threat and the domestic purges; in 1946, Stalin's conviction of a basic hostility toward the West and the domestic decision again to give the Soviet society a taste of War Communism (radical political and economic policies); in 1956, the general situation in the Soviet bloc and the anti-Stalin campaign. In some ways, however, it could be argued that the relationship is becoming increasingly significant. In the past, Stalin's regime was basically inward-oriented and isolationist, but today the U.S.S.R. is deeply involved both in world politics and in the complex process of running an international Communist empire. On the one hand, this involvement strengthens the role of the ruling party since it seems to demonstrate its claim that it is leading the U.S.S.R. to greatness. At the same time, what happens abroad is now much more relevant to domestic Soviet politics. That is why Kennan's thesis that political containment could lead to a domestic mellowing or breakdown of the Soviet system was at least premature. It assumed a relationship between external affairs and domestic politics that did not exist in Stalin's time. It exists today, however, but in a much different way.

The emerging diversity within the Communist orbit, and the necessary Soviet adjustment to it, means that increasingly the hitherto uniform ideology tends to be expressed and emphasized in different ways. Furthermore, the recent admonitions that war is not inevitable and that a nuclear war would be a universal catastrophe necessarily challenge the conception of an immutable and objective historical process and make a purely subjective and perhaps even an irrational factor—someone's decision to start a war—a deciding issue in the historical process. Both tend to threaten the domestic ideological uniformity of the system either by its penetration by competitive ideas or by the relativization of the ideology in view of its varied interpretations in different Communist states. In either case, there is a danger of the gradual domestic erosion of the absolutist ideological commitment. The officially admitted fear of war, stemming in large part from the objective factor of the destructiveness of nuclear weapons, is closely related to the increasing domestic social desire to enjoy the "good life." In the history of the regime, there has always been a tension between a genuine desire of the regime to improve the lot of society and its fear of doing it too quickly, which would be politically and economically disastrous. With the "victory" of socialism in the U.S.S.R. finally assured, the regime finds itself increasingly able to respond to social pressures for a better life. However, it would be politically very dangerous if both at home and abroad a mood of general social relaxation were to prevail. The sense of dynamism must be preserved. The continuous need for the Party's dictatorship and, therefore, for its ideology-action must be demonstrated.

The present response is a compromise both at home and abroad. It is no longer a matter of violent large-scale social revolution at home, but "the extensive transition to Communism," with its hopes for the good life, does mean that the march forward is being continued. And abroad, it is not a matter of outright violent hostility toward the enemy, since that carries with it the danger of total destruction. Rather, it is again a compromise: peaceful coexistence, but an ideological offensive, translated into the encouragement of radical nationalist revolutions made possible by the peaceful and paralyzing mutual nuclear blackmail of the U.S.S.R. and the United States. Peace with victories will serve to strengthen the Party's claim that history is still unfolding, that it must continue its mission, that there is no fraternization with the enemy —but all without war.

Nevertheless, relativization of the ideology is implicit in such adjustments and carries with it dangerous internal implications. The domestic power of the totalitarian system depends on the commitment to an absolutist ideology. But an ideology that is right only in some places, for some people, and at some times cannot provide that conviction. If the ideology becomes a relative one, it will be deprived of the fanaticism and dogmatic conviction that have provided the momentum for sacrifice, forceful action, and internal unity. History teaches that relativization is the first stage in the erosion of the militancy of any system of dogmatic ideas.

The appearance of diversity within international Communism, a diversity that the Soviet regime initially desired to limit only to the institutional side while retaining ideological uniformity, carries with it the danger that varying ideological emphases may result either in splits or in the development of a silent agreement to disagree. This is a novel situation for a movement that has matured in the belief that ideological unity and organizational unity are absolutely essential. It also suggests that if such gradual erosion is to take place and if, in its wake, the Soviet political system is to change fundamentally, the change will have to come primarily from the outside and not from the inside. Originating in bona fide Communist states and formulated within the framework of the common ideology, alternative and more tolerant notions might gradually penetrate the ruling elite and only afterward affect the society as a whole.* However, if one considers what and how long it took for foreign ideas to penetrate the far less controlled Czarist Russia, to merge with domestic trends, and eventually to emerge supreme, and if one weighs all this against the internal power of the Communist regime, one may well be justified in cautioning that this erosion should be awaited with a great deal of patience.

---

* There might be an analogy here to the political history of religiously oriented societies. It was only after the Protestant and Catholic states learned to coexist with one another and, for that matter, with non-Christian states that Protestants, Catholics, and others learned to live with one another *within* given states. An "interfaith council" in the United States is thus not only an example of conscious toleration but also of a decline in absolutist commitment.

4. Transformation or Degeneration

The Soviet Union will soon celebrate its fiftieth anniversary. In this turbulent and rapidly changing world, for any political system to survive half a century is an accomplishment in its own right and obvious testimony to its durability. There are not many major political structures in the world today that can boast of such longevity. The approaching anniversary, however, provides an appropriate moment for a critical review of the changes that have taken place in the Soviet system, particularly in regard to such critical matters as the character of its top leadership, the methods by which its leaders acquire power, and the relationship of the Communist Party to society. Furthermore, the time is ripe to inquire into the implications of these changes, especially in regard to the stability and vitality of the system.

THE LEADERS

Today, Soviet spokesmen would have us believe that the quality of the top Communist leadership in the U.S.S.R. has been abysmal. Of the forty-five years since Lenin, according to official Soviet history, power was exercised for approximately five years by leaders subsequently unmasked as traitors (although later the charge of treason was retroactively reduced to that of deviation); for almost twenty years, it was wielded by a paranoiac mass-murderer, who irrationally slew his best comrades and ignorantly guided Soviet war strategy by pointing his finger at a globe; and, most recently, it was held for almost ten years, by a "harebrained" schemer given to tantrums and wild organizational experimentation. On the basis of that record, the present leadership claims to represent a remarkable departure from a historical pattern of singular depravity.

While Soviet criticism of former Party leaders is now abundant, little intellectual effort is expended on analyzing the implications of the changes in leadership. Yet that, clearly, is the important question in so far as the political system is concerned. Lenin was a rare type of political leader, fusing in his person several functions of key importance to the working of a political system: He acted as the chief ideologist of the system, the principal organizer of the Party (indeed, the founder of the movement), and the top administrator of the state. It may be added that such personal fusion is typical of early revolutionary leaderships, and today it is exemplified by Mao Tse-tung. To his followers, Lenin was clearly a charismatic leader, and his power (like Hitler's or Mao Tse-tung's) depended less on institutions than on the force of his personality and intellect. Even after the Revolution, it was Lenin's personal authority that gave him enormous power, while the progressive institutionalization of his rule (the Cheka, the appearance of the *apparat*, etc.) reflected more the transformation of a revolutionary party into a ruling one than any significant change in the character of his leadership.

Lenin's biographers[1] agree that he was a man characterized by total political commitment, by self-righteous conviction, by tenacious determination, and by an outstanding ability to formulate intellectually appealing principles of political action as well as popular slogans suitable for mass consumption. He was a typically revolutionary figure, a man whose genius can be consummated only at that critical juncture in history when the new breaks off—and not just evolves—from the old. Had he lived a generation earlier, he probably would have died in a Siberian *taiga;* a generation later, he probably would have been shot by Stalin.

Under Stalin, the fusion of leadership functions was continued, but this was due less to his personal qualities as such than to the fact that, with the passage of time and the growing toll of victims, his power became nearly total and was gradually translated also into personal authority. Only a mediocre ideologist—and certainly inferior in that respect to his chief rivals for power—Stalin became institutionally the ideologue of the system. A dull speaker, he eventually acquired the "routinized charisma"[2] which, after Lenin's death, became invested in the Communist Party as a whole (much as the Pope at one time acquired the infallibility that for a long time had rested in the collective church). But his power was increasingly institutionalized bureaucratically, with decision-making centralized at the apex within his own Secretariat, and its exercise involved a subtle balancing of the principal institutions of the political system: the secret police, the Party, the state, and the army (roughly in that order of importance). Even

97

the ostensibly principal organ of power, the Politburo, was split into minor groups, "the sextets," the "quartets," etc., with Stalin personally deciding who should participate in which subgroup and personally providing (and monopolizing) the function of integration.

If historical parallels for Lenin are to be found among the revolutionary tribunes, for Stalin they are to be sought among the Oriental despots.[3] Thriving on intrigue, shielded in mystery, and isolated from society, his immense power reflected the immense tasks he succeeded in imposing on his followers and subjects. Capitalizing on the revolutionary momentum and the ideological impetus inherited from Leninism and wedding it to a systematic institutionalization of bureaucratic rule, Stalin could set in motion a social and political revolution that weakened all existing institutions save his own Secretariat and his chief executive arm, the secret police. His power grew in proportion to the degree to which the major established institutions declined in vitality and homogeneity.[4]

The war, however, as well as the postwar reconstruction, produced a paradox. While Stalin's personal prestige and authority were further enhanced, his institutional supremacy relatively declined. The military establishment naturally grew in importance; the enormous effort to transfer, reinstall, and later reconstruct the industrial economy invigorated the state machinery; the Party *apparat* began to perform again the key functions of social mobilization and political integration. But the aging tyrant was neither unaware of this development nor apparently resigned to it. The Byzantine intrigues resulting in the liquidation of the Leningrad leadership and Voznesensky, and the "doctors' plot," with its ominous implications for some top Party, military, and police chiefs, clearly augured an effort to weaken any institutional limits on Stalin's personal supremacy.

Khrushchev came to power ostensibly to save Stalinism, a task he defined as safeguarding the traditional priority of heavy industry and restoring the primacy of the Party. In fact, he presided over the dismantling of Stalinism. He rode to power by restoring the predominant position of the Party *apparat*. But the complexities of governing (as contrasted with the priorities of the power struggle) caused him to dilute the Party's position. While initially he succeeded in diminishing the political role of the secret police and in weakening the state machinery, the military establishment grew in importance with the continuing tensions of the cold war.[5] By the time Khrushchev was removed, the economic priorities had become blurred because of pressures in the agriculture and consumer sectors, while his own reorganization of the Party into two separate industrial and rural hierarchies in November, 1962, went far toward undermining the Party's homogeneity of outlook, apart from splitting it institutionally. Consequently, the state bureaucracy recouped, almost by default, some of its integrative and administrative functions. Khrushchev thus, perhaps inadvertently, restored much of the institutional balance that had existed under Stalin, but without ever acquiring the full powers of the balancer.

Khrushchev lacked the authority of Lenin to generate personal power or the power of Stalin to create personal authority, and the Soviet leadership under him became increasingly differentiated. The top leader was no longer the top ideologist, in spite of occasional efforts to present Khrushchev's elaborations as "a creative contribution to Marxism-Leninism." The ruling body now contained at least one professional specialist in ideological matters, and it was no secret that the presence of the professional ideologue was required because someone had to give professional ideological advice to the Party's top leader. Similarly, technical-administrative specialization differentiated some top leaders from others. Increasingly, Khrushchev's function—and presumably the primary source of his still considerable power—was that of providing political integration and impetus for new domestic or foreign initiatives in a political system otherwise too complex to be directed and administered by one man.

The differentiation of functions also made it more difficult for the top leader to inherit even the "routinized charisma" that Stalin had eventually transferred to himself from the Party as a whole. Acquiring charisma was more difficult for a leader who (even apart from a personal style and vulgar appearance that did not lend themselves to "image building") had neither the great "theoretical" flare valued by a movement that still prided itself on being the embodiment of a Messianic ideology nor the technical expertise highly regarded in a state which equated technological advance with human progress. Moreover, occupying the posts of First Secretary and Chairman of the Council of Ministers was not enough to develop a charismatic appeal, since neither post has been sufficiently institutionalized to endow its occupant with the special prestige and aura that, for example, the President of the United States automatically gains on assuming office.

Trying to cope with this lack of charismatic appeal, Khrushchev replaced Stalin's former colleagues. In the process, he gradually came to rely on a younger generation of bureaucratic leaders to whom orderliness of procedure was instinctively preferable to crash campaigns. Administratively, however, Khrushchev was a true product of the Stalinist school, with its marked proclivity for just such campaigns at the cost of all other considerations. In striving to develop his own style of leadership, Khrushchev tried to emulate Lenin in stimulating new fervor and Stalin in mobilizing energies, but without the personal and institutional assets that each had commanded. By the time he was removed, Khrushchev had become an anachronism in the new political context he himself had helped to create.

Brezhnev and Kosygin mark the coming to power of a new generation of leaders, irrespective of whether they will for long retain their present positions.[6] Lenin's, Stalin's, and Khrushchev's formative experience was the unsettled period of conspiratorial activity, revolution, and (in Khrushchev's case) civil war and the early phase of Communism. The new leaders, beneficiaries of the Revolution but no longer revolutionaries themselves, have matured in an established political setting in which the truly large issues of policy and leadership have been decided. Aspiring young bureaucrats, initially promoted during the purges, they could observe but not suffer from the debilitating consequences of political extremism and unpredictable personal rule. To this new generation of clerks, bureaucratic stability—indeed, bureaucratic dictatorship—must seem to be the only solid foundation for effective government.

Differentiation of functions to these bureaucrats is a norm, while personal charisma is ground for suspicion. The new Soviet leadership, therefore, is both bureaucratic in style and essentially impersonal in form. The curious emphasis on *kollektivnost' rukovodstva* (collectivity of leadership) instead of the traditional *kollektivnoe rukovodstvo* (collective leadership)—a change in formulation used immediately after Khrushchev's fall—suggests a deliberate effort to achieve not only a personal but also an institutional collective leadership, designed to prevent any one leader from using a particular institution as a vehicle for obtaining political supremacy.

The question arises, however, whether this kind of leadership can prove effective in guiding the destiny of a major state. The Soviet system is now led by a bureaucratic leadership from the very top to the bottom. In that respect, it is unique. Even political systems with highly developed and skillful professional political bureaucracies, such as the British, the French, or that of the Catholic Church, have reserved some top policy-making and hence power-wielding positions for non-bureaucratic professional politicians, presumably on the assumption that a free-wheeling, generalizing, and competitive political experience is of decisive importance in shaping effective national leadership.

To be sure, some top Soviet leaders do acquire such experience, even in the course of rising up the bureaucratic Party ladder, especially when assigned to provincial or republican executive responsibilities. There they acquire the skills of initiative, direction, and integration, as well as accommodation, compromise, and delegation of authority, which are the basic prerequisites for executive management of any complex organization.

Nonetheless, even when occupying territorial positions of responsibility, the *apparatchiki* are still part of an extremely centralized and rigidly hierarchical bureaucratic organization, increasingly set in its ways, politically corrupted by years of unchallenged power, and made even more confined in its outlook than is normally the case with a ruling body by its lingering and increasingly ritualized doctrinaire tradition. It is relevant to note here (from observations made in Soviet universities) that the young men who become active in the Komsomol organization and are presumably embarking on a professional political career are generally the dull conformists. Clearly, in a highly bureaucratized political setting, conformity, caution, and the currying of favor with superiors count for more in advancing a political career than personal courage and individual initiative.[7]

Such a condition poses a long-range danger to the vitality of any political system. Social evolution, it has been noted, depends not only on the availability of creative individuals, but on the existence of clusters of creators who collectively promote social innovation. "The ability of any gifted individual to exert leverage within a society . . . is partly a function of the exact composition of the group of those on whom he depends for day-to-day interaction and for the execution of his plans."[8] The revolutionary milieu of the 1920's and even the fanatical Stalinist commitment of the 1930's fostered such clusters of intellectual and political talent. It is doubtful that the CPSU schools and the

Central Committee personnel department encourage, in Margaret Mead's terms, the growth of clusters of creativity, and that is why the transition from Lenin to Stalin to Khrushchev to Brezhnev probably cannot be charted by an ascending line.

This has serious implications for the Soviet system as a whole. It is doubtful that any organization can long remain vital if it is so structured that in its personnel policy it becomes, almost unknowingly, inimical to talent and hostile to political innovation. Decay is bound to set in, while the stability of the political system may be endangered if other social institutions succeed in attracting the society's talent and begin to chafe under the restraints imposed by the ruling but increasingly mediocre *apparatchiki.*

The Struggle for Power

The struggle for power in the Soviet political system has certainly become less violent. The question is, however: Has it become less debilitating for the political system? Has it become a more regularized process, capable of infusing the leadership with fresh blood? A closer look at the changes in the character of the competition for power may guide us to the answer.

Both Stalin and Khrushchev rode to power by skillfully manipulating issues as well as by taking full advantage of the organizational opportunities arising from their tenure of the post of Party First Secretary. It must be stressed that the manipulation of issues was at least as important to their success as the organizational factor, which generally tends to receive priority in Western historical treatments. In

Stalin's time, the issues facing the Party were, indeed, on a grand scale: world revolution versus socialism in one country; domestic evolution versus social revolution; a factionalized versus a monolithic Party. Stalin succeeded because he instinctively perceived that the new *apparatchiki* were not prepared to sacrifice themselves in futile efforts to promote foreign revolutions but, being for the most part genuinely committed to revolutionary ideals, were becoming eager to get on with the job of creating a socialist society. (Moreover, had the NEP endured another ten years, would the Soviet Union be a Communist dictatorship today?)

Stalin's choice of socialism in one country was a brilliant solution. It captivated, at least in part, the revolutionaries; and it satisfied, at least partially, the accommodators. It split the opposition, polarized it, and prepared the ground for the eventual liquidation of each segment with the other's support. The violence, the terror, and finally the Great Purges of 1936–38 followed logically. Imbued with the Leninist tradition of intolerance for dissent, engaged in a vast undertaking of social revolution that taxed both the resources and the nerves of Party members, guided by an unscrupulous and paranoiac but also reassuringly calm leader, governing a backward country surrounded by neighbors that were generally hostile to the Soviet experiment, and increasingly deriving its own membership strength from first-generation proletarians with all their susceptibility to simple explanations and dogmatic truths, the ruling Party easily plunged down the path of increasing brutality. The leader both rode the crest of that violence and controlled it. The terror never degenerated into simple anarchy, and Stalin's power grew immeasurably because he effectively practiced the art of leadership according to his own definition:

> The art of leadership is a serious matter. One must not lag behind the movement, because to do so is to become isolated from the masses. But neither must one rush ahead, for to rush ahead is to lose contact with the masses. He who wants to lead a movement and at the same time keep in touch with the vast masses must wage a fight on two fronts—against those who lag behind and those who run ahead.[9]

Khrushchev, too, succeeded in becoming the top leader because he perceived the elite's predominant interests. Restoration of the primary position of the Party, decapitation of the secret police, reduction of the privileges of the state bureaucrats while maintaining the traditional emphasis on heavy industrial development (which pleased both the industrial elite and the military establishment)—these were the issues which Khrushchev successfully utilized in the mid-1950's to mobilize the support of officials and accomplish the gradual isolation and eventual defeat of Malenkov. But the analogy ends right there. The social and even the political system in which Khrushchev came to rule was relatively settled. Indeed, in some respects it was stagnating, and Khrushchev's key problem, once he reached the political apex (but before he had had time to consolidate his position there), was how to get the country moving again. The effort to infuse new social and political dynamism into Soviet society, even while consolidating his power, led him to a public repudiation of Stalinism which

certainly shocked some officials; to sweeping economic reforms which disgruntled many administrators; to a dramatic reorganization of the Party, which appalled the
apparatchiki; and even to an attempt to circumvent the
policy-making authority of the Party Presidium by means
of direct appeals to interested groups, which must have
both outraged and frightened his colleagues. The elimination of violence as the decisive instrumentality of political
competition—a move that was perhaps prompted by the
greater institutional maturity of Soviet society, and which
was in any case made inevitable by the downgrading of the
secret police and the public disavowals of Stalinism—
meant that Khrushchev, unlike Stalin, could not achieve
both social dynamism and the stability of his power. Stalin
magnified his power as he strove to change society; to
change society, Khrushchev had to risk his power.

The range of domestic disagreement involved in the
post-Stalin struggles has also narrowed with the maturing
of social commitments made earlier. For the moment, the
era of grand alternatives is over in Soviet society. Even
though any struggle tends to exaggerate differences, the
issues that divided Khrushchev from his opponents, though
of great import, appear pedestrian in comparison with
those over which Stalin and his enemies crossed swords. In
Khrushchev's case, they pertained primarily to policy alternatives; in the case of Stalin, they involved basic conceptions of historical development. Compare the post-Stalin
debates about the allocation of resources among different
branches of the economy, for example, with the debates of
the 1920's about the character and pace of Soviet industrialization; or Khrushchev's homilies on the merits of

corn—and even his undeniably bold and controversial virgin-lands campaign—with the dilemma of whether to collectivize 100 million reticent peasants, and if so, at what pace and with what intensity in terms of resort to violence.

It is only in the realm of foreign affairs that one can perhaps argue that grand dilemmas still impose themselves on the Soviet political scene. The nuclear-war-or-peace debate of the 1950's and early 1960's is comparable in many respects to the earlier conflict over "permanent revolution" or "socialism in one country." Molotov's removal and Kozlov's political demise were to a large extent related to disagreements concerning foreign affairs; nonetheless, in spite of such occasional rumblings, it would appear that on the peace-or-war issue there is today more of a consensus among the Soviet elite than there was on the issue of permanent revolution in the 1920's. Although a wide spectrum of opinion does indeed exist in the international Communist movement on the crucial questions of war and peace, this situation, as far as one can judge, obtains to a considerably lesser degree in the U.S.S.R. itself. Bukharin versus Trotsky can be compared to Togliatti versus Mao Tse-tung, but hardly to Khrushchev versus Kozlov.

The narrowing of the range of disagreement is reflected in the changed character of the cast. In the earlier part of this discussion, some comparative comments were made about Stalin, Khrushchev, and Brezhnev. It is even more revealing, however, to examine their principal rivals. Take the men who opposed Stalin: Trotsky, Zinoviev, and Bukharin. What a range of political, historical, economic, and intellectual creativity, what talent, what a diversity of personal characteristics and backgrounds! Compare this diversity with the strikingly uniform personal training, narrowness of perspective, and poverty of intellect of Malenkov, Kozlov, and Suslov.* A regime of the clerks cannot help but clash over clerical issues.

The narrowing of the range of disagreement and the cooling of ideological passions mean also the waning of political violence. The struggle tends to become less a matter of life or death, and more one in which the price of defeat is simply retirement and some personal disgrace. In turn, with the routinization of conflict, the political system develops even a body of precedents for handling fallen leaders. By now there must be a regular procedure, probably even some office, for handling pensions and apartments for former Presidium members, as well as a developing social etiquette for dealing with them publicly and privately.†

More important is the apparent development in the Soviet system of something which might be described as a regularly available "counter-elite." After Khrushchev's fall, his successors moved quickly to restore to important positions a number of individuals whom Khrushchev had purged,‡ while some of his supporters were demoted and

---

* One could hardly expect a historian to work up any enthusiasm for undertaking to write, say, Malenkov's biography: *The Apparatchik Promoted, The Apparatchik Triumphant, The Apparatchik Pensioned!*

† Can Mikoyan, for example, invite Khrushchev to lunch? This is not a trivial question, for social mores and political style are interwoven. After all, Voroshilov, who had been publicly branded as a military idiot and a political sycophant, was subsequently invited to a Kremlin reception. Zhukov, against whom the Bonapartist charge still stands, appeared in full regalia at the twentieth anniversary celebration of the Soviet victory in World War II.

‡ F. D. Kulakov, apparently blamed by Khrushchev in 1960 for agricultural failings in the R.S.F.S.R., was appointed in 1965 to direct the Soviet

transferred. Already for a number of years now, it has been fairly common practice to appoint Party officials demoted from high office either to diplomatic posts abroad or to obscure, out-of-the-way assignments at home. The total effect of this has been to create a growing body of official "outs," who are biding their time on the sidelines and presumably hoping someday to become the "ins" again. Moreover, they may not only hope; if sufficiently numerous, young, and vigorous, they may gradually begin to resemble something of a political alternative to those in power, and eventually to think and even act as such. This could be the starting point of informal factional activity, of intrigues and conspiracies when things go badly for those in power, and of organized efforts to seduce some part of the ruling elite in order to stage an internal change of guard.* In addition, the availability of an increasingly secure "counter-elite" is likely to make it more difficult for a leader to consolidate his power. This, in turn, might tend to promote more frequent changes in the top leadership, with policy failures affecting the power of incumbents instead of affecting only retroactively the reputation of former leaders, as has hitherto been the case.

Union's new agricultural programs; V. V. Matskevich was restored as Minister of Agriculture and appointed Deputy Premier of the R.S.F.S.R. in charge of agriculture; Marshal M. V. Zakharov was reappointed as Chief-of-Staff of the Armed Forces; even L. G. Melnikov re-emerged from total obscurity as chairman of the industrial work safety committee of the R.S.F.S.R.

* Molotov's letter to the Central Committee on the eve of the Twenty-second CPSU Congress of October, 1961, which bluntly and directly charged Khrushchev's program with revisionism, was presumably designed to stir up the *apparatchiki* against the First Secretary. It may be a portent of things to come.

The cumulative effect of these developments has been wide-ranging. First of all, the reduced importance of both ideological issues and personalities and the increasing weight of institutional interests in the periodic struggles for power—a phenomenon which reflects the more structured quality of present-day Soviet life as compared with the situation under Stalin—tends to depersonalize political conflict and to make it a protracted bureaucratic struggle. Secondly, the curbing of violence makes it more likely that conflicts will be resolved by patched-up compromises, rather than by drastic institutional redistributions of power and the reappearance of personal tyranny. Finally, the increasingly bureaucratic character of the struggle for power tends to transform it into a contest among high-level clerks, and it is therefore not conducive to attracting creative and innovating talent into the top leadership.

Khrushchev's fall provides a good illustration of the points made above, as well as an important precedent for the future. For the first time in Soviet history, the First Secretary has been toppled from power by his associates. This was done not in order to replace him with an alternative personal leader or to pursue genuinely alternative goals, but in order to depersonalize the leadership and to pursue more effectively many of the previous policies. In a word, the objectives were impersonal leadership and higher bureaucratic efficiency. Khrushchev's removal, however, also means that personal intrigues and cabals can work, that subordinate members of the leadership—or possibly, someday, a group of ex-leaders—can effectively conspire against a principal leader, with the result that any future First Secretary is bound to feel far less secure than Khrushchev must have felt at the beginning of October, 1964.

The absence of an institutionalized top executive officer in the Soviet political system, in conjunction with the increased difficulties in the way of achieving personal dictatorship and the decreased personal cost of defeat in a political conflict, create a ready-made situation for group pressures and institutional clashes. In fact, although the range of disagreement may have narrowed, the scope of elite participation in power conflicts has already widened. Much of Khrushchev's exercise of power was preoccupied with mediating the demands of key institutions, such as the army, or with overcoming the opposition of others, such as the objections of the administrators to economic decentralization or of the heavy industrial managers to non-industrial priorities. These interests were heavily involved in the Khrushchev-Malenkov conflict and in the "anti-Party" episode of 1957.

At the present time, these pressures and clashes take place in an almost entirely amorphous context, without constitutional definition and established procedures. The somewhat greater role played by the Central Committee in recent years still does not suffice to give this process of bureaucratic conflict a stable institutional expression. As far as we know from existing evidence, the Central Committee still acted during the 1957 and 1964 crises primarily as a ratifying body, giving formal sanction to decisions already fought out in the Kremlin's corridors of power.[10] It did not act as either the arbiter or the supreme legislative body.

The competition for power, then, is changing from a death struggle among the few into a contest played by many more. But the decline of violence does not, as is often assumed, automatically benefit the Soviet political system; something more effective and stable has to take the place of violence. The "game" of politics that has replaced the former maffia-style struggles for power is no longer murderous, but it is still not a stable game played within an established arena, according to accepted rules, and involving more or less formal teams. It resembles more the anarchistic free-for-all of the playground and therefore could become, in some respects, even more debilitating to the system. Stalin encouraged institutional conflict below him so that he could wield his power with less restraint. Institutional conflict combined with mediocre and unstable personal leadership makes for ineffective and precarious power.

PARTY AND GROUP INTERESTS

In a stimulating study of political development and decay, Samuel Huntington has argued that stable political growth requires a balance between political "institutionalization" and political "participation," that merely increasing popular mobilization and participation in politics without achieving a corresponding degree of "institutionalization of political organization and procedures" results not in political development but in political decay.[11] Commenting in passing on the Soviet system, he therefore noted that "a strong party is in the Soviet public interest" because it provides a stable institutional framework.[12]

The Soviet political system has certainly achieved a high index of institutionalization. For almost five decades the ruling Party has maintained unquestioned supremacy over the society, imposing its ideology at will. Traditionally, the Communist system has combined its high institutionalization with high pseudo-participation of individuals.* But a difficulty could arise if division within the top leadership of the political system weakened political "institutionalization," while simultaneously stimulating genuine public participation by groups and institutions. Could this new condition be given an effective and stable institutional framework and, if so, with what implications for the "strong" Party?

Today, the Soviet political system is again oligarchic, but its socio-economic setting is now quite different. Soviet society is far more developed and stable, far less malleable and atomized. In the past, the key groups that had to be considered as potential political participants were relatively few. Today, in addition to the vastly more entrenched institutional interests, such as the police, the military, and the state bureaucracy, the youth could become a source of ferment, the consumers could become more restless, the collective farmers more recalcitrant, the scientists more outspoken, the non-Russian nationalities more demanding. Prolonged competition among the oligarchs would certainly accelerate the assertiveness of such groups.

* The massive campaigns launching "public discussions" that involve millions of people, the periodic "elections" that decide nothing, were designed to develop participation without threat to the institutionalized political organization and procedures. The official theory held that as Communist consciousness developed and new forms of social and public relations took root, political participation would become more meaningful and the public would come to govern itself.

By now some of these groups have a degree of institutional cohesion, and occasionally they act in concert on some issues.* They certainly can lobby and, in turn, be courted by ambitious and opportunistic oligarchs. Some groups, because of institutional cohesion, advantageous location, easy access to the top leadership, and ability to articulate their goals and interests, can be quite influential.† Taken together they represent a wide spectrum of opinion, and in the setting of oligarchical rule there is bound to be some correspondence between their respective stances and those of the top leaders. This spectrum is represented in simplified fashion by the following chart, which takes cumulative account of the principal divisions, both on external and on domestic issues, that have per-

* A schematic distribution of these groups is indicated by the following approximate figures: (A) amorphous social forces that in the main express passively broad social aspirations: workers and peasants, about 88 million; white collar and technical intelligentsia, about 21 million; (B) specific interest groups that promote their own particular interests: the literary and artistic community, about 75,000; higher-level scientists, about 150,000; physicians, about 380,000; (C) policy groups whose interests necessarily spill over into broad matters of national policy: industrial managers, about 200,000; state and collective farm chairmen, about 45,000; commanding military personnel, about 80,000; higher-level state bureaucrats, about 250,000. These groups are integrated by the professional *apparatchiki,* who number about 150–200,000. All of these groups in turn could be broken down into sub-units; e.g., the literary community, institutionally built around several journals, can be divided into hard-liners, centrists, progressives, etc. Similarly, the military. On some issues, there may be cross-interlocking of sub-groups, as well as more or less temporary coalitions of groups. For further discussion, see Z. Brzezinski and S. Huntington, *Political Power: USA-USSR* (New York: Viking Press, 1964), chap. 4.

† An obvious example is the military command, bureaucratically cohesive and with a specific *esprit de corps,* located in Moscow, necessarily in frequent contact with the top leaders, and possessing its own journals of opinion (where strategic and hence also—indirectly—budgetary, foreign, and other issues can be discussed).

plexed Soviet political life during the last decade or so.*
Obviously, the table is somewhat arbitrary and also highly
speculative. Individuals and groups cannot be categorized
so simply and some, clearly, could be shifted left or right
with equal cause, as indeed they often shift themselves.
Nonetheless, the chart illustrates the range of opinion that
exists in the Soviet system and suggests the kind of alliances, group competition, and political courtship that
probably prevail, cutting vertically through the Party organization.

Not just Western but also Communist (although not as
yet Soviet) political thinkers are coming to recognize more
and more openly the existence of group conflict even in a
Communist-dominated society. A Slovak jurist recently observed:

> The social interest in our society can be democratically
> formed only by the integration of group interests; in the
> process of this integration, the interest groups protect
> their own economic and other social interests; this is in no
> way altered by the fact that everything appears on the
> surface as a unity of interests.[13]

---

* The categories "systemic left," etc., are adapted from R. R. Levine, *The
Arms Debate* (Cambridge, Mass.: Harvard University Press, 1963), which
contains a suggestive chart of American opinion on international issues. By
"systemic left" is meant here a radical reformist outlook, challenging the
predominant values of the existing system; by "systemic right" is meant an
almost reactionary return to past values; the other three categories desig-
nate differences of degree within a dominant "mainstream."
In this chart (unlike Levine's), the center position serves as a dividing
line, and hence no one is listed directly under it. Malenkov is listed as
"systemic left" because his proposals represented, at the time, a drastic
departure from established positions. Molotov is labeled "systemic right"
because of his inclination to defend the essentials of the Stalinist system in
a setting which had changed profoundly since Stalin's death.

Policy Spectrum USSR

Systemic Left	Left		Centrist		Right		Systemic Right
		◄———	Marginalist	———►			
Malenkov	Khrushchev Podgorny		Kosygin Mikoyan	Brezhnev	Kozlov Suslov Voronov		Molotov Kaganovich
Consumer Goods Industry	Light Industry	Regional Apparat	Military Innovators	Shelepin / Central Apparat	Conventional Army	Agitprop	Heavy Industry
	Agronomists				Ministerial Bureaucrats		Secret Police
Scientists	Economic Reformers (Liberman)			Economic Computators (Nemchinov)			
Moscow-Leningrad Intellectuals							

The author went on to stress that the key political problem facing the Communist system is that of achieving integration of group interests.

Traditionally, this function of integration has been monopolized by the Party, resorting, since the discard of terror, to the means of *bureaucratic arbitration*. In the words of the author just cited, "the party as the leading and directing political force fulfills its functions by resolving intra-class and inter-class interests." In doing so, the Party generally has preferred to deal with each group bilaterally, thereby preventing the formation of coalitions and of informal group consensus. In this way the unity of political direction as well as the political supremacy of the ruling party have been maintained. The Party has always been very jealous of its "integrative" prerogative, and the intrustion on the political scene of any other group has been strongly resented. The Party's institutional primacy has thus depended on limiting the real participation of other groups.

If, for one reason or another, the Party were to weaken in the performance of this function, the only alternative to anarchy would be some *institutionalized process of mediation,* replacing the Party's bureaucratic arbitration. Since, as noted, group participation has become more widespread, while the Party's effectiveness in achieving integration has been lessened by the decline in the vigor of Soviet leadership and by the persistent divisions in the top echelon, the creation and eventual formal institutionalization of some such process of mediation is gaining in urgency. Otherwise participation could outrun institutionalization and result in a challenge to the Party's integrative function.

Khrushchev's practice of holding enlarged Central Committee plenums, with representatives of other groups present, seems to have been a step toward formalizing a more regular consultative procedure. (It also had the politically expedient effect of bypassing Khrushchev's opponents in the central leadership.) Such enlarged plenums provided a consultative forum, where policies could be debated, views articulated, and even some contradictory interests resolved. Although the device remained essentially non-institutionalized and only *ad hoc,* consultative and not legislative, still subject to domination by the Party *apparat,* it was nonetheless a response to the new quest for real participation which Soviet society has manifested and which the Soviet system badly needs. It was also a compromise solution, attempting to wed the Party's primacy to a procedure allowing group articulation.

However, the problem has become much more complex and fundamental because of the organizational and ideological crisis in the Party over its relevance to the evolving Soviet system. For many years the Party's monopoly of power and hence its active intervention in all spheres of Soviet life could indeed be said to be "in the Soviet public interest." The Party provided social mobilization, leadership, and a dominant outlook for a rapidly changing and developing society. But, in the main, that society has now taken shape. It is no longer malleable, subject to simple mobilization, or susceptible to doctrinaire ideological manipulation.

As a result, Soviet history in the last few years has been dominated by the spectacle of a party in search of a role. What is to be the function of an ideocratic party in a relatively complex and industrialized society, in which the structure of social relationships generally reflects the Party's ideological preferences? To be sure, like any large sociopolitical system, the Soviet system needs an integrative organ. But the question is, What is the most socially desirable way of achieving such integration? Is a "strong" party one that dominates and interferes in everything, and is this interference conducive to continued Soviet economic, political, and intellectual growth?

In 1962, Khrushchev tried to provide a solution. The division of the Party into two vertically parallel, functional organs was an attempt to make the Party directly relevant to the economy and to wed the Party's operations to production processes. It was a bold, dramatic, and radical innovation, reflecting a recognition of the need to adapt the Party's role to a new state of Soviet social development. But it was also a dangerous initiative; it carried within itself the potential of political disunity as well as the possibility that the Party would become so absorbed in economic affairs that it would lose its political and ideological identity. That it was rapidly repudiated by Khrushchev's successors is testimony to the repugnance that the reorganization must have stimulated among the professional Party bureaucrats.

His successors, having rejected Khrushchev's reorganization of the Party, have been attempting a compromise solution—in effect, a policy of "muddling through." On the one hand, they recognize that the Party can no longer direct the entire Soviet economy from the Kremlin and that major institutional reforms in the economic sphere, pointing toward more local autonomy and decision-making, are

indispensable.[14] (Similar tendencies are apparent elsewhere
—e.g., the stress on professional self-management in the
military establishment.) This constitutes a partial and implicit acknowledgment that in some respects a party of
total control is today incompatible with the Soviet public
interest.

On the other hand, since obviously inherent in the trend
toward decentralization is the danger that the Party will be
gradually transformed from a directing, ideologically oriented organization to a merely instrumental and pragmatic
body specializing in adjustment and compromise of social
group aspirations, the Party functionaries, out of a sense of
vested interest, have been attempting simultaneously to re-
vive the ideological vitality of the CPSU. Hence the renewed stress on ideology and ideological training; hence
the new importance attached to the work of the ideological
commissions; and hence the categorical reminders that
"Marxist education, Marxist-Leninist training, and the
ideological tempering of CPSU members and candidate
members is the primary concern of every party organization and committee."[15]

However, it is far from certain that economic decentralization and ideological "retempering" can be pushed forward hand in hand. The present leadership appears ob-
livious to the fact that established ideology remains vital
only when ideologically motivated power is applied to
achieve ideological goals. A gradual reduction in the directing role of the Party cannot be compensated for by an
increased emphasis on ideological semantics. Economic
decentralization inescapably reduces the scope of the polit-
ical-ideological and increases the realm of the pragmatic-

instrumental. It strengthens the trend, publicly bemoaned by Soviet ideologists, toward depolitization of the Soviet elite.[16] A massive indoctrination campaign directed at the elite cannot operate in a "de-ideologized" socio-economic context, and major efforts to promote such a campaign could, indeed, prompt the social isolation of the Party, making its dogmas even more irrelevant to the daily concerns of a Soviet scientist, factory director, or army general. That, in turn, would further reduce the ability of the Party to provide effective integration in Soviet society, while underscoring the Party *apparatchik*'s functional irrelevance to the workings of Soviet administration and technology.

If the Party rejects a return to ideological dogmas and renewed dogmatic indoctrination, it unavoidably faces the prospect of further internal change. It will gradually become a loose body, combining a vast variety of specialists, engineers, scientists, administrators, professional bureaucrats, agronomists, etc. Without a common dogma and without an active program, what will hold these people together? The Party at this stage will face the same dilemma that the fascist and falange parties faced and that currently confronts the Yugoslav and Polish Communists: In the absence of a large-scale domestic program of change, in the execution of which other groups and institutions become subordinated to the Party, the Party's domestic primacy declines and its ability to provide social-political integration is negated.

Moreover, the Soviet Party leaders would be wrong to assume complacently that the narrowed range of disagreement over domestic policy alternatives could not widen again. Persistent difficulties in agriculture could some day prompt a political aspirant to question the value of collectivization; or the dissatisfaction of some nationalities could impose a major strain on the Soviet constitutional structure; or foreign affairs could again become the source of bitter internal conflicts. The ability of the system to withstand the combined impact of such divisive issues and of greater group intrusion into politics would much depend on the adaptations that it makes in its organization of leadership and in its processes of decision-making. Unless alternative mechanisms of integration are created, a situation could arise in which some group other than the top *apparat*—a group that had continued to attract talent into its top ranks and had not been beset by bureaucratically debilitating conflict at the top—could step forth to seek power; invoking the Soviet public interest in the name of established Communist ideals, and offering itself (probably in coalition with some section of the Party leadership) as the only alternative to chaos, it would attempt to provide a new balance between institutionalization and participation.

THE THREAT OF DEGENERATION

The Soviet leaders have recognized the need for institutional reforms in the economic sector in order to revitalize the national economy. The fact is that institutional reforms are just as badly needed, and even more overdue, in the political sector. Indeed, the effort to maintain a doctrinaire dictatorship over an increasingly modern and industrial society has already contributed to a reopening of the gap that existed in pre-revolutionary Russia between the political system and the society, thereby posing the threat of the degeneration of the Soviet system.

A political system can be said to degenerate when there is a perceptible decline in the quality of the social talent that the political leadership attracts to itself in competition with other groups; when there is persistent division within the ruling elite, accompanied by a decline in its commitment to shared beliefs; when there is protracted instability in the top leadership; when there is a decline in the capacity of the ruling elite to define the purposes of the political system in relationship to society and to express them in effective institutional terms; when there is a fuzzing of institutional and hierarchical lines of command, resulting in the uncontrolled and unchanneled intrusion into politics of hitherto politically uninvolved groupings.[17] All of these indicators were discernible in the political systems of Czarist Russia, the French Third Republic, Chiang Kai-shek's China, and Rakosi's Hungary. Today, as already noted, at least several are apparent in the Soviet political system.

This is not to say, however, that the evolution of the Soviet system has inevitably turned into degeneration. Much still depends on how the ruling Soviet elite reacts. Policies of retrenchment, increasing dogmatism, and even violence, which, if now applied, would follow almost a decade of loosening up, could bring about a grave situation of tension, and the possibility of revolutionary outbreaks could not be discounted entirely. "Terror is indispensable to any dictatorship, but it cannot compensate for incompetent leaders and a defective organization of authority," observed a historian of the French revolution, writing of the Second Directory.[18] It is equally true of the Soviet political scene.

The threat of degeneration could be lessened through several adaptations designed to adjust the Soviet political system to the changes that have taken place in the now more mature society. First of all, the top policy-making organ of the Soviet system has been traditionally the exclusive preserve of the professional politician, and in many respects this has assured the Soviet political system of able and experienced leadership. However, since a professional bureaucracy is not prone to produce broad "generalizing" talents, and since the inherent differentiation of functions within it increases the likelihood of leaders with relatively much narrower specialization than hitherto was the case, the need for somewhat broader representation of social talent within the top political leadership, and not merely on secondary levels as hitherto, is becoming urgent. If several outstanding scientists, professional economists, industrial managers, and others were to be coopted by lateral entry into the ruling Presidium, the progressive transformation of the leadership into a regime of clerks could thereby be averted, and the alienation of other groups from the political system perhaps halted.

Secondly, the Soviet leaders would have to institutionalize a chief executive office and strive to endow it with legitimacy and stability. This would eventually require the creation of a formal and open process of leadership selection, as well, probably, as a time limit on the tenure of the chief executive position. The time limit, if honored, would depersonalize power, while an institutionalized process of selection geared to a specific date, and therefore also limited in time, would reduce the debilitating effects of unchecked and protracted conflict in the top echelons of power.

The CPSU continues to be an ideocratic party with a strong tradition of dogmatic intolerance and organizational discipline. Today less militant and more ·bureaucratic in outlook, it still requires a top catalyst, though no longer a personal tyrant, for effective operations. The example of the Papacy, or perhaps of Mexico, where a ruling party has created a reasonably effective system of presidential succession, offers a demonstration of how one-man rule can be combined with a formal office of the chief executive, endowed with legitimacy, tenure, and a formally established pattern of selection.

Any real institutionalization of power would have significant implications for the Party. If its Central Committee were to become, in effect, an electoral college, selecting a ruler whom no one could threaten during his tenure, the process of selection would have to be endowed with considerable respectability. It would have to be much more than a mere ratification of an *a priori* decision reached by some bureaucratic cabal. The process would require tolerance of the expression of diverse opinions in a spirit free of dogmatism, a certain amount of open competition among rivals for power, and perhaps even the formation of informal coalitions, at least temporary ones. In a word, it would mean a break with the Leninist past, with consequences that would unavoidably spill over from the Party into the entire system and society.

Thirdly, increased social participation in politics unavoidably creates the need for an institutionalized arena for the mediation of group interests, if tensions and conflicts, and eventually perhaps even anarchy, are to be avoided. The enlarged plenums of the Central Committee were a right beginning, but if the Committee is to mediate effectively among the variety of institutional and group interests that now exist in Soviet society, its membership will have to be made much more representative and the predominance of Party bureaucrats watered down. Alternatively, the Soviet leaders might consider following the Yugoslav course of creating a new institution for the explicit purpose of providing group representation and reconciling different interests. In either case, an effective organ of mediation could not be merely a front for the Party's continued bureaucratic arbitration of social interests, as that would simply perpetuate the present dilemmas.

Obviously, the implementation of such institutional reforms would eventually lead to a profound transformation of the Soviet system. But it is the absence of basic institutional development in the Soviet political system that has posed the danger of the system's degeneration. It is noteworthy that the Yugoslavs have been experimenting with political reforms, including new institutions, designed to meet precisely the problems and dangers discussed here. Indeed, in the long run, perhaps the ultimate contribution that the CPSU can make to Soviet political and social development is to adjust gracefully to the desirability, and perhaps even inevitability, of its own gradual withering away. In the meantime, the progressive transformation of the bureaucratic Communist dictatorship into a more pluralistic and institutionalized political system—even though still a system of one-party rule—seems essential if its degeneration is to be averted.

Part II

FOREIGN AFFAIRS

5. Communist Ideology and International Affairs

My purpose here is to discuss briefly the nature of the Soviet ideology, its impact on the Soviet approach to international affairs, and the prospects for ideological erosion.

THE NATURE OF THE IDEOLOGY

A reformist social doctrine ceases to be an intellectual abstraction and becomes an active social agent, or an ideology, when it is applied to concrete situations and becomes a guide to action. No doctrine, however elaborate or sophisticated, can provide answers and guidelines to fit all aspects of historical development. The shaping of events necessarily involves situations that are either unforeseen or dictate a logic of their own, even if initially fitting the theoretical assumptions. Doctrine is then "creatively" extended, new principles are extrapolated from the original set of assumptions, new generalizations crystallize, and, finally, the identity of the ideology emerges. Ideology is, in effect, the link between theory and action. (See the Introduction for a working definition.)

The persisting and important role of ideological assumptions in the thinking and actions of Soviet leaders (which, it is argued here, is essential to an understanding of their conduct) can be appreciated only if it is seen in a perspective that takes into consideration the various factors that go into the shaping of an ideology. The triumphant assertions that the Soviet leaders are abandoning their Marxism or Communism, voiced in the West with such monotonous regularity and persistent ignorance,* might possibly be dismissed more quickly if the usual image of an abstract and arid Marxist dogma were to give way to a better appreciation of the inextricably close linkage between the Soviet social environment and the Soviet ideology. It is precisely because the ideology is both a set of conscious assumptions and purposes and part of the total historical, social, and personal background of the Soviet leaders that it is so pervading and so important.

Without undertaking a comprehensive review of the development and substance of Soviet Communist ideology, it may be useful to recall in "capsule" form some of the

* To cite just a few such assertions: Stalin has returned to true Russian nationalism (he was not even a Russian); Soviet Russia is interested in Czarist territorial ambitions only; Stalin is a skillful practitioner of power, but is not interested in ideology; Malenkov is essentially a spokesman of pragmatic managers; Khrushchev is a level-headed experimenter; Mikoyan is really no different from our businessmen; the Soviet Union is accepting incentives and efficiency and is chucking "doctrinaire" Communism.

factors that have gone into molding it (or perverting it, as the purists would claim), thereby making it much more a part of the Russian reality and infusing it with genuine social vitality. Such variables as the general historical context, the role of personalities, the manner in which a foreign doctrine was understood and absorbed,[1] the emergence of the Party and its special organizational experience, and finally, the process of shaping a new society—all interacted dynamically to give the ideology its particular flavor and emphasis. No one of these factors alone can be said to have determined the character of the Soviet ideology; taken together, they do help us to understand how it emerged and developed. In summary form, the following assumptions and principles may be said to be part of the ideological framework within which the Soviet leaders evaluate and organize their perception of the outside world: Marxist doctrine is the basic source of their commitment to economic and dialectical determinism in history, and of their persistent conviction that the vehicle of history is the class struggle. (These themes were often reflected by Mr. Khrushchev in his little homilies on American television.[2]) Closely related to this "scientific" conception of history is the apocalyptic image of the future and the belief in the inevitable triumph for their form of social organization. The basic organizational principles that they apply to society are rooted in the conviction that most social evils are derived from private ownership; under certain circumstances, even an inefficient public or state ownership is to be preferred to private ownership. (Countless examples of this basic prejudice are available from past and present Soviet experience, as well as from Eastern Europe and China.)

The experience of the Bolshevik leaders in pre- and post-Revolutionary Russia resulted in the emergence of a series of further basic postulates, which together with the above categories constitute the Soviet ideological framework. Probably the most important of these is the Soviet conviction that the construction of socialism anywhere requires that power be wielded solely by the Communist Party. This belief, in part rooted in the Russian experience and in part reflecting the institutionalized vested interest of the ruling elite, has become a fundamental thesis of the Soviet leaders. Its impact on their vision of the world should not be underestimated, for it colors particularly their appreciation of changes occurring in the underdeveloped parts of the world. Similarly, the Leninist concepts of the seizure of power, with their emphasis on violent revolution, went far in the direction of establishing the supremacy of "conciousness" over "spontaneity" in historical processes, in turn consolidating the importance of the organized and conscious agent of history. The Soviet commitment to monolithic dictatorship and intensified class struggle as necessary attributes of the socialist construction thus again reflects the combination of doctrine and practice becoming ideology. Similarly, Lenin's discussion of the nature of imperialism reflected his pragmatic awareness that theory must always be related to a given reality; in the case of his historical era, it was to provide a meaningful insight into the inner dynamics of the underdeveloped and restless part of the world. The Marxist approach was the basis for the Leninist theory of imperialism and gave Lenin his point of departure as well as his basic analytical tools. However, the combination of Marxist doctrine, Russian revolutionary experience, social-economic backwardness, and the vested interest of the ruling Bolshevik Party resulted in the notion that social developments throughout the world operate on the basis of a sharply definable dichotomy—a dichotomy that is proof per se of an unbridgeable hostility between the emerging socialist state (later a system of socialist states) and the rest of the world.[3] A paranoiac image of the world conspiring against socialism easily followed.

All these conceptual and analytical factors combined serve to organize the Soviet vision of international affairs, to define goals, and to evaluate reality. These aspects should not be confused with the utopian elements of the ideology, which are necessary as part of a long-range vision and which perform essentially a rationalizing and legitimizing function. Confusing these two, or failing to distinguish between Marxist theory and the ideology, can lead to the simplistic conclusion that Soviet ideology is merely a cynical sham, consciously manipulated by the Soviet leaders. Similarly, it can result in the opposite and extreme conclusion that the Soviet approach to reality can be understood merely by consulting a Marxist handbook. I have already tried to show that the Soviet Communist ideology must be viewed as combining certain doctrinal assumptions with principles derived from the theory but closely reflecting the specific reality of those who subscribe to the ideology. It then becomes part of the reality and an autonomously existing factor, conditioning behavior through the selection of the various policy alternatives that may exist at any particular moment.

Its Role and Impact in International Affairs

How, then, does the Soviet Communist ideology affect the Soviet approach to international affairs?[4] Here, a distinction must be drawn between short-range and long-range prospects. The former are naturally much more often determined by the imperatives of the moment. For example, on the matter of choice of international friends, Soviet freedom of action was severely circumscribed in June, 1941, quite unlike the situation in the summer of 1939. In the latter case, the essentially ideologically determined conclusion that the objective of the West was to embroil the U.S.S.R. in a war with Germany dictated a policy of creating the conditions for conflict among the capitalist powers—that is, giving the Germans the freedom of action they considered necessary for the commencement of hostilities.* However, Soviet short-range moves are only in part a function of the situation as created by outside forces. They are also the consequence of certain long-range commitments made by the Soviet Union itself, and in that sense they are the product of the factors that shape the nature of that long-range com-

---

* A strong case could be made that Soviet behavior in the fall of 1938 had the same objective. Soviet aid to Czechoslovakia was conditioned on France moving first; if war had broken out, it is quite possible that the U.S.S.R. would then have used the Polish and Rumanian refusal to let Soviet troops through as an excuse to stay on the sidelines. In the meantime, the conflict between the capitalist powers would have been precipitated.

mitment. From that standpoint, they do feel the impact of ideology on Soviet external behavior and policy.*

The general Soviet approach to international affairs is strongly affected by the fundamental Soviet assumption that all material reality changes continuously through the clash of antagonistic contradictions. This conflict is said to be the basic law of social development until such time as socialism becomes a world system. As a result, the Soviet approach to international affairs is characterized by an intense preoccupation with change. This awareness of continuing change, and the conviction that the inner nature of that change is understood only by them, creates the basis for the faith of the Soviet leaders that they have unraveled the internal logic of history and that their policies are not merely an aspiration but a "scientific" calculation.

The preoccupation with change results in a continuing concern with the question: At what point do quantitative changes become qualitative? Communists have not always been successful in answering it, but there is at least a persistent awareness among them of the problem. The following sequence of questions is usually examined by the Communists when defining their policy: What is the nature of the present historical phase? What is the meaning of the relationships prevailing between economic forces and political institutions? What direction are they taking? Who is our major enemy? Is the enemy subjective

---

* For instance, the Marshall Plan may be seen as a consequence of certain ideologically influenced moves by the Soviet Union in 1946–47. However, it created immediate problems to which the Soviets had to respond and about which they had relatively little choice.

or objective? (For instance, Japan at one time was "objectively" hostile in its policy while "objectively" a progressive force since its industrialization was subverting the feudal order.) Who are our allies, subjectively and/or objectively? At what point will we part with our allies? What ought to be the pace of our efforts to stimulate further change?

At almost every important turning point in Communist policy, such questions have come to the forefront and have often resulted in heated debates and conflicts. But once understanding and evaluation have been achieved, the debate ceases and the policy is set. Understanding, evaluation, action—these are the stages of policy formulation. Such was the case, for example, with the concept of the people's democracy in Eastern Europe in the years 1945–47. Applied to specific instances, ideology thus defines first of all the ultimate purposes to which policy must aspire. In that sense, it has remained basically unchanged throughout Communist history. Second, to the Soviets it makes possible the understanding and evaluating of various historical phases that serve as stages on the way to the final goal. In policy-making, these phases are not so broad as the general Marxist historical stages (e.g., feudalism or capitalism). Rather, they identify the basic character of the specific phase within the present epoch— as, for instance, a revolutionary phase, a quiescent phase, a phase dominated by aggressive imperialism, or a phase in which the essential force changing history is "the liberation struggle of the colonial peoples." Once properly understood, the nature of a particular phase reveals who the main enemy is and what measures ought to be adopted.

Preoccupation with proper "phasing" reflects a distinctive kind of continuous and conscious effort to identify, dissect, and reconstruct reality. Ideology thus infuses Soviet foreign policy with a keen appreciation of the close relationship between international affairs and domestic developments. Rejecting the conception that international affairs involve principally the interplay of various nation-states attempting to promote their national objectives, the Soviets view the world as a continuing struggle among a variety of interests—domestic, social, economic, political, as well as national. The interplay between nation-states is merely one, and often only a formal, aspect of international affairs. In the Soviet view, for true understanding, one must seek to establish the correlation of the various forces that are dynamically coexisting within a given society and chart their likely pattern of behavior as well as their likely influence in the future. For instance, much of the recent Soviet foreign policy toward the United States appears to be based on the calculation that forces at work within American society are bent on achieving a modus vivendi with the U.S.S.R. and are willing to pay a relatively high price for it.[5]

The preoccupation with change, the willingness to adjust to the particular "historical" phase, and the quest to understand the inner dynamics of other societies has not, however, prevented the ideology from infusing Soviet foreign policy with a sense of continuity in purpose. This sense of continuity is derived from the militant conception of relations, in which reality is viewed as being a continuing conflict. In the Soviet view, occasional equilibriums result in international *détentes;* they do not, however, halt the fundamental process of change and therefore cannot create enduring conditions of stability. This means that any political arrangement is binding only until it ceases to interpret accurately that reality. For this reason, no long-range commitments to the status quo can be contemplated except in terms of communicating with those who are accustomed to thinking in terms of the present and who regard the changing reality as part of a vaguely definable, free-flowing, and gradual historical process. Given that, the over-all purpose of Soviet foreign policy is to remain associated with, and to stimulate, the evolution of these processes of change in the direction of ultimate consummation. The ideological commitment inherent in this attitude permits the Soviet leaders to remain persistent in their task, transcending reversals and failures that inevitably occur and despite shifts in their own policies.[6]

An absolute certitude of self-righteousness is also an inherent aspect of the ideological influence. Compromises and adjustments can never be ends in themselves and are only accepted by the Soviet leaders if they appear to be warranted in terms of their pursuit of higher ends. While in practice this may appear to differ little from the attitude of those nations that view such compromises in a favorable light and are prepared to consider them as ends of policy, the significant factor is the built-in element of transiency involved in any such compromise as far as the Soviet leaders are concerned. Indeed, Soviet policy-makers face a continuing dilemma of having always to differentiate between tactical expediency and concession of principle in order to be able to make such compromises.* This difficulty, however, is minimized by the Soviet conviction that, in the final analysis, Soviet foreign policy is always objectively correct since it is geared to history. From this it follows that, since war is a violation of the basic pattern of historical development (i.e., an effort to stop or reverse history), the Soviet Union is always for peace, even at a time when waging war. The capitalist concept of peace being essentially static, and therefore antiprogressive, is objectively against peace.[7]

In addition, despite the shifts and turns in Soviet foreign policy in the last several decades, a persisting attribute of its long perspective is the sense of compulsive obligation to assist the spread of Communism throughout the world. This universality of goal makes Soviet foreign policy something altogether different from Czarist foreign policy or, for that matter, from the relatively vague and rather generalized American desire to see a "free" but otherwise undefined world. (However, there are some striking parallels between the Soviet view and the tradi-

---

* Khrushchev alluded to this difficulty in a speech on October 31, 1959:

But one must not confuse mutual concessions in the interest of peaceful coexistence with the concessions of principle, in matters that concern the actual nature of our socialist system, or ideology. In this there cannot be any question of concessions or any adaptation. If there are concessions of principles, in questions of ideology, it will mean an incline toward the position of our foes. It will mean a qualitative change in policy. It will be a betrayal of the cause of the working class. Whoever adopts such a course will take the course of betraying the cause of socialism, and, of course, the fire of merciless criticism must be opened upon him.

tional American image of America as an active symbol of certain universal norms.) Admittedly, Soviet foreign policy, especially in its short-term aspects, is concerned with national security, frontiers, national power, etc.[8]—factors that inherently introduce similarities with Russia's traditional concerns.[9] Quite unlike their predecessors, however, the Soviet leaders view these issues in terms of certain long-range perspectives and not as ends in themselves. Indeed, the Soviet conception of their own security is inherently offensive; as long as alternative political systems exist, there is continued need to be preoccupied with security issues.[10] Because they see themselves as part of a historical process toward a defined end, the Soviet leaders are compelled to view any effort to "stabilize" or to "normalize" the international situation as a hostile design.[11]

The universality-of-goals aspect of Soviet foreign policy also makes it clear that, while the concept of "national interest" may not be irrelevant to an understanding of Communist foreign policy, to be useful it must be linked to the ultimate ideological objective. As far as Communist leaders are concerned, Soviet national interest is that which increases the power and the capability of the U.S.S.R. to promote Communism. Communist ideology, therefore, does not raise the dilemma of national versus international objectives—at least, it did not until such time as a series of other Communist states came into being. Dovetailing of national and international interests is hence another important ideological element and permits the Soviet leaders to strengthen their power without

142

power becoming the sheer end of their actions. Ideology that makes power both a tool and an end allows the Soviet leaders to be continuously concerned with the maximization of their power but without that power becoming an impediment to the fulfillment of ideological values.

For instance, even if the reason for enforcing dramatic and, indeed, revolutionary changes in Eastern Europe were merely the desire to strengthen Soviet power over the area and not to construct Communism per se, the mere fact that the method of strengthening that power was conceived in terms of large-scale social and economic changes showed the underlying ideological bias. One can certainly argue that a more moderate program would have created much less resistance and hence would have favorably affected the Communist power situation. The standard Communist answer—Communism is not safe without creating a social upheaval that uproots the existing interest groups—in itself reveals an approach to problems of political power that is strongly tinged with ideological assumptions. Similarly, in economics, the issue of collectivization is a case in point. Also, as far as the international Communist movement is concerned, ideology permits the Soviet Union to enjoy an additional operational advantage without always having the actual power to control the behavior of the various Communist parties throughout the world. Ideology, as a binding system of belief, thereby translates itself into a factor of power.

Admittedly, the ideological factor can and often does create difficulties. It can lead to excessive dogmatic evaluation of the situation, stimulate premature optimism, or simply mislead.* Furthermore, as far as the Soviet leaders are consciously aware of the ideology's role as a unifying bond for international Communism, it may tend to limit their freedom of action lest this unity be strained. This consideration was less important during Stalin's days than before and after the dictator's rule.

However, on balance, the various roles of the ideology cannot be viewed merely as a liability. There is a tendency in the West to view ideology as something irrational and to counterpoise it against pragmatism and empiricism.

---

* The strict application of Marxist theory to an examination of world affairs occasionally leads the Soviet leaders to make some extraordinary mistakes, such as their belief in the revolutionary Marxist nature of the world proletariat. The Russians were bitterly disillusioned to discover that the working classes of Germany and the East European countries were by no means either solidly pro-Soviet or the source of power they expected.

See R. S. Tarn, "Continuity in Russian Foreign Policy," *International Journal*, 1950; reprinted in R. A. Goldwin (ed.), *Readings in Russian Foreign Policy* (London: Oxford University Press, 1959), pp. 689-705:

> Another important miscalculation stemming from the application of Marxist theory has been the Soviet belief in the inevitability of American economic depression after the war, and the belief that because of the contradictions in capitalism the two principal capitalist powers, the United Kingdom and the United States, would soon fall out. The appreciation in the Kremlin of Marshall aid was also based on the belief that the United States must acquire new markets in Europe in order to postpone the coming depression in the United States. Even as regards colonial theories they have had a difficult task in reconciling the peaceful handing over of power by Britain in India and Burma—though Indo-China and Indonesia have provided plentiful ammunition for the Soviet theorists. Finally, a supreme miscalculation has been the failure to gauge properly the continuing force of nationalism, particularly in Eastern Europe.

Other examples might be the Soviet policy in China, both in the 1920's and the mid-1940's; in Yugoslavia in 1947-58; and in Eastern Europe in general in 1956-57.

From what has already been said, it would appear that ideology is not incompatible with rational behavior, once the basic assumptions are granted. While these assumptions may or may not be rational, they are at least so far removed from immediate concerns that they do not produce a conflict between the ideology and a rational approach to reality. The goal of an ultimate world-wide Communist society, allegedly determined by history, may be irrational, but it does not necessarily impose irrational conduct.

Secondly, and perhaps more significant, some of the concepts of the ideology do offer meaningful insights into international affairs. The preoccupation with the nature of the domestic dynamics of other societies and the realization that economic processes create political problems that are international can result in a more meaningful appreciation of reality than arguments about traditional national goals or moralistic pontifications to the effect that democracies are inherently peaceful and more powerful, while dictatorships are warlike and ultimately doomed. For all its limitations, Soviet ideology at least seems to point to some of the inner mechanisms of international affairs. The approach of Western statesmen is still often derived from an image of international affairs shaped by the emergence of nation-states. As long as these states operated in an environment in which mass emotionalism, particularly nationalism, was not politically determinant, international politics could function relatively stably on the basis of certain commonly accepted rules.[12] The intervention of mass public opinion, rallying around first nationalist symbols and then ideological ones (democratic or totalitarian), necessarily transforms interstate political conflicts into national ones, with profound social-economic overtones. The differences between the Vienna Congress of 1815 and the Versailles Treaty of 1919 are symptomatic.

The Soviet Communist ideology has made an important contribution toward the transformation of international politics from a "game" with certain commonly accepted rules into a profoundly intense conflict, insoluble without a major social transformation either of some of the participating societies or at least of the outlook of some of their elites. However, given the fact that modernization, particularly industrialization, has produced a world-wide awakening of the political consciousness of the masses, the Communist ideology, even while serving to intensify conflicts, underscored the necessity to base international conduct less and less on legal and diplomatic devices and more and more on political-sociological insights that cut across state frontiers. The Communist realization, even though often not successfully exploited in policy, that the key to the future of our era lies in the transformation of the colonial and underdeveloped parts of the world preceded similar recognition on the part of Western chancellories by several decades. The focusing on certain long-range social-economic and political trends, a matter increasingly accepted in the West since World War II, has doubtless contributed to a more sophisticated appreciation of certain international issues than efforts to operate international affairs on the somewhat artificial plane of legal-diplomatic interaction between nation-states increasingly charged with blinding emotional content.

For the time being, that same ideology distorts its own insight by viewing international affairs through a perspective that sees them as operating on the basis of a hostile dichotomy between two rigidly, abstractly, and simplistically conceived social-economic systems. The Soviet Communist ideology, even while consciously grappling with certain social problems, introduces into international affairs an element of profound instability and conflict by rejecting the notion that social-economic change might be *unconsciously* taking place in all societies faced with certain similar difficulties, thereby reducing the degree of their diversity. Soviet insistence (derived from the conceptual elements of ideology already noted and from their general impact on Soviet foreign policy) that ultimate peace depends on the total victory of a particular social system led by a particular political party injects into international affairs an element of a fundamental struggle for survival not conducive to conflict resolution.

PROSPECTS OF IDEOLOGICAL EROSION

There is a difference between ideological change and ideological erosion, although the two are closely related. Change has to take place if ideology is to continue to respond to social needs. However, when the ideology begins to lose its social vitality, either by becoming so dogmatic that it no longer corresponds to reality or because reality has so changed that even the widest stretching of the ideology can no longer encompass it, the change develops into erosion. The ideology becomes merely declamatory or simply fades away. These verbal

147

dialectics can perhaps be made meaningful by a discussion of the impact on the ideological framework that shapes the Soviet foreign policy of the following three sets of factors: (1) the interaction of Communist objectives and domestic change; (2) the emergence of the Communist bloc; and (3) the impact of international affairs.

Communist objectives and social change. The development of the Soviet ideology has been closely linked with the various phases of the activity of the political movement that embodies the ideology and, beyond that, with the various men who have stood at the helm of that movement. A recent and perceptive analysis of these stages characterized them as that of transplantation, adaptation, and implementation.[13] To the extent that it is possible to compartmentalize social development into neat phases, the first two may be said to have been closely associated with the name of Lenin, and the third with Stalin. Each of these phases was dominated by some central objective that necessarily magnified or minimized some of the ideological principles to which the movement subscribed. For instance, the emergence of the Party as the central, indispensable agent of history has been a crucial ideological ingredient of the entire span of Soviet development, a necessity interdependent with the changing central objective. On the other hand, the stage of transplantation permitted or maybe even required a measure of internal dialogue that gradually became incompatible with the subsequent stages of adaptation and implementation and with the character of the movement that such a dialogue bred. Increasingly, the anti-authoritarian and democratic

elements of the doctrine gave way to ideologically sup-
ported discipline, ending finally with the physical liquidation of all those who by their mere presence reminded
the Party or its leader of the movement's former diversity.
Similarly, the essentially antistate orientation of the early
revolutionaries gradually gave way to the acceptance and
then to the enshrinement of the state as a central and
positive factor in effecting the desired socio-economic
change. The building of a new industrial society also
meant that the principle of egalitarianism had to be aban-
doned and be replaced by a highly stratified social system.[14] The emphasis on a mounting class struggle during
the difficult phase of implementation again reflected both
the dynamics of the central objective and the impatient
disposition of the Party leadership that came to power
in that particular phase. Finally, even after the seizure
of power the Party continued to view itself as a conspiratorial movement, and this also helped to define the
character of its relations with the society subject to it
and with the world at large.

The process of shaping new principles or changing old
ones is not without its tensions. One could almost say
that there is a kind of "dialectical" relationship between
an ideologically oriented party and reality. The ideological party attempts to change reality and, in this way, is a
revolutionary force; the new, changed reality for a while
corresponds to the ideology even while gradually changing itself; in time, the ideology may become a conservative
force; a new adjustment is eventually forced, and the
ideology may then again become a revolutionary force.

The varying stages of Soviet Communist ideology—Leninism, Stalinism, Khrushchevism—and the relatively violent transitions from one to the other can be seen as part of this dialectical relationship between ideology and reality. Yet, it is exactly this adaptability that permits the ideology to exercise a continuing influence and prevents it from becoming sterile and irrelevant, thereby allowing it to retain a certain identity of its own.

However, in the present period two factors threaten to translate this process of change into erosion. The raising of the banner of Communist construction, proclaimed by the Twenty-first CPSU Congress in an effort to revitalize the ideological sense of purpose, will produce much sooner than hitherto might have been expected a confrontation between reality and ideology. This confrontation might threaten the role of the Party as the agent of history and undermine the validity of the ideology. As long as the Party was actively shaping Soviet society and as long as that society was mere putty in the hands of the leaders of the Party, the position of the Party could not be contested. But a highly industrialized Soviet society, increasingly conscious of its achievements, could cease to be a passive object and could begin to exert pressures even on the Party. These pressures now seem to be most timid, but so are the initial stirrings of life. Even most restrained social pressures—as, for instance, those in favor of a higher rate of consumption or more freedom in the literary arts—would augur a changing relationship and, as a result, a somewhat changing conception of the ideology. Some alert Communists, more alert perhaps than

Khrushchev, have already signaled warnings that excessive emphasis on industrial indexes and on material well-being as the expression of the achievement of socialism-Communism could result in the unconscious acceptance of many "bourgeois" values by the Communists themselves.[15]

In the meantime, with the passage of years and with the changed social conditions, the very factors that shaped Marxism into Soviet-Communist ideology—the specific historical conditions, the personal background of the Bolshevik revolutionaries, and the manner in which they perceived their Marxism, the dynamics of the movement and its early experience, or, in other words, the objective and subjective factors that shaped the ideology—will have receded into the past. (To a freshman class entering a Soviet university in 1961, Stalin is already a historical figure.) The impact on the ideology of a policy designed to achieve material well-being for a society that has already gone through the most difficult phase of industrialization is bound to differ from the impact of a policy of violent industrialization applied to a backward society. Both the objective and its context are different. What might then happen to the ideology?

A delicate hint of this dilemma is revealed to us by Khrushchev's efforts to return to Leninism. Compared even to Stalin, Khrushchev is a crude thinker whose ideological views are more a matter of a series of preconceptions than a conscious search for relevant formulations, as was still the case with Stalin. But even Khrushchev came to feel that somehow the Stalinist ideology and the Stalinist movement got out of tune with reality. His

151

emphasis on Leninism represents an effort to return to something that seems to evoke a positive echo in the Soviet society of his day. He hopes in this way to recapture the old spirit of the ideology. But little does he realize that these positive echoes are evoked by elements that were "lags" even from the pre-Leninist phase and that Leninism was increasingly combatting: internal democracy, dialogue, doctrinal discussions, not autocracy, dogma, and ideological dictation. None of these need threaten the basic Marxist postulates concerning the nature of reality, to which both the ruling movement and Soviet society could continue to subscribe. However, even a gradual and unconscious return to the original doctrinal assumptions would involve an eventual erosion of the ideological trappings and, with it, of the dogmatic perspectives on world affairs.

The impact of the Communist bloc. In the initial phase of its existence, the Communist bloc served to strengthen the ideological conviction that history is on the side of Communism (or vice versa). The expansion of Communism to include one-third of the globe, effected by force of arms or by revolution, seemed to recapture some of the old revolutionary fervor that had been denied the Russian Communists since the 1920's. History was again in its dynamic phase. To this day, the Soviet leaders glory in the size and population of the camp and frequently cite these as proof that "the east wind is now blowing over the west wind." Furthermore, as long as Stalin lived, the expansion of the camp did not raise insurmountable ideological difficulties. Even the old theory of capitalist encirclement was still maintained, to be attacked, finally, only as late as 1958.* However, this dismissal of capitalist encirclement did not involve an important ideological reconsideration; rather, it was a matter of reassessing the relationship of forces in the international arena and reaching a more optimistic (and as it happens, a more correct) conclusion.

As far as new Communist-ruled states were concerned, after a brief transition period, they adopted an essentially Stalinist pattern of domestic restructuring and conceptions. The Soviet experience in "construction of socialism" was adjudged to have universal validity, and consequently a complex of methods and beliefs, which formed the Soviet ideology and reflected the Soviet adaptation of Marxism, was grafted onto all the ruling Communist elites, whatever their intellectual and political heritage. Stalin's death soon revealed the inadequacy and the fundamental instability of this application. And the subsequent search for new forms of ideological and political unity within the camp underscored the full complexity of the problem of applying Soviet ideology, with its universal aspirations, to varied national conditions.[16]

Without retracing the involved series of attempted solutions and without discussing their relative merits, it can be observed that the efforts to develop common ideological prescriptions for the post-Stalin Soviet bloc came face to

---

* Addressing the Twenty-first Party Congress on January 27, 1959, Khrushchev stated: "The situation in the world has fundamentally changed. Capitalist encirclement of our country no longer exists." On August 15, 1951, *Bolshevik*, reaffirming that capitalist encirclement still exists, stated the following: "Capitalist encirclement is a political term. Comrade Stalin has stated that capitalist encirclement cannot be considered a geographic notion."

face with two obvious and related difficulties: the matter of different social contexts within which an ideology matures and the problem of varying stages of "socialist" development. The first of these could be ignored as long as Stalinist power and Stalinist prestige were available and could be applied so as to universalize the Soviet outlook. Furthermore, the early stage of Communist rule in the newly subject nations meant that the main thrust of Communist efforts was directed at consolidating their power and at destroying the old society. These essentially negative tasks did not raise ideological problems as acute as the later one of building new social institutions.

However, Stalin's death and the dissipation of Stalinism took place when the attention of the Communist leaders was increasingly turning to the latter objective. Within the context of relative relaxation, faced with domestic problems peculiar to their own societies, some of them increasingly eschewed Soviet solutions and step by step began to feel the full weight of their own social traditions and their own "apperception" of the ideology. A general consequence of this was the emerging ideological diversity that characterized the bloc in 1956–57 and potentially exists even today, despite conscious and essentially expedience-motivated efforts by the ruling elites to re-establish ideological uniformity.*

Moreover, the varying stages of social-economic development of the various countries within the Soviet bloc inherently produced different problems requiring different solutions. China, going through an economic and

---

* The high point of these efforts was the November, 1957, conference of the ruling Communist parties and its declaration.

social revolution at a pace even more rapid than the
Soviet Union did in the most violent Stalinist phase,*
could not escape drawing primarily on those aspects of
the ideology that justified the application of violence,
maximized the power of the Party, simplified international issues into simple relations of hostile dichotomy,
and viewed with profound suspicion any voices of moderation.[17] The Soviet Union—on the brink, if not of a Communist fulfillment, then at least of reaping a partial
harvest of several decades of social sacrifice—was becoming
increasingly concerned with rationalizing the operations
both of its own society and of the bloc. Many Communists
in Poland, Hungary, and Rumania, countries suffering
the pangs of transition from a rural society to an industrial one and lacking the indigenous support that both
the Russian and Chinese Communists enjoyed, were increasingly coming under the influence of "revisionism"—
that is, abandoning the simplifications of the Soviet ideological outlook, increasingly viewing the problems of social
transformation as organic worldwide processes, requiring
also a gradual and continuous transformation of social consciousness. On the other hand, the leaders of industrially
advanced East Germany and Czechoslovakia, not faced
by social-economic tribulations, were increasingly sympathetic to the Chinese outlook, since it provided the
political justification for their politically unstable regimes.
Striking evidence of this was provided by the Chinese
tenth-anniversary celebration in Peking in October, 1959:
On foreign-policy issues and on Chinese domestic policies,

* This can be readily seen from comparative data on economic development, for instance, for analogous periods of their "socialist" development.

including the "Great Leap Forward" and the communes, the East Germans and the Czechs adopted the most enthusiastic line, quite in contrast to the Poles and the Russians.

The consequence of this differentiated ideological conditioning, of the different stages of development of the respective socialist states, as well as of different interests of the ruling elites, has been an occasional diversity of outlook on a variety of important issues. In the case of China and the Soviet Union, this diversity seems to involve an issue not new to the Soviet Communists: To what extent can a Marxist revolutionary cooperate with the existing social forces and merge himself with the observable trends in the direction of the inevitable victory? To what degree must he remain alienated from the world, rejected, and strive to alter it by first destroying it? Perhaps it would not be too gross an oversimplification to say that the crux of the problem was whether peaceful coexistence with the enemy was transitionally possible. There are interesting historical precedents for questions such as these. At one time, Mensheviks believed that the historical stage had arrived when they could face the forces of reaction on their own ground and that victory was within their reach. As Haimson has stated it:

Absolutism stood already on the brink of extinction. . . . Plekhanov no longer had any serious reason to be concerned over the preservation of orthodoxy in social democracy. . . . Axelrod no longer had much cause to worry over the task of organizing forces capable of overthrowing absolutism; and Martov could look forward confidently to a moment in the not-too-distant future when the power of the hostile forces reigning in the world would at least be significantly reduced.[18]

The Bolsheviks rejected such views, feeling that Menshevik policy could only dull the sharp edge of the revolutionary trend and allow the enemy to create the preconditions for even more durable, albeit more subtle, oppression. In some ways, however, the Soviets could be viewed today by the Chinese as adopting an essentially Menshevik position in international affairs. Overconfident of their strength, they seem to overlook the danger that premature optimism can only lead to a demobilization of revolutionary zeal. And, conversely, the Soviets might well feel that the Chinese overlook the decisive, objective fact of the contemporary phase of international affairs—that of Soviet power, which allows the Communist bloc to adopt the policies of coexistence from positions of strength.[19] Nevertheless, the presence of a more *revolutionary* state in the camp cannot help but be disconcerting to the Soviet claim of ideological "virtue" and must certainly cause ideological uneasiness in the Soviet ranks. Indeed, it is this capacity to adopt more radical policies than the Soviet Union that is the major source of Chinese ideological leverage within the camp.

Quite a different challenge to ideological unity is raised by some of the East European Communist states. The most extensive statement of contemporary East European revisionism is contained in the program adopted by the Yugoslav Communist Party in April, 1959.[20] The general response of the camp to it has been to anathematize the Yugoslavs. But within all the ruling European Communist parties, such views are entertained by many members, particularly among the intellectuals, and provide the underpinning for potential ideological disunity.[21] The reason for this is simply that the Soviet ideology will not meaningfully reflect or shape reality in the Eastern European context unless Soviet force is available to back it. Anyone familiar with the ideological traditions of Polish left-wing socialism, with the cultural climate of the country and its "political style," or with the role played by the populist writers in Hungary in the shaping of Hungarian radicalism would agree that forceful measures would be necessary to prevent the dilution and revision of Marxism-Leninism when that ideology comes to be embodied by large mass movements within these countries. Such forceful measures were undertaken by the small, dedicated Marxist-Leninist minorities existing in these countries, but even they found it difficult to remain immune to their environment. Much the same could be said for some of the other Communist-ruled states.

It was this environmental influence that was at the root of the 1956 crisis, and the same consideration has recently forced the Soviet leaders to equivocate on the old issue of the class struggle after the seizure of power. In response to the needs of Soviet society and attempting to explain the "aberrations of Stalinism," Khrushchev negated and condemned the principle of the mounting class struggle as a Stalinist distortion of Marxism-Leninism. In 1959, however, faced in Eastern Europe with the dilemma of social opposition to socialist construction and fearful that his abandonment of this Stalinist principle might strengthen the hands of the revisionists there, he modified it "dialectically":

> The Twentieth Congress of our Party rightly criticized Joseph Stalin's mistaken proposition that the class struggle grows sharper with progress in socialist construction. But criticism of this proposition certainly does not mean that we can deny the inevitability of class struggle in the period of socialist construction. . . . This development does not proceed along a straight line. Class struggle in the epoch of building socialism can intensify at certain periods in connection with some of the changes in the internal and external situation and assume an extremely sharp form, up to and including the armed clash, as was the case in Hungary in 1956.[22]

Khrushchev's efforts were symbolic of the growing necessity to adjust the ideology to varying national conditions. In spite of his efforts, however, the radically different conditions that the ruling Communist elites encountered in Eastern Europe as compared to Russia in 1917 or to China in 1949 pose a continuing dilemma to the unity of Communist practice and, therefore, to the unity of the ideology.

Despite Soviet efforts to maintain an ideological equilibrium, the consequence of this growing diversity, and the Soviet elasticity in response to it, is to *relativize* the meaning of the ideology. For forty years, the Soviet leaders have been accustomed to rejecting those who talk a different "language" than they and to ejecting those who use the same language to disagree. Now, for the first time, they have to tolerate fellow Communists who use similar concepts to reach different conclusions. Even today, one should increasingly speak not of Communist ideology but of Soviet Communist ideology, Chinese Communist ideology, Yugoslav Communist ideology, etc. And since it was the Marxist-Leninist ideology's claim to universality that originally stimulated such intense Soviet involvement not only in the domination of its neighbors but particularly in directing the character of their domestic transformation, the increasing diversity in ideological emphases threatens the universal validity of even the Soviet ideology itself and thereby undermines one of the factors that shape the Soviet approach to the world. It also threatens the domestic legitimacy of this Soviet ideology by denying its central claim—that is, its universal validity—which is used as a justification for its domestic application. Efforts to reassert unity in response to this threat can further divorce the ideology from reality, while the toleration and resulting extension of such diversity threatens to introduce elements of relativism dangerous to the cohesion of the ideology.

This vicious circle also brings up the problem of the relationship of the Soviet Union to international Communism. In the immediate post-Revolutionary phase, the new Soviet leaders were quite prepared to sacrifice what traditionally has been considered Russian national interest in order to promote the spread of the revolution. They were thus willing to sanction Polish independence and to cede territory in the hope of stimulating a revolutionary chain reaction.[23] The failure and disappointments experienced in the 1920's resulted in the convenient merger of ideology and national interest, and the defense and ex-

pansion of the revolutionary base, Russia, became synony-
mous with the interests of Communism. The same applied
to international Communists in their relations with the
U.S.S.R. The emergence of several Communist states
could challenge this identification, despite continuous
efforts to assert Soviet primacy and confluence of interests.
After forty years, even a marriage of convenience can
develop a measure of stability, and certainly the social
pressures within the highly nationalistic U.S.S.R. would
oppose policies designed to promote international Communism at the expense of the U.S.S.R. One may even assume that Soviet leaders would think automatically that
any policy harmful to the Soviet Union would harm international Communism and would oppose efforts to transform their "universal insight" into a mere parochial
perspective. Yet, it is not too much to assert that differing
viewpoints could crystallize in Warsaw or Peking, or even,
for that matter, in East Berlin. The divorce of Communist ideology from Soviet national interest would not
strengthen the ideology within the U.S.S.R., while their
continued linkage is likely to breed resentment and
weaken that ideology elsewhere.

The impact of international affairs on ideology. After
the seizure of power, the Soviet leaders had to adjust
to an international reality that did not quite fit their
earlier expectations. The adjustment was not easy and
involved a series of conflicts between reality and ideology
(e.g., the controversy generated by the Brest-Litovsk negotiations with Germany). Even after their power had been
consolidated, the spread of the revolution was both expected and artificially stimulated by Moscow. Gradually

and painfully, however, ideology began to correspond to reality, and the principle of "socialism in one country" emerged.[24] It took a long time for this principle to lapse, and many Soviet actions after the war with respect to their new Communist neighbors were rooted in this principle lagging behind the new political situation.

As far as Soviet conduct in the international arena was concerned, given the weakness of the new Soviet state, ideology could not exercise a wide latitude in action. The number of policy alternatives open to the Soviet Union was relatively limited, if one excludes political suicide as an alternative; and Communist ideology, unlike the Nazi one, lays the greatest emphasis on self-preservation. Faced with international politics that operated essentially on the balance-of-power principle, the Soviet Union, in order to pursue its ideological objectives, had no choice but to attempt "to play the game," employing the openings that the game provided to its best advantage.* In summing up his evaluation of the role of ideology in Soviet foreign policy, Moore correctly concluded that, as far as the Soviets were concerned, "the choice of antagonists or allies has been determined not primarily by ideological factors, but by the structure of the balance of power system itself." [25]

The situation has changed with growing Soviet power and with the even more rapidly growing Soviet sense of confidence. For the first time since the 1920's, the Soviet leaders seem to feel again that the day of their victory

* Symbolic of this was the acceptance, after some reservations, of the Western diplomatic techniques, rituals, and protocol trappings.

is not far away.[26] However, balancing this are also several factors related to international affairs that eventually could serve to modify this Soviet sense of ideological fulfillment. These may be treated under three headings: stability in Western society, patterns of development in the underdeveloped societies, and the nature of modern weapons systems. With respect to the first, it would appear that in 1947 the Soviet leadership still entertained some hopes that revolutionary upheavals might take place in France, Italy, and/or Greece, and they were counting on the expansion of Communism into Western Europe. Failure of these attempts, followed .by a remarkable West European recovery, seems to have convinced the Soviet leaders that in the foreseeable future they cannot count on the duplication of either the Leninist (seizure of power) or the Stalinist (military occupation) form of Communist development. Beyond that, they increasingly appear to be willing to concede that in such stable, prosperous, and democratic societies, an altogether different form of transition from the bourgeois stage to the socialist stage must be contemplated. Khrushchev finally articulated this when he stated at the Twentieth Party Congress that, Lenin to the contrary, a peaceful takeover by the Communist Party was possible and that parliamentary devices could be used to that end. Such a conception comes dangerously close to an abandonment of Leninism, and the Soviet leaders were not unaware of it. Therefore, they refrained from taking the next step (taken by the Yugoslavs)—that of conceding that socialism may be built by social-democratic parties—and they continued to insist that only the

163

Communist Party could effect such a true transition. Nevertheless, the importance of the change should not be underestimated. The change does involve an important modification of their outlook.

The relevance of this change, furthermore, is not limited only to the West; similar considerations could apply in the East, although the Soviet leaders consider it much less likely (Kerala may be an example). It is, however, not the theory of the peaceful transition to socialism per se that poses a threat to Soviet ideology in the East. Rather, it is the related matter of the general method of building socialism. In Soviet thinking the following is required in order to build socialism:

> . . . the leadership of the masses of the working people by the working class, the core of which is the Marxist-Leninist Party, in bringing about a proletarian revolution in one form or another and establishing one form or another of the dictatorship of the proletariat; alliance of the working class with the bulk of the peasantry and other strata of the working people; the abolition of capitalist ownership and the establishment of public ownership of the basic means of production; gradual socialist reorganization of agriculture; planned development of the national economy with the aim of building socialism and Communism, raising the working peoples' standard of living; the accomplishment of a socialist revolution in the sphere of ideology and culture and the creation of a numerous intelligentsia devoted to the working class, the working people, and the cause of socialism; the elimination of national oppression and the establishment of

164

equality and fraternal friendship among peoples; defense
of the achievements of socialism against encroachments
by external and internal enemies; solidarity of the working class of a given country with the working class of
other countries—proletarian internationalism.[27]

The end result is to be a centrally planned, nonexploita-
tive society with a relatively high standard of living. The
Soviets are convinced, given their dichotomic image of
the world divided into socialism and capitalism, that only
through socialism can industrialization be achieved and a
prosperous society constructed.

The new and still underdeveloped states therefore pose
the challenge of claiming by and large to be building
societies of a socialist type and of actually doing it through
democratic political means and highly pragmatic and
certainly not Soviet (nor capitalist) economic methods. If
they should succeed, and they possibly might with both
Soviet ("socialist") and American ("capitalist") aid, the
consequence will have to be a major redefinition of the
processes of social-economic change, whatever the Soviet
ideologues may choose to call the new society.[28] Such a
development would strike not only at the ideology and
its dichotomic image of social change but even at its
doctrinal foundations. It would pose a threat to the
entire historical structure of the ideology and would
strengthen the appeal of revisionism within the Communist ranks.

The third and probably the most important aspect of
international affairs that could promote the erosion of

ideology pertains to the weapons systems. The Soviet Union has always considered its strength to be an important determinant of its policy, dictating caution or warranting action. In so far as military strategy is concerned, the Soviet leaders, particularly Stalin, have considered their society to be especially well equipped for lengthy wars of attrition—given its size, morale, endurance, and discipline. That remained the prevailing Soviet doctrine even after World War II, which was not surprising, given the nature of the Soviet experience in it. After Stalin's death, however, following a period of internal strategic debate, the primacy of nuclear weapons in Soviet military thinking was established, with the consequent emphasis on striking power and the element of surprise.[29] As this conception gained the upper hand in Soviet thinking, it was only a matter of time before the converse came to be recognized—that similar strategies might be equally decisive if used by the opponent.

This had immediate bearing on the Soviet thinking concerning the inevitability of war. For a long time, the basic Soviet conception had been that wars were inevitable as long as capitalism, and particularly imperialism, created the economic basis for war. Stalin restated this principle as late as 1952. However, if such a war should occur and if the Soviet Union were drawn into it, there could be only one result: the end of capitalism. Gradually, with the mounting possibility of mutual destruction, the Soviet leaders have been forced to conclude that war is no longer, as Khrushchev put it at the Twentieth Party Congress, "a fatalistic inevitability." The further extension of this shift has involved an increasing willingness to concede that war would be mutually destructive and that it would not benefit either side.[30] The formal explanation for this change in position was that the strength of the socialist bloc, and of the Soviet Union in particular, has become, so to speak, a sufficiently powerful political-military superstructure balancing the economic necessity for war.

Of course, it could be argued that this change reflects increased Soviet confidence that history's scales have finally been tipped in favor of Communism and that rash action, therefore, is to be avoided. In other words, the adjustment is the product not merely of necessity but also of Soviet interest. Furthermore, there can be little doubt that if the military situation were to become one-sidedly favorable to the U.S.S.R., making it invulnerable, the Soviet viewpoint might change again. However, the important point is that, under the impact of the concrete factor of admittedly decisive importance—the problem of survival—the Soviet ideology had to gradually adjust again, modifying a hitherto important ideological assumption. Peaceful coexistence as an alternative to mutual destruction cannot easily be squared with some of the historical inevitabilities inherent in the ideology, even if such peaceful coexistence is defined as competition.* By implication, at least, it does seem to elevate nuclear weapons into a force capable of interfering with history. It would be naïve, of course, to assume that Soviet commitment to such peaceful coexistence is irreversible; but

* As if to compensate for this, the Soviet press has recently been stressing the need for intensified ideological struggle against alien concepts and against the capitalist system.

given a general fear of war, the Soviet leaders would have to think twice before restoring "the inevitability of war" principle. However, a necessary precondition for the maintenance of the new formulation is the perpetuation by the West of its destructive capability. Without it, the objective reason for peaceful coexistence will have disappeared.

The cumulative effect of the various processes discussed in the preceding pages could be the gradual erosion of certain ideological aspects of the Soviet perspective on international affairs. The ideological syndrome, containing an oversimplified conception of an antagonistic confrontation between two social systems and of historical change in general, the commitment to conflict, the universality of goals, the sense of self-righteousness, and the belief in the imminence of victory—all could be threatened by the combined impact of domestic change, the emergence of ideological relativism due to the spread of Communism, and the stark threat of nuclear extinction. A growing willingness to accept some common and overt rules of behavior could follow, buttressing the existing informal and undefined restraints on violence that both sides have tacitly recognized. But this process of erosion is at the present time balanced by certain pressures in the opposite direction, which reassert and even revitalize the ideology. The final outcome of these clashing tendencies depends on too many variables to be safely predicted, but uncertainty about the outcome should not obscure the certainty about conflicting pressures.

SOURCES OF IDEOLOGICAL VITALITY

The experience of the German Social Democratic movement with Marxism might serve as a general lesson that one should not expect such an erosion to occur rapidly. It took the German Party a very long time to shed its relatively rigid Marxist orientation, and the final act of liberation from the Marxist doctrine did not take place until its Congress of 1959.* In part, this might be explained by the delaying impact of the Nazi experience and the reaction against the revival of laissez-faire capitalism in Germany. In part, it also reflected the delaying influence of the Party as an organization with a vested interest in its doctrine and of that organization's action commitment, which necessarily stimulated opposition to its Marxism and thereby also intensified belief in it. That this belief was strong and persisted for many years should need no documentation. It does offer, however, a striking illustration of an ideology's capacity to survive even under conditions increasingly remote from those to which the ideology was relevant. It is also to be remembered that this ideology finally began to fade when a democratic political process and democratically accepted changes in socio-economic organization made possible a peaceful re-evaluation of the Party's views and did not pose before it the alternative of disintegration.

In the Soviet Union, several established commitments

* Compare the basic program of Bad Godesberg with the Heidelberg program of 1925.

act as powerful counterforces and protect the ideology from erosion. The most important of these is the institutional commitment in the form of the ruling party. Not much needs to be said about this most important factor. If the ideology were to fade, particularly among the membership, the power of the Party would be threatened, even though ritualization could delay the disintegration. The upper echelons of the Party are very conscious of this. The steps taken by Khrushchev to re-establish the role of the Party in Soviet society and the recent measures adopted to invigorate the ideological indoctrination of the population at large suggest that the Party is determined to maintain ideological consciousness in its ranks. In the foreseeable future, there is little reason to doubt its capacity to do so.

The institutional commitment to ideology is backed by a personal commitment. To individuals like Khrushchev, the ideology is the source of their insight into reality, a conscious treasure to be guarded against pollution (unless by themselves, which is a different problem), the basic course of their education (*Rabfak,* in Khrushchev's case), and the emotional source for their personal sense of life. The present generation of Soviet leaders—men in their early sixties—came of age during the latter stages of the civil war and matured during the NEP and the Stalinist transformation of Russia. Their first contact with the ideology came at a time when the Party was still intensely preoccupied with ideological issues and was attempting—through debate, deviations, and purges—to determine what course to pursue in building a new society. Even a simple young member like

Khrushchev, for example, could not avoid involvement and had to make his choice. Ideology in the 1920's was an important matter, even if one were to focus merely on the power struggles that were taking place. Khrushchev's experience in this period was bound to leave with him a lasting awareness that there is a "correct" and an "erroneous" path and that the Party must always remain conscious of this. In a decade or so from now, and maybe sooner, a new generation of Soviet leaders will come to the fore. The men who are now in their fifties—e.g., Brezhnev and Kozlov—were twenty when Stalin undertook his collectivization drive and defeated all opposition, and they were in their mid-twenties when the Party experienced its great purge. They faced no alternatives. To them, power equaled ideology. The road forward was simple, firmly charted, and not subject to discussion. To such a generation, ideology may be less a matter of conscious preoccupation. This may make them in some ways much more defenseless against unarticulated social processes that quietly erode the ideology. Nevertheless, the habits of thought and the personal experience of the Soviet leaders will act as a braking element on the force stimulating erosion.

Broad social commitment is another "defensive" element. As values become socially ingrained, they resist new values. The reconstruction of Soviet society on the basis of the ideology and the indoctrination of many decades has created a social residue that will resist the intrusion of new ideas, even though the intellectually alert elements may be drawn by them. The influence on the latter can be effective only if they either penetrate the Party or succeed in infusing the society with new notions. Given the nature of the Soviet society, the task for the carriers of new ideas is not easy, unless a major crisis should shake its stability. In some ways, it can even be argued that urbanization and industrialization, achieved within an ideological context and by an ideologically motivated movement, will tend to perpetuate the role of ideology. First, they institutionalize an environment that is based on the ideological aspirations and in time begins to act as a buffer for that ideology; second, through a very tangible sense of achievement, they create a widespread acceptance of the ideology, which, even if lacking its original revolutionary zeal, becomes gradually more pervading; third, the nature of a modern industrial society, which is based on social ownership and has severely limited individual initiative, requires a continuous articulation of societal goals to help preserve the broadly accepted purpose. These factors together are inimical to a rapid erosion of the ideology. Finally, action commitment revitalizes the ideology. Action provokes reaction and breeds hostility and conflict and thereby intensifies belief, steeled by trial. Action crowned by success strengthens the ideology even more. In so far as the masses are concerned, the Soviet leadership has been making strenuous efforts to identify its successes in launching Sputniks or achieving a higher rate of growth with its ideology. Indeed, it may be one of the ironies of the Soviet version of Communism that Soviet military preponderance might become an element that retrenches and intensifies ideological belief.

To the Party membership, Soviet international achieve-

ments are increasingly becoming the "ersatz" method of
establishing the correctness of the ideology, thereby preserving the inner sense of ideological purpose without
which the Party could decay. This ersatz method of
revitalizing the ideology is not entirely a matter of conscious design. Having become a great power, at a rate
certainly not expected in the West and possibly not even
by the Kremlin either, the Soviet Union has a degree
of involvement in the rapidly changing world that by itself tends to create conflicts with other powers. Such
conflicts can easily be translated into ideological terms,
especially as some of the competing units do differ in
values and social systems.

In a sense, therefore, the very act of involvement on
a massive scale—an involvement that in part is also a
function of size and power and would continue to generate
conflicts between the U.S.S.R. and the United States even
without ideology—tends to revitalize the ideology and to
translate even simple issues into broader conflicts. For
instance, one could see the Berlin problem as a proper
matter of international dispute among several parties,
comparable to the Saar. However, quite unlike the Saar
problem, the disputing parties differ sharply in political
and socio-economic conceptions, and any change in the
status of Berlin has immediate implications for the stability of some of the disputing parties. Beyond that, the presence of other Communist states, some possibly more
ideologically radical than the Soviet Union, as well as
the Soviet interest in maintaining unity in the Communist bloc, is likely to intensify the action commitment of
the ideology. The Soviet leaders have recently been mak-

ing strenuous and generally successful efforts to re-establish ideological ties throughout the bloc.

It is these forces that impede the erosion of the ideology and inhibit the Soviet leadership from accepting international affairs as a game with a series of rules; instead, these forces make them insist on treating international affairs as a conflict with only *one* solution. For the moment, possibly the least hazardous conclusion would be to suggest that, while the pressures for the erosion of ideology are gradually building up, the "conservative" forces of the ideology are still well entrenched and have not lost their capacity to exert influence. In the near future, an international "conflict resolution" is unlikely.

6. Deviation Control:
The Dynamics of Doctrinal Conflict

This essay is a comparative study in the dynamics of doctrinal conflicts. It deals with two organized international movements overtly committed to spreading and carrying out a doctrinal program of action, theological or ideological, on the basis of both the individual commitment of their respective members and their collective goals as organized bodies. Its purpose is to generalize from the experience of these organizations in handling deviations involving a unit of the movement that differed or clashed either with the acknowledged center or with another unit of the movement, in both cases over theological or ideological issues, but within the common doctrine and accompanied by mutual doctrinal recriminations. A brief and selective analysis of the historical experience of one such movement, Catholicism, might contribute to a more sophisticated understanding of some recent developments within a contemporary international movement, Communism.

More specifically, this study will seek some implications from the doctrinal clashes between Rome and the Jansenists and from the Jesuit missionaries' disputes with their Franciscan and Dominican critics in the seventeenth cen-

tury for the problems of unity and diversity which international Communism has recently encountered.[1] Since the
issue of Jansenism involved the relations between the
French kingdom, with its strong emphasis on the Gallicanism of the French Church, and Rome, the first case has
elements of a conflict between a nationally based doctrinal
deviation and the center. The second instance pertains to
doctrinal-strategic conflicts between component units of
the international movement.

In both cases we are dealing with theological or ideological movements which are action-oriented; thus, a theological or ideological dispute among their respective units
is more than just a discussion of philosophical abstractions.
Factors of political power and control inevitably become
involved. Also, since in any doctrinal* bargaining there is
no firm, "objective" way of determining the correctness of
conflicting positions, a doctrinal dispute has a dynamic
quality to it. Once such a dispute breaks out, a doctrinal
compromise is extremely difficult to arrange. Splitting the
difference as in financial transactions, selecting a river or
a mountain range as in border disputes, accepting the line
held when firing ceased as in armistices—all these devices
are simply not applicable. Barring an outright split, the
usual solutions tend to be more extreme: the agreement
of one protagonist to become doctrinally silent, although
not necessarily retracting his original views; or the doctrinal subordination of one to the other. A third solution,
a mutual agreement to become silent, is not stable if one

---

* For the purpose of brevity, henceforth the word "doctrinal" will be
used to cover both theological and ideological disputes, even though there
are obvious differences between doctrine, theology, and ideology.

of the parties involved is the center, since a doctrinally oriented movement cannot remain doctrinally silent in the face of continually changing reality.

The same consideration makes the commitment to silence on the part of a deviation-inclined unit difficult to sustain. In time, the unit involved must make doctrinal judgments, just as the movement as a whole cannot become silent, because doctrine rationalizes and justifies its program. When that happens, the unit is faced with the choice either of saying what it was earlier unwilling to say—in effect, thereby capitulating—or of reopening the dispute. By way of example, Gomulka's 1956 implicit agreement to remain doctrinally silent was gradually translated into doctrinal capitulation. Tito and Khrushchev, after attempting in 1955–56 to effect something amounting to an agreement for mutual silence, both soon discovered that they were compelled to speak up, and so they clashed again. The Jansenists during the seventeenth century faced the same dilemma, since they also were attempting to wage a doctrinal conflict within the framework of a common doctrine and a common international organization.

Power is heavily involved in these disputes. A concession on a doctrinal issue automatically magnifies the power and strengthens the prestige and even authority of one protagonist at the expense of the other. Furthermore, a doctrinal dispute very frequently generates related conflicts. These may stir up, for instance, jurisdictional, organizational, or personal issues, which then also intensify the doctrinal conflict. Indeed, in doctrinally oriented organizations, such conflicts in themselves usually stimulate doctrinal differences, since there is a strong temptation among doctrinally sensitive organizations to use the charge of doctrinal laxity (or some other imperfection) as a means of scoring a point in any disagreement. The term doctrinal deviation or conflict is used here whenever such doctrinal recriminations are exchanged, irrespective of their cause, within the common doctrinal and organizational context.

In spite of its inherent dynamism, doctrinal conflict also possesses certain elements of stability. Usually, until quite some time after a deviation has become a defection or a defiance, the conflict tends to be limited by the mutual acceptance of a common value-system inherent in the doctrine, which tends to confine that conflict within the organization and precludes alliances outside of it. For instance, the sharing of animosity toward the "nonbelievers" is a persisting characteristic of doctrinal conflict. Furthermore, the common doctrine facilitates communication, both explicit and implicit, between protagonists. Certain moves are not only understandable but easily deciphered—hence the ambiguity inherent in conflicts between doctrinally antithetic protagonists (e.g., "the enigma" of Communism in the eyes of the West) is limited.[2] Doctrinal conflict thus involves agreement and disagreement at the same time.

The Comparative Framework

With the foregoing setting the general framework, it may now be appropriate to outline those aspects of the Church's history in the sixteenth and seventeenth centuries[3] and of Communism today which provide the point of contact for this comparative treatment of deviation control. The analogies that will be suggested are not meant to establish a rigid identity in behavior, but rather to unfold certain parallel trends, given the structural-functional similarities of the two movements. Perhaps it need not be added that the pace of events in our age is so rapid that changes involving mere decades must be equated with processes which, in the past, took several centuries to mature.

No general equivalence between Catholicism and Communism can be implied by this study. Indeed, a most vital and distinctive aspect of the activity of the Catholic Church, the spiritual, which defines the unique character of the Church as both a spiritual and a temporal institution, is altogether excluded from consideration. However, certain aspects of the social-political functions of the two movements are both sufficiently similar and unique to them to justify a joint analysis. Both movements see themselves as the exclusive standard-bearers of an absolutely correct and normatively all-embracing vision of reality; both have been frequently tested in the defense of the purity of their doctrine; and, since almost nothing that occurs on this earth is seen as irrelevant to the doctrines of these organizations (although Catholicism recognizes the realm of the morally neutral), both have been faced with the difficult task of developing their doctrinal storehouse to take into account changing social conditions. Both are inherently committed to proselytization and are expansion-oriented: A static or defensive outlook is contrary to their internal nature, while their value-systems make the success of any one unit of the movement the source of satisfaction to the entire membership. This membership is exclusive, and both movements have jealously protected themselves against the free influx of groups claiming alleged identity of views.[4] Both are international, yet both have been frequently faced with the challenge of having to reconcile their claim to universality with the often intense impact of nationalism on their various memberships. It would be incorrect to think of them simply as homogeneous units. Precisely because of their universal scale, their internal organization has to reflect the complexity of the human condition, and they must take into account various national and functional needs. Hence these movements possess only relatively homogeneous international organizations,[5] composed of usually more homogeneous units. Finally, both movements have a highly developed hierarchical power structure, they stress internal discipline, and they possess a sophisticated bureaucratic apparatus which in itself generates an organizational compulsion toward application of the doctrine in practice.

Deviation involving the relations among some of these units, and not deviation within any one of them, is the object of this study. In the case of Catholicism in the sixteenth and seventeenth centuries (the choice of this period is justified below), the principal units were, first of all, the center of the organization, the Papacy, with its highly developed bureaucratic apparatus and its far-flung Papal nuncios; the various Catholic kingdoms, which in general accepted the principle of universal Catholic unity, but with varying degrees of actual Papal intervention in their church matters;[6] the established Catholic universities, such as Louvain or the Sorbonne, which were very active in doctrinal discussions, and which operated as corporate entities; the dioceses, particularly those ruled by strong-willed bishops anxious to assert the principle of internal episcopal independence from Rome; and the various orders of the Church, such as the Jesuits, the Dominicans, the Franciscans, etc.

A systematic classification of the component units of international Communism would presumably include the various Communist-governed nation-states and the national Communist parties as well as the center of the movement, the CPSU.[7] These states differ in national power and are in various stages of doctrine-fulfillment (i.e., some are still building "socialism," while others are more or less ahead); some are truncated states, hence the expansion-orientation of their Communist elites is more intense; and some are indigenous Communist regimes, while some are entirely dependent on Soviet support.* Within the various ruling parties, different shades of ideological orientation, the extremes of which are generally described under the terms revisionist and dogmatist, have developed in recent years. There are also strictly international, functional Communist undertakings, such as the WFTU, etc. Thus, both international movements are composed of various political entities of asymmetrical strength, interacting and sometimes clashing within a common organizational-doctrinal framework.

Perhaps it is not entirely accidental that these organiza-

---

* A fuller classification of Communist states might have the following categories: stages of doctrine-fulfillment; stages of social-economic development; unified or truncated states; indigenous or imposed Communist regimes; stable, popular regimes; stable, unpopular regimes; unstable, unpopular regimes. It would be interesting to see whether there is any relationship between the above and the doctrinal attitudes of the ruling elites. However, that is subject matter for a separate study.

tional-functional analogies are also matched by certain parallels in historical experience. By the late sixteenth and early seventeenth centuries, the Church, and particularly the Papacy, was seeking new formulas for doctrinal and organizational unity. Badly shaken by the Reformation, which had split Christian unity, the Church was exposed to various crosscurrents of reform, some seeking salvation in new forms of organization and behavior, others turning to a fundamentalist, literalist reaffirmation of the doctrine. The emergence of absolutism, furthermore, meant that the Catholic world was increasingly becoming a composite of units, each claiming domestic sovereignty. The universal Church, in effect, had become an international one, i.e., composed of national units. The direct physical scope of Papal power became much more limited, and the problem of defining its limits and of somehow translating it into authority was a source not only of concern but also of tension within the Catholic world.

Communism has faced similar problems in the course of the last decade. Communism in one country expanded to twelve countries, thus becoming international. But the split with Tito, then Stalin's death, the crisis of 1956, and the self-assertion of China have limited the direct scope of Soviet power,[8] despite nuclear weapons. The problems of defining the role of the CPSU within the changing bloc and of coping with the revisionist and the dogmatist remedies for some of its ills have been preoccupying Communist leaders over the last few years. In both cases, perhaps the two most important antecedent developments, which subsequently shaped the histories of both Communism and Catholicism in the periods under discussion, were (1) the emergence of highly centralized power within each, and (2) the crisis of unity, prompted in part by the internal deformations generated by the arbitrary and increasingly corrupt practices employed in the exercise of that power.

Papal power, including its use of physical coercion, grew rapidly in the late Middle Ages. Many factors contributed to its growth. The doctrine itself generated pressures, with the Petrine Texts of the Gospel of St. Matthew, chapter 23, providing the authoritative source, for Papal supremacy over the other bishops.[9] The Crusades, with their mobilization of doctrinal zeal, reinforced the special position of the Papacy, while the diplomatic initiatives of the Popes in gaining the support of European monarchs and in raising the necessary financial backing through indulgences and other means enhanced their special status. The appearance of military orders, independent of local parishes and dioceses, acknowledging only the sovereignty of the Pope, likewise contributed to Papal power. These were followed, on a larger and more enduring scale, by various mendicant orders, whose ordained members, traveling around Europe, gradually undermined the autonomy of the local bishops. Two great Catholic universities, Bologna and Paris, helped to develop the intellectual underpinnings of the Papal system.[10] Under Pope Gregory IX, the principles of Papal supremacy were fully developed, while in the Roman Curia the nucleus of an efficient and centralized bureaucracy was established. More generally, perhaps, these developments can be viewed as a centralizing drive inherent in any action-oriented organization committed to an absolutist value-system.

Doubtless, the Inquisition also contributed to the consolidation and expansion of Papal power. The use of physical violence, frequently wielded by members of one of the mendicant orders, delegated by Rome directly, was vigorously applied against those accused of doctrinal error, which was defined in practice as deviation from the principles of faith laid down by the center.[11] Much of the Inquisition was directed at the members of the movement itself. In spite of the opposition of some bishops, who warned that its practices would harm the Church,[12] in time the Inquisition, especially in Spain, mounted in intensity, employing tortures, requiring confessions, rendering judgment by administrative trials without defense for the accused, and applying sanctions against families of the accused.

In the Communist case, too, an inherent tendency toward centralization was operating, given the doctrines and the early organizational inclinations of the ruling group.[13] The launching of the internal revolution in 1928–29, much like the Crusades, intensified internal zeal, while the gradual absorption of the Comintern and the purges of foreign Communists made the universally oriented movement a Soviet-centralized one. In both cases, the centralization and the application of physical violence led to corruption and internal decay.

Indeed, there are striking parallels between the processes and the effects of the Inquisition and of the Soviet purges of the 1930's. Some Communist leaders, like Kirov, warned against the use of physical violence within the movement, but were overruled. The purges which followed swept the Communist Party, using techniques similar to those cited above.[14] Just as the Inquisitors made ample use of the charge of witchcraft to mobilize popular ignorance and suspicion and particularly to take advantage of the susceptibility of the masses to prejudice, so too the Soviet secret police charged many purge victims with *vreditel'stvo*, or wrecking.* While it would be interesting to speculate at what stage a doctrinal movement undergoes such internal convulsions (might it be when exhausted patience and growing skepticism prompt in some members a renewed quest for utopian fulfillment?), the effect of the purges was a further concentration of power at the center. The fear of opposition intensified the violence, and the violence, in turn, intensified the fear.

In the case of the Church, internal decay led to a challenge to centralized power and subsequently to the fracturing of the unity of the organization. In the case of Communism, the two events were telescoped closer together: The organization's unity was fractured while centralized power still existed, but that centralized power was challenged shortly after disunity appeared. The Council of Constance (1414–18), already reflecting strong national differences, was a major effort to upset the power of the Curia, although its actual purpose was to elect one Pope in place of the three claimants. Its consequence was the doctrine of conciliar supremacy, which shortly afterward was tested at the Council of Basle (1431). Although Papal

* Many credulous and semi-literate Soviet citizens, baffled by the dislocations caused by the first impact of the social revolution, probably swallowed the charge that some distinguished old Bolsheviks were derailing Soviet trains with the same seriousness with which their thirteenth- and fourteenth-century counterparts accepted the accounts of "nocturnal meetings, where the devil appeared in the form of a toad, a pale spectre, and a black tomcat, [with] wicked abominations . . . practiced." Janus, *The Pope and the Council* (London, 1869), pp. 252–53.

power had been badly shaken, in that contest the Pope still prevailed. The split in Christian unity, effected a century later by the Reformation, thus came at a time when the movement was still basically centralized, although beneath the surface secular absolutism was setting the stage for the transformation of the Church from a single homogeneous unit into an international one. The Stalin-Tito break was, in that sense, remarkably similar, for it took place when Communism was outwardly united, but in reality it, too, was becoming international, having absorbed a number of nation-states and having set up nationally based Communist regimes in them.

Neither organization handled its first major crisis of unity well, but each was to derive valuable lessons from it. At first, both apparently thought that past methods would suffice to repel the challenge posed, respectively, by Luther in 1518 and Tito in 1948. The Pope seems to have expected that branding Luther's views heretical and ordering him to appear in Rome (Papal citation of August, 1518) would dispose of the German cleric; Stalin, with the purges presumably still fresh in his memory, assumed that a mere condemnation of Tito's regime would topple the recalcitrant Yugoslav revolutionary. It is particularly striking that, in both cases, the prospective deviants did not wish to deviate and at first went to considerable pains to reassure the center of their continued loyalty. However, the center's insistence on continuing the dialogue with the deviating member[15] resulted in the further crystallization of the deviant position as well as in an increase in the would-be deviant's personal stake in not becoming physically subject to the center's power.

The open defiance and the actual split came rather quickly in both cases. An attempted compromise, engineered by von Miltitz, the Papal nuncio, and based in part on Luther's promise to observe silence if his opponent did also, failed in late 1518, for the reasons outlined earlier in this essay. Luther continued his defiance, and in June, 1520, a Bull of Condemnation was issued. It was followed six months later by personal excommunication. Allowing for problems of communication, the split was about as rapid as in the 1948 Stalin-Tito case.

Both Luther and Tito found a haven for their doctrinal defiance in national power, and in both cases, the center, not accurately interpreting the changes that had taken place in their respective international movements, had not foreseen this contingency. Instead of either arranging for a quiet liquidation, followed by an open condemnation of the improper views, or merely ignoring the alleged deviant, the centers in both cases moved precipitously, personalized the conflicts, thereby making conciliation more difficult, and then found themselves unable to cope with the alerted and properly entrenched defiers. It is likely that greater patience on the part of the centers, and particularly refusal to engage in open dialogue, might have been more productive, especially since both Luther and Tito viewed their actions merely as attempts to invigorate their respective movements, were in some ways doctrinally more orthodox and more radical than their centers, and would have been unlikely to effect a split on their own. With time, and particularly with their deaths, the centripetal pressures inherent in the combination of absolutist doctrine and action might have sealed whatever breaches Luther's or Tito's excessive zeal could have effected.

The splits, accompanied by the profound transformation of both organizations, resulted in a quest for a new balance of unity and diversity and for new bases of central power. With Stalin's death, Communism also experienced a crisis of leadership, and it has since been seeking some enduring definition of the center's doctrinal authority. Like the Kremlin until 1956, the Papacy had not needed an explicit and formal affirmation of its infallibility, as long as it was enjoying some temporal power. With the decline of its physical power, pressures developed from within the Church, particularly from some of the orders (e.g., the Jesuits), for an explicit doctrinal assertion of Papal authority to protect the movement's organizational unity, which further doctrinal divergences, like the one with Luther, could rupture. Furthermore, the tactical lessons of the Luther experience were not lost on the Church: In the handling of subsequent deviations, it displayed far more sensitivity to the dangers inherent in doctrinal conflict and far greater skill in deviation control.

THE PAPAL EXPERIENCE

The Church's "deviation consciousness," acquired at the price of deviation transformed into open defiance, became apparent when Jansenism came to threaten Catholic unity and to defy the Pope's leadership throughout most of the seventeenth century.[16] Jansenism can be seen as a fundamentalist reaction both to the internal decay which had caused the doctrinal split (the Reformation) and to some of the reform movements within the organization, particularly the Jesuit movement, that became active after the split. Thus, the Jansenists bear a strong resemblance to the dogmatists who were active in international Communism after the difficulties prompted by de-Stalinization: They reacted furiously against the remedies suggested by the revisionists,* and used their attacks on the revisionists as a form of criticism of the center.

When Jansenism first appeared in the Lowlands, with the posthumous publication in 1640 of Cornelis Jansen's (Jansenius) major opus, *Augustinus, seu Doctrina* . . . ,[17] which stirred a lively discussion in the circles associated with the University of Louvain (as well as a prompt Jesuit rejoinder), the official attitude of the center was to discourage any doctrinal debates on the complex subjects of Grace and Communion. [18] Thus, both the Jansenist publications and the Jesuit attacks on them were criticized by Papal decree without, however, an explicit condemnation or affirmation of either.[19] The center's position was clearly one of avoiding a new doctrinal debate. However, the Jansenists were quick to exploit this restraint—much as the revisionists and the dogmatists did before the unity conference of 1957—as proof of the orthodoxy of their position. Frequently citing Saint Augustine, the Jansenists argued that their views represented the true principles of Christianity, as contrasted with the alleged doctrinal elasticity of the Jesuits.

* It is interesting to note that much of the reform criticism came from the peripheries both in the case of Catholicism and of Communism. Jansenism originated in the Lowlands. Compare with the criticisms of Communism by the Yugoslav Djilas, or the Hungarian Nagy, etc.

Although the Louvain debates were vexing to the Church, Jansenism became a serious problem only when its principles were shortly afterwards adopted by a gifted French theologian, Antoine Arnauld, and popularized by him within the French church and influential French court circles. Sympathetic members of the clergy, including several bishops and at least one convent, in turn found support in the government, always ready to protect the Gallican Church (with its French way to heaven) against the encroachments of the center.[20] Arnauld and his adherents avoided attacking Rome, but concentrated their ire especially on the Jesuits,[21] who were said to be gradually undermining the true doctrinal foundations of the movement. Formally proclaiming their obedience to the Pope,[22] the Jansenists thus made use of what we might call the "indirect-dialogue technique" and the "enemy-by-analogy" device to challenge the doctrinal interpretations of the center—again, much like some of the recent Chinese and Albanian polemics against Moscow by way of the Yugoslav revisionists. Similarly, some of the French bishops, in the course of assuring Rome of their loyalty and of Arnauld's, hinted that "certain persons" within the movement, "instead of applying the true remedies to the decay of manners, had recourse to attenuations and palliations."[23]

As Jansenism spread in France, the doctrinal debate over Grace inevitably led to a challenge to the authority and doctrinal infallibility of the center. Both sides were still anxious to limit their rift. Thus, anti-Jansenist critics avoided making explicit charges of heresy. Instead, they pointed to the operational harm of Jansenist views; for instance, Jansenist priests, because of their severity, were accused of having become divorced from the masses.[24] This charge is strikingly similar to that often made against the contemporary dogmatists.[25] Beyond that point, the center was loathe to go. Thus, when in 1654, Pope Alexander VII, was urged by some of his advisors to publish a new Bull against Jansenism, he delayed, explaining that, as long as the Jansenists did not explicitly defend the errors of Jansenius, he "was unwilling . . . to drive them to fresh subterfuges and to a denial of Papal infallibility."[26] The center was not anxious to create a new heresy, which could conceivably prompt rash reactions from the most influential Catholic monarchy in Europe.

Papal restraint gave the Jansenists some margin for maneuver. Enjoying at least the passive support of the French government, which viewed favorably those developments that might limit the Papacy's influence over French life, the Jansenists had no intention of detaching themselves from the Church.[27] A defection on their own initiative would have posed a difficult dilemma for many French Catholics otherwise favorably inclined to them. Jansenism was thus more influential when it was still part of the organized movement. Its fundamentalist attitude had won over numerous sympathizers, who pleaded their cause with the center. Many concerned believers viewed them as dedicated reformers, anxious to restore a zealous church.[28] (Doubtless, the same arguments among others have operated recently in criticizing precipitous Soviet action against their Albanian or Chinese critics.) The Jansenists, furthermore, in spite of their doctrinal zeal, did not hesitate to point to the specter of the Inquisition whenever Papal sanctions threatened, just as the contemporary dogmatists, whenever pressed, are quick to insist that true internationalism must prevail in the internal affairs of the Communist bloc. But above all, the Jansenists' major stress was on denying any novelty in their views; indeed, they frequently used the Dominican Order to prove the orthodoxy of their interpretations,[29] and Arnauld kept reiterating that he was merely expounding the views of Saint Augustine, not of Jansenius. (The dogmatists rarely cite Stalin; they rely primarily on Lenin.) Even when Arnauld took the imprudent step of openly questioning Papal infallibility,[30] and the center's sense of concern for organizational unity led the Pope (in August, 1656) to condemn explicitly Arnauld's writings, an outright rupture did not occur. A new spokesman for the Jansenists, Blaise Pascal, eloquently pleaded that there was no real disagreement with the center, because the allegedly heretical principles were in fact never uttered by either Jansenius or Arnauld, and that the whole affair was a Jesuit plot. The Jansenists thus simply refused either to submit or to leave the organization.

At this point, the issue, already grown from the realm of doctrine to that of discipline, became complicated by the intrusion of the factor of national sensitivity. "Gallicanism became Jansenism's strongest ally,"[31] just as Chinese or Albanian nationalism doubtless buttresses the dogmatists' stand against Moscow. Thus, "the Papal decisions were received with docility insofar as they concerned the sphere of faith, but as soon as the Pope attempted to intervene in any other way, Gallican susceptibilities were at once aroused in most alarming fashion."[32] The center's efforts to place before its tribunal four French bishops who had espoused Jansenism were effectively sidetracked by the

French insistence that instead they be tried by twelve French bishops, who could be expected to reflect a polycentric organizational orientation.[33] The matter thus dragged on for years, until the death of Alexander VII in 1667. Bitterness built up on both sides, and each hinted that the other had, in effect, betrayed the true faith.

The change in central leadership (which usually is handled more efficiently in Catholicism than in Communism) created a new situation. Alexander's successor, Clement IX, elevated with French support, was quickly approached by the deviant churchmen who, while formally apologizing, promptly blamed the rift on Alexander. In effect, they seized the opportunity to try to reduce the quarrel posthumously to a mere personal issue.* Since both Rome and Paris were predisposed to compromise (and the Jansenists, as deviants, could only welcome it, since it would keep them within the organization), an arrangement involving the *pro forma* submission of the recalcitrant bishops to Rome was hammered out in 1668–69. However, Rome was advised by its delegate not to publish anything which would make it appear as a total capitulation and to ignore evidence which suggested that the bishops' submission was insincere and very limited.[34] "In the end, Rome had to be content with the subscription of the four and to take its sincerity for granted. 'The Pope only judges of external actions,' Cardinal Rospigliosi observed. . . ."[35] Khrushchev might have said the same after obtaining Liu Shao-chi's signature to the December, 1960, declaration. The strategy

* This is what Khrushchev did in 1955–56, when he blamed Stalin for the quarrel with Tito; and this the Chinese might do after Khrushchev's death, or the Soviets, after Mao's.

of conciliation thus involved a deliberately staged, reciprocal ritual.[36]

The short-range effect of the "Clementine peace" was to legitimize continued Jansenist activity in France and even to facilitate its growth.[37] The center, however, persevered in its policy of moderation,[38] maintaining silence while still fully encouraging various other units of the organization (in this case, the Spanish and Hungarian clergy) to condemn the French deviation.[39] Skirmishes and occasionally bitter clashes continued, but the Jansenists were fighting a losing battle. With Arnauld's death in 1694, the doctrinal mantle passed to Pasquier Quesnel, but even pro-Jansenist writers concede that Jansenism was in its decline.[40] With the doctrinal vigor of the deviation weakened by the death of its most vigorous spokesman and with its influence on the French monarchy waning, more energetic measures of suppression could be applied. Early in the eighteenth century, two Papal bulls condemned Jansenism, and the French royal authorities no longer opposed their enforcement. The issue was simply no longer a crucial one, and the fundamentalist zeal had expended itself. Isolated pockets of Jansenism persisted, but on a socially insignificant scale.

It could be argued, perhaps, that the center's policy of restraint and covert manipulation had weakened the doctrinal cohesion of the movement's organization, but the alternative which had been avoided was that of a split. It had been skirted because the highly doctrinaire deviant had an inherent inclination not to cast himself out of the common fold, while the center, aware that France might be lost if the deviation became defiance, played the game in such a manner as not to destroy all the binding elements. This meant, of course, that the deviant enjoyed a measure of impunity, but at the same time his oft-proclaimed loyalty to the center was bound to become politically operative when the divisive issues ultimately lost their conflict-fed sense of urgency.

Before turning to the general implications of the foregoing, a briefer survey of another aspect of the Church's history in that period is revealing. Catholicism in the sixteenth and seventeenth centuries, much like Communism today, seemed to have reached its zenith in Europe and increasingly saw its fulfillment in what today would be called the underdeveloped lands. Missionary work, particularly in the Orient, seemed full of promise. The Chinese Empire offered a particularly appealing target, and late in the sixteenth century the first Jesuit missionaries succeeded in penetrating its hitherto sealed frontiers.[41]

Conscious of the intense Chinese self-esteem and xenophobia, the Jesuits proceeded with utmost caution and discretion. Since foreigners were generally not allowed to settle within the Empire, and since foreign proselytizers were certain to be kept out, the Jesuit fathers carefully avoided any specific identification with Christianity and, in petitioning the Chinese authorities for the right to settle in China, they (in the words of Father Ricci) "explained that they were members of a religious order, who had left their native land over distant seas, attracted by the fame of the Chinese Empire . . . that they intended to remain here for the rest of their lives, and that all they wanted was a small plot of ground to build a house, and also a church in honor of the King of Heaven. . . . Neither in this request nor in any other way was any mention made of Christianity. . . ."[42]

The Jesuits were quick to adapt themselves to Chinese customs, applying their founder's injunction that "we may *ad bonum* approve or agree with someone in regard to some one thing that is good, passing over other bad points, and thus by winning his confidence we further our good object; by going in with him we come out with ourselves."[43] They tolerated Chinese ancestor-worship, on the grounds that it merely involved filial veneration, and they praised Confucius as a wise philosopher.[44] After a quick appraisal of the Chinese social-political structure, the Jesuits adopted the dress, the customs, and the status of the *literati* and cultivated the upper classes. In their appeal to them, the Jesuits at first avoided outright proselytization, but instead attempted to impress the Chinese with European science and gadgets. For example, they gained the right to establish residence in the province of Canton by presenting a mechanical clock (a device unknown in China) to the governor.[45] Having gained entry into Peking through the presentation of similar gifts to the king, "the esteem which the Jesuits enjoyed at the Imperial Court grew still further when, in 1610, they foretold the date of an eclipse of the moon with greater accuracy than the native astronomers."[46] Father Ricci himself, at various stages of his remarkable mission, overcame Chinese suspicions by making for them detailed maps and globes of the world (and carefully putting China in the middle so as not to hurt Chinese self-esteem); by presenting their dignitaries with clocks and watches; by installing a large clock on the outside of his mission so that people could admire it; by teaching advanced astrology and mathematics to the Chinese scholars. In his memoirs, in a chapter entitled "Mathematics and Converts," he states that "whoever may think that ethics, physics and mathematics are not important in the work of the Church, is unacquainted with the tastes of the Chinese, who are slow to take a salutary spiritual potion, unless it be seasoned with an intellectual flavoring."[47]

It is evident from the foregoing that the "soft sell" technique of the Soviet technical missions is not original. Contemporary Soviet policy toward the underdeveloped lands is clearly premised on a similarly sophisticated appreciation of the depth of national sensitivities. The Soviets, by and large, have toned down direct ideological propagandization, and they calculate that Communist doctrinal advances will be a function of demonstrated Soviet technical skill. They have been de-emphasizing the revolutionary ethic and concentrating on winning over the "national bourgeoisie," i.e., the intellectual-political elite. Not revolutionary peasant armies, but rather Soviet-trained intellectuals, mesmerized by Soviet technical achievements, will lead these nations into socialism. The similarity in the relationship of Father Ricci's clocks and astrology to Catholicism and of the sputniks and cosmonauts to Communism is striking.

The parallel goes farther, since these moves provoked severe charges of doctrinal laxity within both international movements. Just as the Chinese Communists have given evidence of their displeasure with the Soviet approach toward the neutralist and underdeveloped lands,[48] so the Franciscan and Dominican missionary orders looked askance at the Jesuit methods in China and India, and, traditionally emphasizing other aspects of the common doctrine, they saw in these methods dangerous signals of heresy. Their suspicions were especially easily aroused, since the orders had earlier differed (as the Soviets and Chinese recently have) on matters pertaining to internal reforms within the movement's organization. Thus, for example, the Dominican Alfonso de Avendano had spent seventeen years (1577–94) preaching that the Jesuits were "secret heretics, hypocrites, and pharisees."[49] Some Dominicans, furthermore, had been sympathetic to the Jansenists. The feeling was widespread among many Catholics that the Jesuits "adapted their teachings too freely to the spirit of the world. . . ."[50] Moving into the Orient, the Franciscans, therefore,. proceeded to apply their own more direct strategy: "Crucifix in hand they preached in the open streets and public places, condemned to the deepest hell Confucius . . . and proclaimed that every kind of veneration of ancestors was unlawful; the Jesuits' caution with regard to Confucius and the veneration of ancestors they condemned as connivance at idolatry."[51] It may be assumed that the predominance of the Spanish Conquistador tradition among the Franciscans and Dominicans had something to do with their attacks on the predominantly Portuguese and Italian Jesuit missionaries. National differences thus probably intensified the tension.

Although the Franciscan methods quickly backfired by provoking Chinese violence (one is tempted to think of possibly varying Soviet and Chinese Communist guidelines to the Iraqi Communists and of the ill-fated Kirkuk uprising),[52] the debate persisted. In effect, the center was faced with the now familiar question of determining the proper balance between the universal and the particular. Wisely, however, no quick decisions were reached. The matter was deliberated; missions traveled to and from the Orient (consuming years in the process); and commissions were appointed. The formal solutions finally adopted by Rome tended toward compromise: In 1645, the Jesuits suffered a setback; in 1651, they recouped some of their losses.[53] However, just as the Jesuits effectively argued after 1645 that the center had not been apprised of all the relevant facts, so after 1651 the other orders similarly felt that the concessions now granted to the Jesuits were based on improper information, and they simply would not take advantage of such doctrinal shortcuts. But with time, they gradually relented, as practice showed the advantages of Jesuit efforts.

Several factors helped to contain the dispute, even though some outraged spokesmen at times had already charged heresy. (It is to be remembered that the issues involved were of very great doctrinal import, even though superficially they may have seemed only matters of tactics.) The acceptance by the parties involved of the center's judgment on doctrinal issues established a certain common frame of reference, even if the respective parties subsequently tried to evade surreptitiously the center's decisions. Recognition of Papal authority automatically meant the acceptance of arbitration as the method for resolving doctrinal issues. Secondly, the *esprit de corps* of the organization and the dedication of its member units to a common value system, in which the specific success of one unit reflected glory on the movement as a whole, meant that doctrinal issues which could be tested in action (as contrasted to purely abstract ones) were not easily translatable into overt doctrinal ruptures. Thirdly, the center's handling of the problem (in part due to the slowness of communications and to bureaucratization) was deliberate, which created a safety valve and made compromises possible. Lastly, the passage of time demonstrated quietly the superiority of one method over another, thereby also helping to control potential deviationism.

A seventeenth-century outside observer might have expected a different outcome. An imaginary analyst, employed either by an interested non-Catholic power in, for instance, A-CIA (The Anti-Catholic Information Association) or, let us say, by the Constantinople CAND (Catholic Analysis and Development Center), might have quickly dismissed the common doctrine as irrelevant to his analysis, especially since, being external to it, he would find it difficult to grasp the doctrine's special, universalizing function of self-identification. The analyst, furthermore, would have been very conscious of the relatively recent split in Catholicism, and might hence have tended to interpret every limited scrap of evidence, culled from Jansenist pamphlets or from discreet Jesuit or Franciscan "leaks," as signaling the likelihood of a new rupture. Internal doctrinal deviation coupled with evidences of internal strategic differences, based in part on nationalism, would have seemed to augur a dark future for the international movement's organizational unity.

Toward a "Manual" on Deviation Control

Perhaps certain lessons relevant to analysis of developments within contemporary Communism are to be learned from this very brief survey, and they may even serve as a modest point of departure toward a "doctrinal conflict and deviation-control manual." International Communism, a doctrinally oriented movement composed of various nationally based Communist parties, is inevitably involved in perpetual internal bargaining designed to establish common doctrines and strategies and to resolve conflicting interests or views. Since the CPSU is still by far the most powerful and authoritative party,* it follows that its basic preoccupation is with minimizing doctrinal divisions and with preventing any one unit from assuming the stance of outraged doctrinal self-righteousness. Harmonious unity avoids situations which could lead to a challenge to that primacy. On the other hand, the various other units, and particularly those which have some claim to speaking authoritatively, especially the CCP, by adopting doctrinally deviant positions and arguing about them with the center, indicate clearly that their purpose is to persuade the center to change its position, even while preserving internal organizational unity. The very fact of argument indicates absence of a desire to defect, but also signals the possibility of a challenge to unity. However, the dynamic of argument can subsequently generate sufficient heat to cause defiance, defection, or condemnation, i.e., escalation.

---

* There is an inclination in some quarters to exaggerate the present power of the CCP. It is to be remembered that China's general backwardness, overpopulation, economic difficulties, etc. all place it in a position vis-à-vis the U.S.S.R. analogous, in many respects, to that of India vis-à-vis the United States in the non-Communist world. It is curious that, when India is discussed, its overpopulation is normally mentioned as a factor of weakness. When talk shifts to China, however, the same factor is normally mentioned as proof of China's power.

The weaker but skillful deviant, therefore, especially in the beginning, acts as if there is no distinction between his and the center's doctrinal position, even if he suspects that the center has strayed from the "truth." On the contrary, he studiously and monotonously reiterates his allegiance to the movement, appealing to some earlier and mutually respected source of its doctrine. This forces the center either to tolerate the deviation, allowing it perhaps to spread, or to take the first step in joining the issue, in effect launching a process of argument which it naturally would prefer to avoid. The skillful deviant makes the choice difficult by his strategy of ambiguity, always implying the possibility of his return to the position of doctrinal subordination, while gradually consolidating his position and probing the international movement for other sources of support. This prevents the center from issuing public threats, since the issuance in itself implies conflict and, with the center presumably wishing not to precipitate conflict, forces the center into silence. Informal threats, on the other hand, can be deflected by the deviant through equivocation, requests for further explanation, etc.

The deviant, furthermore, may protect himself against the center by using his assets of weakness or of fanaticism or both. The "asset of weakness" involves pleading sympathy with the center's doctrinal position but inability to enforce it. Thus, the center is faced with a situation in which the alleged deviant pleads doctrinal orthodoxy in principle, but deviates doctrinally in practice. The choice, then, is whether or not to punish the deviant for a situation which he, indeed, perhaps truly may not be able to control.

For instance, the University of Louvain pleaded lack of competence to enforce a Papal Bull against the Jansenists, while not questioning the validity of the Bull.[54] Similarly, Gomulka accepted in principle socialism in agriculture, but pleaded that he could not enforce collectivization.*

The "asset of fanaticism," i.e., being more doctrinally extreme than the center, restrains the center by implying to it that the deviant "has his heart in the right place but is a little extreme."† The effect is similar to that achieved by the advantage of ignorance in a mixed-motive game, "if it is recognized and taken into account by an opponent."[55] Furthermore, within a doctrinally oriented movement, the fanatic usually can protect himself by "literalism," i.e., by citing texts, thereby forcing the center into the more difficult position of having to prove that its own novel interpretations, often necessitated by changing social conditions, are still in "the proper spirit" of the doctrine.[56] The fanaticism, furthermore, carries with it a degree of commitment which may inhibit the center's reaction for fear of

* The center can also use this dodge to protect itself against claims. For instance, the public Soviet emphasis on achieving a higher standard of living can be seen as a form of commitment to a third party (i.e., its own people), which makes it difficult for the Soviet Union to respond fully to the demands of its allies for economic aid. For example, when China demands greater aid, the Soviet leadership can point to its public commitment as an excuse for not giving it.

† This generalization was indirectly confirmed in 1965, when the Soviet leadership, commenting on the Sino-Soviet dispute, conceded that "at the beginning of the controversies . . . one might have received the impression that we were dealing with the CCP leaders as ideologically mistaken people who were trying, without understanding the real situation of the world, 'to speed up the world revolution' and who are willing, in pursuit of this aim, to risk a 'general war' and sacrifice their own and other people." (Circular letter of the CPSU, as published in *Die Welt*, March 21, 1966.) Author's note, 1966.

prompting an irrational defiance by the deviant.* Indeed, under certain circumstances, it may even be advantageous for one of the protagonists, usually the weaker, to acquire some uncertainty about himself in order to minimize predictability: e.g., the alleged Jesuit reputation for "duplicity," or the inscrutability and vagueness of the Chinese Communists. (Apparently the Soviets have complained that the Chinese use of aphorisms is complicating "comradely" discussions.)

Lastly, the deviant, in order to support his position, can mobilize non-doctrinal commitments, which then are cloaked in the doctrinal mantle. It is noteworthy that Luther, Arnauld, Tito, Mao, and Hoxha, all of whom would consider themselves strict exponents of the doctrine, used nationalism as a source of power to buttress their doctrinally deviant positions.

In responding skillfully, the center must be careful to

---

* This gives the physically weaker but more extreme deviant a bargaining advantage. If, for instance, in the Sino-Soviet dispute the Soviet and Chinese preferences were as follows:

Soviet

(1) Only Moscow speaks for the movement on doctrinal issues.
(2) Neither speaks, i.e., agreement to silence.
(3) Both speak, i.e., open dispute.
(4) Only Peking speaks, i.e., capitulation.

Chinese

(1) Only Peking speaks. . . .
(2) Both speak, i.e., open dispute.
(3) Neither speaks.
(4) Only Moscow speaks, i.e., capitulation.

then, using game theory, the advantage would rest with the Chinese. See R. D. Luce and H. Raiffa, *Games and Decisions* (New York: John Wiley & Sons, 1957), pp. 146–49, for alternative mathematical calculations, on the basis of a payoff matrix, of relative scales of advantage. (The above example is adapted from their use of two individuals resolving a problem of conflicting choices.)

take advantage of those factors in the posture of the deviant which inhibit the potentially dynamic escalation of deviation into defiance or defection.[57] As long as the deviant acknowledges the principle of organizational unity, the organization enjoys a long-range advantage. Deviants die, the organizations go on.[58] But if the center abandons self-restraint and cuts off the heretical limb before waiting for it to wither, the limb may sprout its own roots and grow into a tree. That was Stalin's mistake with Tito, which Khrushchev has so far avoided with Mao. An open condemnation, furthermore, involves an irrevocable doctrinal commitment, creating a gulf which subsequently may be very difficult to bridge without the outright capitulation of one of the parties. Khrushchev discovered this when seeking a reconciliation with Tito.

Restraint, furthermore, is more advisable in the case of fanatical, fundamentalist deviants than in the case of those who wish to moderate and dilute the doctrine. The fundamentalists, in the final analysis, can still be counted as adherents to the common doctrine in terms of still being *against* (and even more so) the common enemy. In the case of the moderates, the shift is toward the camp of the enemy, but even then, the deviant is normally very careful to avoid any identification with the enemy. As long as this is the case, the internally unifying doctrinal self-identification still exercises pressures for unity.[59]

An open condemnation of doctrinal heresy should either accompany or follow the physical liquidation of the deviant. Issuing it in the expectation that it will cause his liquidation or submission is not likely to be effective, if the deviant enjoys local, nationally based organizational backing and is given no choice but to mobilize it for the defense of his position and of his life.* Rather, since early in the game the deviant normally wishes to avoid a schism,† but is also concerned with proving to his own local organization that it must sink or swim with him, and since, furthermore, there are normally groups within his organization which would like to displace him and can take advantage of the friction with the center to attempt to do so, it is to the center's advantage to pose as the moderate party seeking reconciliation. Doctrinal arguments, even if covert, lead to the doctrinal crystallization of the deviant's position, which tends to be quite rigid once it has taken shape. Restraint gives opposition elements within the deviating local unit an opportunity to argue that their deviant leadership is recklessly and unnecessarily rupturing the international organization's unity. A useful device here might be to invite the deviating leader for conversations with the center: This puts the option up to him—to refuse to go is to take the initiative in splitting; to go is to take a certain personal risk.‡ The desirable quality of ambivalence in this invitation would be increased if the past record could not provide the deviant with much certainty of either a safe return home or an untimely demise.§

* Alternatively, it might be issued when the opponent is already in the process of being defeated. Presumably this was why Abraham Lincoln, who had insisted earlier that preservation of the Union, not slavery, was the issue in the Civil War, delayed the Emancipation Proclamation until after he had significant victory on the battlefield to give it weight. (I am indebted to Professor Mansfield for this observation.)

† Luther, Arnauld, Tito, Hoxha, all apparently started off with no desire to split.

‡ Arnauld, Luther, Tito refused; Gomulka went in 1956; Hoxha apparently hesitated. Many of Gomulka's friends urged him not to go.

§ This might be called the center's asset of inconsistently uncivilized behavior.

As long as the deviant still sees himself as part of a doctrinally bound family, fear of isolation is a powerful restraining factor available to the center. Just as Rome took advantage of the loyalty of the peripheries subtly to restrain the French, so Moscow, in 1960, attempted to isolate the Chinese and the Albanians. Here, the fanatics are more vulnerable than the moderates, since they have nowhere else to go. For this reason, an outright condemnation should be delayed, while the fear of it, to which even a deviant is susceptible, since he still sees himself as sharing in the common undertaking, should not be diluted by threats. Besides, partial direct reactions (e.g., counterarguments) on the center's part have the double disadvantage of suggesting weakness and of stimulating further disagreement; thus, the suspended and undiluted fear of condemnation is a better deterrent in a situation which has no easy way out. This may be true even if the deviant, aware of his importance (e.g., China), doubts that the center would take such an extreme step: He may doubt it, but he cannot be certain.[60] Dilution increases his security and, hence, impunity.

Indirect and ostensibly irrelevant reactions are another weapon of doctrinal conflict, in addition to the techniques of "indirect-type dialogue" and "enemy-by-analogy" already mentioned. Avoiding any *direct* relevance to the issues at stake and formally maintaining the position that no disagreement is involved, such reactions can convey the center's displeasure, without permitting the deviant to assume the pose of the aggrieved party and to mobilize local support, which becomes convinced that it has no choice but to resist the center. Slowing down economic aid, granting fewer honors (but still granting *some*), addressing anniversary greetings to the unit, but failing to mention its leaders, downgrading the deviant's doctrinal standing—these are insufficient to provoke a rupture, but they can weaken the internal position of the deviant and provoke factional struggle within his realm.* Furthermore, if the issue is sufficiently acute, it may be advisable to select some insignificant section of the international movement for forceful condemnation and destruction as a lesson to others. Failure to liquidate rapidly and physically the moderate Gomulka in 1956 (which presumably could have been done, although at unpredictable risks) gave the fanatical Hoxha a certain amount of security in 1961.[61] And Hoxha's condemnation in 1961 or 1962, while creating a new split, would at least have the effect of increasing credibility for Soviet seriousness, while putting before the Chinese the difficult option of responding, or not, to an accomplished fact which ostensibly does not concern them.†

But even if the center decides to take such an indirect, but extreme, step as condemning Hoxha to influence the behavior of the more important Mao, it is still desirable to find a means of giving Mao some advance warning, sufficiently ambiguous to prevent a counterwarning, but clear enough so that the step itself cannot be subsequently interpreted as an effort to take him by surprise. Irrevocable sur-

* Thus, for example, the general theme that no country can build socialism alone (with its implied threat of isolation of China) was certainly more credible when quietly accompanied by illustrative steps—gradual shutting off of her supplies, etc.

† This paper was submitted for publication prior to the open Soviet attack on Albania in October, 1961, and not revised in the light of subsequent events.

prise moves, such as a sudden condemnation, intensify the conflict by eliminating the stabilizing factor of mutual anticipation. They are only desirable in a post-defiance or defection situation, i.e., in a case of outright conflict.*

The foregoing "praxeology"[62] of deviation control is derived from the mixed-motives character of doctrinal conflict. Significantly, in such conflict the opponents have generally tried to keep their disagreements confidential; and sometimes, even after a doctrinal rupture, they have cooperated in protecting the internal secrets of the movement from "outsiders."† Secrecy not only gives them a certain flexibility and allows them room for maneuver; its cause is more deep seated than that. It is rooted in their shared sense of distinctiveness as compared to the rest of the world and in the self-restraint imposed on them also by the very existence of that world. Both China and the U.S.S.R. think of the United States every time they exchange mutual accusations, and the existence of the United States cannot help but restrain deviationist tendencies within Communism. Furthermore, if the movement as a whole is experiencing the self-invigorating sense of fulfillment in its mission of world expansion,[63] the divisive tendencies within tend to be submerged by the political momentum of its forward thrust and by the emotional satisfaction of personal triumph on the part of its individual members.

The stabilizing effects inherent in the common doctrine, which provides a mutually understood framework for com-

---

* The sudden Soviet move against the Chinese in Bucharest in the summer of 1960 did much to intensify the bitterness.
† The Yugoslavs are a good example.

munication,* and in the conflict-limiting factor of distinctiveness, which makes alliances outside the doctrine very difficult, are at their greatest if the international organization possesses an acknowledged doctrinal arbiter. An organization built around an absolute dogma requires this arbiter to avoid splits. The church as an organization sought him by rooting Papal authority in the doctrine of infallibility. Indeed, Catholicism probably preserved itself as a major unified force by taking that step. Otherwise, it might have become a loose federation of various national units, with very differing doctrinal commitments. Stalin's infallibility derived only from an authority which rested primarily on power, and the remaining vestiges of both were destroyed by Khrushchev in 1956. One may justifiably speculate (leaving Soviet domestic considerations apart) whether Khrushchev's position with *international* Communism would not have been stronger today if he had not destroyed the element of legitimacy inherent in his own past Stalinism and in his successorship to Stalin.

As it is, the recent divisions between the Chinese and the Soviets, while still restrained by the factors mentioned above, necessarily become contests for doctrinal primacy. The relationship is thus different from the Franciscan-Jesuit conflict, which could ultimately be resolved through their mutual recognition of Papal authority, just as the 1957 tensions between the East Germans and the Czechs on the one hand, and the Poles on the other, could be arbitrated by Moscow, especially after the November, 1957,

* This was well illustrated by the difficulties encountered by Westerners in deciphering the various moves by Tito in 1955–57 and by the Chinese more recently.

reaffirmation of Soviet leadership. The ability of the Chinese to act in spite of Soviet guidance and the eventual proclamation, in December, 1960, of the CPSU's *non-leadership*[64] mean that doctrinal divisions can no longer be effectively arbitrated, but only negotiated, within the organization. This is a politically grave liability, inhibiting expeditious deviation control.

This liability, however, is balanced by two factors. First, the Communist doctrine is so action-oriented that pure, abstract issues (such as those raised by the Jansenists) do not become the fulcrum of disputes. True, to Western pragmatists, even the discussion of the nature of imperialism or of the transition to Communism, or of the nature of our era, may already appear to involve relatively abstract, unreal issues, and the tendency to discuss them as matters of general principle seems entirely alien to a Western observer. Nevertheless, these issues are far more closely related to material reality than some of the issues raised by the Jansenists, and, furthermore, they do serve as points of departure for action.[65] Thus, while the absence of a recognized arbiter doubtless stimulates acute tensions,[66] at the same time the rapid pace of events in our age permits a much more rapid testing in action of the alternative doctrinal approaches, thereby establishing a somewhat more objective standard of judgment. This seems already to have happened in the Sino-Soviet dispute.[67]

Second, the absence of an arbiter is at least partially offset by the CPSU's constant efforts to establish itself, again through practice, as the unit of the international movement closest to the doctrine-fulfillment stage. Its emphasis on "objective" material demonstration of this proximity is designed to ward off possible challenges based on such "subjective" factors as mass zeal and revolutionary will. At the same time, space achievements help to underline the Soviet Union's primacy by underscoring its technical leadership in an age of technology and science. Both of the foregoing factors tend to compensate for the absence of a formally recognized doctrinal arbiter and to give the U.S.S.R. a privileged position.

Another difficulty which both international movements have experienced involves the tendency already noted in this paper for doctrinal deviations to support themselves on a national base. Since nationalism is still intense, and since international Communism is composed of nation-states and nationally based parties, Communism is particularly exposed to its challenge. Stalin's solution, to put it most simply, was to suppress it. The violent and divisive reaction which this prompted has resulted in a far more sophisticated approach, which aims at providing such close underlying economic and social ties that eventually national interdependence will make national-based deviation much more difficult to sustain. At the same time, all the elites make a great effort to educate their future successors in the common doctrine and strive to develop in them a sense of common identification.

Looking into the future, it may be worth remembering that deviation is the rule in doctrinally oriented international movements. It is difficult to conceive of circumstances in which such an international movement, action-oriented and composed of a variety of homogeneous units, each with a special interest, national perspective, and power, could avoid internal doctrinal conflicts, with some

units deviating one way or another. The ebb and flow of
this persisting condition can be described as a dynamic
state of *divergent unity.* This condition arises because the
movement cannot avoid the process of differentiation,
which is a function both of scale and of the fact that it has
become an international organization. A triumphantly expanding doctrinal movement, with an allegedly universally
valid program, can be said to go successively through a
stage of universalization, with its principles accepted or
imposed almost *in toto* on other societies, and then, when
these societies develop their own doctrinal elites, a stage of
particularization. The clash of the two, with its occasionally painful adjustments, may result in the retention of the
universal doctrine and of unity, but with a far greater
degree of diversity permitted within the international
movement. The alternative is an open split. The common
but originally absolutist doctrine thus gradually becomes
relativized.

This relativization slowly dissipates doctrinal vitality. It
vitiates the sense of distinctiveness from non-members and
weakens the concomitant fanaticism. More than this, it can
cause within some units of the international organization a
process of erosion of the doctrine to the point where the
doctrine gradually becomes an empty, formal vessel, even
if currency is still given to some time-honored slogans. At
the same time, by a process of reaction, it may prompt outraged doctrinal revivals in other units of the organization
and, depending on the nature of the general world context,
cause more or less intense clashes.

Focusing more specifically on international Communism, it is hence most unlikely that the international scene

will soon see a realignment of forces which pits, as some seem to expect, a coalition of the U.S. and the U.S.S.R. against Communist China. For this to happen, a major domestic transformation of the Soviet system would be necessary, with its Communist elite losing all hope of Communist victory, in effect moving over into the doctrinal position of its erstwhile enemies and, consequently, giving up its doctrinal claim to domestic power. This transformation could only occur in conditions of prolonged international stability. A lengthy international stalemate, with its dangerous implications of doctrinal boredom, is the condition most likely to lead to major internal stresses in international Communism, with potentially excessive reactions on the part of the more impatient units. However, such an impasse is very unlikely, since it would have to include not only the so-called Western world but also the underdeveloped areas, which at the moment seem to offer the best revolutionary prospects.

In the more likely condition of dynamic international change, either involving developments which increase the sense of Communist momentum or events which seem to them to imply a turning of the tide against Communism, the pressures for unity may be fed by optimistic feelings of doctrine-fulfillment or by the quest for mutual security. Admittedly, the forward thrust of expansion can produce its own divisive reactions: For instance, the more radical members may begin to urge even more energetic steps to accelerate the process. But it appears highly unlikely that the division would be deep enough to make one of the units take the ultimate initiative of splitting, or eventually even siding with the "historically doomed" enemies. More

214

acute difficulties could occur in the event of sustained defeats, with mutual accusations of ineptness, lack of commitment, etc., generated by the losses. However, it is likely that the very conflict with the outside enemy which led to such defeats would have intensified the hostility of the members of the movement toward their enemies, thus helping to contain the divisive pressures.

Of course, unforeseen factors can intervene in any of these hypothetical projections. Clumsy responses by either side can promote splits, since they contribute to the escalation of conflict. The succession problem is also an unpredictable factor. A sudden change in Moscow or in Peking could intensify the conflict by getting it involved in the succession struggle. On the other hand, to the extent that the existing deviation may be a function of personal animosity among the leaders, the divergence could actually narrow. To predict this, one would have to know much more about the personal relations prevailing among the Communist leaders.[68] On the whole, however, it may be said that the inherent and normal deviations generate acute conflicts (1) least often when the movement is engaged offensively and is successful; (2) more often when the movement is on the defensive; (3) most often in conditions of frustrating stalemate. Furthermore, till now, the relatively rare cases of major defection or expulsion have not only occurred in conditions of relative stalemate but they probably could have been avoided if the parties involved, especially the center, had been less inept and more flexible. Finally, both parties have usually regretted the split, especially since an expansion-oriented doctrinal movement cherishes its dynamic sense of statistical or territorial growth. A break inescapably involves a doctrinally embarrassing retrogression, and experience has shown that it is very hard to repair.

Provided the leaders exercise a minimum of skill in deviation control, along the lines sketched above, splits can be avoided. At the same time, the very appearance of divergent unity, with its reliance on deviation control to prevent splits, is a reflection of the very gradual underlying process of differentiation, relativization, and erosion. Each successful case of deviation control involves perhaps only a small measure of further doctrinal relativization, but it still always involves some. Through this relativization, the doctrinal movement as a whole eventually may lose some of its overt militancy. Hence it appears that deviations, contained but not crushed, are the handmaidens of history, stimulating the inevitable internal evolution of doctrinal movements.

7. Threat and Opportunity in the Communist Schism

In ten short years since Joseph Stalin's death, a once potent revolutionary force has disintegrated into two mutually hostile phalanxes, linked only by ritualistic proclamations of unity: an orthodox international Communism headed by Mao Tse-tung, and a revisionist international Communism led by Nikita Khrushchev. There is no cooperation between the Soviet and the Chinese leaders, no collaboration in actual policies, no coordination of a general outlook. The alliance as an active political force is dead.

CAUSES AND IMPLICATIONS

The failure of international Communism to prevent the schism appears to be rooted in certain generic peculiarities of Communism itself. First of all, the importance attached by Communists to ideology means that there must always be a "general line," guiding the tactics and the strategy of the movement. Setting the line was an easy matter when Stalin was alive. Today, it involves dealings among many parties and regimes, while the preoccupation of Communists with their alleged monopoly on the only "true" and

217

"scientific" understanding of reality results in the quick transformation of differences into matters of principle, with mutual accusations of "dogmatism" or "revisionism" inevitably following. In addition, commitment to the ideology resulted in a general delusion that, by definition, there could be no conflict among Communist states. Thus, there was no predisposition to develop the tradition of agreeing to disagree or to build up the institutions for collective decision-making.

Second, the common emphasis on the Marxist-Leninist ideology became a liability when the movement expanded to embrace some forty per cent of the world's population. A single doctrine simply could not encompass the complex, highly diverse, and rapidly changing world-wide processes of change. This was especially so since that doctrine was derived from an early stage of industrial development and later adjusted to rural societies experiencing the first impact of industrialization and nationalism. Thus, the ideology was particularly inadequate to cope with the problems both of the leading Communist state, the Soviet Union, and of the Communist parties of the more developed societies. Irresistible pressures toward doctrinal innovation (i.e., "revisionism") were created, and these, in turn, provoked a fundamentalist reaction from those parties whose conditions were still adequately served by orthodox Marxism-Leninism.

Thirdly, the nationalism of the Communist rulers prevented effective "deviation control." This was not the conventional nationalism of nineteenth-century Europe, but Communism interpreted in terms of the interests of the state power wielded by particular Communist regimes, i.e., national Communism. The so-called international Communism of Stalin was based on one leader (Stalin), on the primacy of one Party (the CPSU), and on the acceptance of one program (the Soviet). In effect, it meant the supremacy of Soviet national Communism. Neither Stalin nor his successors ever adjusted to the requirements of an international Communist community, nor have they been willing to subordinate Soviet interests to it. They mechanically identified the interests of international Communism with those of the U.S.S.R. That worked only as long as the CPSU was the effective leader. But the eventual emergence of independent or semi-independent Communist regimes, especially in China, gave rise to demands that their interests also be considered, with the Chinese even suggesting (very much in the Leninist tradition) that only their interpretation was the correct one. It should be remembered that nationalism is a phenomenon of early development, and most Communist elites reflect the peculiar self-righteousness which comes with it. This made compromise and adjustment difficult, and indeed, eventually prevented them altogether.

Moreover, the polarization of the Communist parties throughout the world into either the orthodox or the revisionist fronts is taking place in part on the basis of racial differences, pitting the Occidentals against the Afro-Asians, and in part on the basis of differences in stages of development. In a true Marxist, these considerations should prompt some unhappy reflections, refuting Khrushchev's claim that only "subjective" differences are involved.

In many parties, factional conflicts are now in progress. Irrespective of how they are resolved, they contribute to further hostility between the two sides. At the same time, the appeal of Communism as the only scientific guide for our age has been badly discredited, and its claim to absolute truth undermined. The Chinese assertion that they are the only true "Marxist-Leninists" is certainly not helped by the fact that most parties have sided with the Soviets. On the other hand, the Soviets, in their efforts to gain support, have watered down considerably the binding tenets of the doctrine, and they now accept many models of "socialism" and more diversity in the relations among Communist states. As Khrushchev put it in a speech December 12, 1962:

> Different interpretations of concrete questions of socialist construction, a different approach to various problems, are not excluded. This is what happens in practice, and it apparently will happen in the future when other peoples take the road to socialism. That is why it would be incorrect to evolve a certain model and to adhere to it in mutual relations with other socialist countries. It would be an error to condemn as renegades all those who do not fit that model.

This means the relativization of the doctrine, the erosion of its binding force. But old habits die hard, and the Soviets have not been able to overcome entirely their traditional conviction that only they are right. Hence, in that very same speech, a mere few sentences later, the Soviet leader charged the Albanians with pursuing "errors" and declared that they are not Marxist-Leninists. Thus, even within revisionist Communism, the conflict between the doctrinal and the pragmatic approach is far from resolved;

it contributes to further tensions and, eventually, to new dissensions, all the while eroding the unifying bonds of the ideology.

In the present phase of the schism, it is likely that there will be a further strengthening of ties between the Soviet Union and its allies on the one hand, and China and its supporters on the other. One sees evidence of that in the growing importance of the Council for Mutual Economic Assistance (CEMA) and in the much more frequent consultations between Soviet and East European leaders. Similarly, the Chinese will probably try to rally more closely the revolutionary parties and eliminate from them the vestiges of Soviet influence. The long-run trend, however, points toward even further diversification: Revolutionary parties, as both the Yugoslavs and the Chinese taught the Soviets earlier, are extremely difficult to control, and it is unlikely that the Chinese hegemony can be effectively maintained, especially in view of the relatively limited Chinese resources; similarly, the ruling Communist parties in Eastern Europe are likely to press gradually for a greater margin of autonomy, and the Soviet wooing of Yugoslavia is bound to intensify these pressures. The Italian Party has already asserted its autonomy. Thus, both the orthodox and revisionist wings are likely to see further erosion of central power.

In the meantime, the two Communisms will be pursuing, openly and often competitively, different strategies against the West. The Chinese have recently spelled out theirs at length. Their statements, particularly the one of December 16, 1962, make it clear that the general line of revolution-

221

ary Communism rests on "slighting imperialism strategically" and on "respecting it tactically":

> On the question of how to deal with imperialism and all reactionaries, the Chinese Communist Party has always maintained that one should slight them strategically but deal seriously with them tactically. That is to say, on the one hand, strategically, from a long-term point of view and taken as a whole, imperialism and all reactionaries, in the final analysis, are doomed to failure and the masses of the people will certainly triumph. Without this understanding it would not be possible to encourage the masses of people to wage with full confidence resolute revolutionary struggles against imperialism and all reactionaries, nor would it be possible to lead the revolution to victory. On the other hand, from the tactical point of view, on each immediate, specific issue, it is necessary to deal with imperialism and all reactionaries seriously, to proceed with care and caution and to pay attention to the art of the struggle. . . .

This means basically a policy of encouraging insurgency, of stimulating popular unrest, of subordinating the national bourgeois governments, and of directing intense propaganda warfare against the West, particularly the United States, but all that without precipitating a direct showdown.

The Chinese have made it clear that they regard Khrushchev's Cuba misadventure as a negative confirmation of the soundness of their line. In their view, because he overestimates the importance of nuclear weapons and assumes that they have a decisive importance, he recklessly involved himself in the export of nuclear weapons to Cuba, i.e., he was tactically an adventurist. And again, because he attaches such importance to these weapons, he then allowed himself to be intimidated by U.S. nuclear power; he pulled back and settled for a "compromise," i.e., he was strategically a "capitulationist." In other words, Khrushchev's short-range gambles are reckless, while his long-range policy involves the abandonment of revolutionary struggles by the masses.

In contrast, the Chinese presumably see their recent policy toward India as a positive confirmation of their strategy. By exercising restraint in capitalizing on their military advantage, they prevented direct Western involvement on India's behalf, thereby displaying "tactical" respect for imperialism. At the same time, the long-range effect of their military victory over India in their view showed the other nations of Asia that China is the number-one power in the region, that it cannot be defied effectively, that it has the ability "to slight imperialism strategically." As the revolutionary Communism gains in strength, the Chinese may eventually expect to be able to "slight" imperialism tactically as well, thereby precipitating a major threat to peace.

The policy of Moscow's revisionist Communism is much more ambivalent. On the one hand, Soviet criticisms of the Chinese are in many ways reminiscent of the criticisms voiced in the early 1920's by the Social Democratic leaders of the Second International against Lenin's Third International. The emphasis on peace; the assertion that "peaceful coexistence" is a reflection of optimism in the victory of Communism, whereas the Chinese are nothing but prophets of doom; the glowing praise for Soviet achievements—

all are repetitions of earlier Socialist criticisms of Communist revolutionary strategy. The European Socialist leaders argued that socialism could be achieved by modifying democratically the bourgeois society, that Bolshevik reliance on revolution was sheer pessimism, that the workers had already achieved too much to risk an open clash with the entrenched but gradually yielding bourgeoisie. As the Socialist-Communist argument mounted, the gap between them widened, and eventually the Socialists participated in coalition governments and adjusted themselves to the notion of very gradual reform. Indeed, by the time of the Communist revolution in Russia, many of the Western Socialist parties were already in a post-revolutionary mood. Their argument with the Communists enabled them to shed the remaining revolutionary myths.

This, too, could happen to the Soviet Union and its allies, none of which any longer believes basically in the feasibility of the "old-fashioned" revolution. They are certainly not ready to make heavy sacrifices for it, even though they still pay lip service to it.

But that is only one side of the picture. What makes the Soviet policy ambivalent and supplies the "on the other hand" of the argument is that the global ambitions of Communist ideology have now been harnessed to a new sense of national self-assertion, intensified by power and achievement. That combination drives the Soviet Union toward global primacy. It would be a mistake to consider the Soviet leaders simply as nationalists, cynically manipulating Communist slogans to gain support. In all probability, they believe themselves to be true Communist internationalists, but they interpret that internationalism in terms of Soviet interests and purposes. Thus, they will use foreign revolutions, such as the Cuban, in their struggle against the United States, and they will even back Cuba with their nuclear weapons; but, again as Cuba showed, in moments of crisis they will be ready to sacrifice the foreign revolution for the sake of the U.S.S.R.

It has been suggested that the Soviet leaders may now concentrate on domestic development, since it is hopeless to surpass America in military power, and push in the direction of a general disarmament which will eventually equalize American and Soviet power. This argument is not entirely convincing. Psychologically, it is hard to see the Soviet leaders accepting passively the idea of prolonged American predominance, and it would certainly be difficult for them to abandon their external aspirations without intensifying domestic pressures for greater freedom. The recent ideological debate in the arts shows clearly the need for an enemy, if the ruling elite is to justify its power. Ideology, nationalism, and the interests of power thus merge, and the competition with America is their natural expression. Moreover, given the Soviet image of America, the very least the Russian leaders will have to do is to keep up with American military development, lest in their view some future "right-wing" American government be tempted to impose its will on a much weaker Soviet Union.

The Soviet leaders are thus likely to continue pressing forward with their military development, hoping perhaps for a "breakthrough" in weapons development, or relying on such military spectaculars as spaceships armed with rockets for military and psychological effect. This will provide them with the necessary minimum for probing for

Western weak spots, in Berlin and elsewhere, for backing revolutions where the danger of a direct showdown is not too high, and for deterring Western moves affecting Soviet interests. In all probability, however, this will not be a crash program of military development, which sacrifices domestic aspirations altogether, or even largely. In fact, the Soviet leaders are probably quite sincere and serious when they argue that in the long run it is the pace of Soviet economic development that will be decisive in tipping the scales of history. An economically dominant Soviet Union could then effectively assert its primacy among the developing nations, while surpassing the United States militarily. The tension between the desire to take advantage of immediate opportunities to give history a push and the longer-range reliance on economic development creates the dangerous ambivalence in Soviet policy.

REVISIONIST COMMUNISM AND THE WEST

In the short run, then, the revisionist Communism is the more dangerous, because it is based primarily on Soviet power, reflects intense Soviet national ambitions, and is backed by a nuclear rocket force. As the Cuban adventure showed, the Soviet leadership is willing to brandish this destructive power in order to assert its interests. However, the gradual decline in the revolutionary orientation of the Soviet leaders, their growing recognition that a nuclear war would not bring about a Communist victory, and their increasing stress on economic competition leave room for some optimism concerning a future adjustment with the West. The orthodox Communism, because of its military

226

impotence, is less of an immediate danger, but it represents the greater long-range threat to peace. One may presume that its Chinese leaders will strive to promote international instability, not only in order to promote revolutionary situations but also to embroil Moscow's revisionist Communism in a more direct conflict with the West.

Our policy in the years to come must accordingly be based on a recognition of these differences in terms of both their short-range and long-range implications. Basically, our task is to eliminate the ambivalence in Soviet policy and to encourage the Soviet Union toward a grand reconciliation with the Western world. For the foreseeable future, it is, therefore, absolutely essential to maintain American military superiority over the Soviet Union, since even parity could tempt the Soviet leaders to engage in brinkmanship on the assumption that our society would be more likely to yield to nuclear blackmail. Similarly, it would be dangerous to make concessions to Khrushchev on the grounds that obstinacy on such issues as Berlin (or Cuba) plays into the hands of the more militant elements. Quite the contrary, anything less than military superiority and firmness actually rekindles the increasingly dormant revolutionary tendencies in the Soviet Union and sets back the process described above. In this connection, it is certainly high time to bury the fashionable notion, assiduously disseminated by Yugoslav and Polish diplomats and eagerly repeated by Western journalists, that Khrushchev's fall would be a major setback to peace. In the unlikely event that he fell because of Western firmness, it is almost certain that his successor would be anxious not to get into a similar difficulty until such time as the Soviet Union was stronger than the West.

This effective American counterweight to Soviet power prevents (to use Chinese parlance) Soviet "tactical adventurism" and consolidates Soviet "strategic capitulationism." Gradually, the U.S.S.R. might come to accept international stability; that is, acceptance of the *status quo* might eventually seem preferable to maintaining the costs of armament at present or even higher levels. For this reason, disarmament should be pursued cautiously. It is only logical to assume that as long as political enmity exists between the West and the U.S.S.R., it is in the interest of the weaker side to use disarmament to obtain, first, greater equality in power and, second, perhaps even the opportunity surreptitiously to change the balance of power. Furthermore, the premature elimination of the mutual nuclear restraint could result in new complications, given the persisting tensions between the two sides and the continued challenge from the orthodox Communist forces.

The maintenance of American military superiority over the Soviet Union would also make possible the political steps designed gradually to attract and absorb the revisionist Communism into the Western world. In Europe, this would involve a peaceful engagement in the affairs of the several Communist states, for the purpose of increasing their margin of autonomy and eventually achieving their return to the European fold. Whenever forces for moderation emerge, such as those in Poland and more recently in Hungary, they should be encouraged with aid and closer contacts. At the same time, the territorial security of such states as Poland and Czechoslovakia should in some form be guaranteed by the West. West Germany could well be advised to abandon the Hallstein Doctrine, so as to permit closer contacts between Eastern Europe and the new and democratic Germany. (The Doctrine could still be applied toward states which exercise a real freedom of choice in their foreign policy, and it could be backed by economic sanctions which, in the final analysis, provide the real deterrent to a recognition of East Germany by many neutral states.) All of these measures would help the trend toward more autonomy and moderation in Eastern Europe. They would also further isolate the East German regime, which, lacking a national base, is unable to moderate itself. Hence, it would become an isolated political anachronism in Eastern Europe and a burden to the U.S.S.R.

In this connection, a word should be said about the special and changing role of Yugoslavia. As long as the Communist world was united and hierarchical, a Yugoslavia outside it was a definite asset to the Free World. But today the situation is quite different. The return of Yugoslavia into the revisionist Communist camp has helped to outrage the more orthodox parties, while within Eastern Europe the participation of the independent Yugoslavs (who certainly are not Soviet-controlled) helps to undermine Soviet supremacy. We should, therefore, not worry too much about Yugoslav friendship for Moscow and the decline in its sympathies for the West. Its "subjective" friendship is far less important than the "objectively" disruptive character of its participation in the revisionist Communist community.

In promoting the evolution of Eastern Europe, an essential role will inevitably be played by Western Europe. As de Gaulle has unintentionally demonstrated, the concept of European unity is perhaps the most potent force on the Continent today, and it is gradually beginning to be felt in Russia also. Western Europe is not likely to remain satisfied with the artificial division of Europe into two parts. It can be assumed that pressures toward "a Europe to the Urals" (de Gaulle's phrase) will increase as Western European power grows. The inevitable acquisition of a nuclear force in some form will give the West Europeans a new sense of power and will create the basis for a foreign policy preoccupied primarily with Europe. By linking itself with the effort to break down the present division of Europe, America can both strengthen its momentum and exercise a restraining influence on those West European powers that may have strong emotional and geographical reasons for challenging Russian domination more forcefully than the United States might think prudent. A joint European atomic force, backed by the United States, would have an entirely different political complexion and would offer a far less dangerous—but more powerful—front to the East than a series of national nuclear powers, including eventually Germany. It is not too farfetched to postulate the possibility of a Europe, dominated by France and Germany, becoming to America what China has become to Russia, unless the United States now takes the lead both in shaping a militarily united Europe and in defining common affirmative—and not merely defensive—goals for all Europe.

The Common Market can be a powerful vehicle for attracting Eastern Europe and eventually Russia, but in the short run there is danger that it will actually intensify the political and economic integration of the Soviet part of the Communist world. By making trade with the West more difficult, it has already forced some of the East European states into greater economic dependence on the Soviet Union. It is, for this reason, important to consider ways in which an economically united and increasingly powerful Europe could eventually extend the hand of cooperation to the states united in CEMA. A new, European-based version of the Marshall Plan could be envisaged as a step toward the unification of all of Europe. Thus, Eastern Europe as a unit, now more industrialized and increasingly integrated in CEMA, could be encouraged to relate itself step by step to an all-European economic development, at first in very loose form, later in a more binding fashion. Over several decades, the open wound on the Elbe might be healed.

To attempt a disengagement in Central Europe at a time of tension between East and West is both useless and dangerous. But in time it may become both possible and useful as a way of bridging the gap between Western Europe (and indirectly America) and the revisionist Communist world. Rather than press for the immediate reabsorption of East Germany into the Federal Republic, one might consider a transitional status, perhaps under United Nations auspices, which would offer reassurance that drawing together with Western Europe means neither the political ascendancy of the West nor immediate deprival of East German industrial resources to the countries of CEMA.

Even more important is the possibility that the present integration of Eastern Europe with the Soviet Union may make Russia increasingly susceptible to the attraction of

Europe. Eastern Europe can serve as a transmission belt reaching ever wider circles of Soviet society, especially the intelligentsia. And as China increasingly repels, it gradually pushes Russia toward Europe and sets the stage for perhaps an entirely new historical relationship. This is not to suggest that the Soviet Union will be transformed into a social democracy or that its internal institutions will soon come to resemble those of the West. But a Russia deprived first of its revolutionary zeal and then of its global Communist ambitions may eventually find a more fruitful place for itself in the European confraternity, provided its way to aggression is first blocked by America and the way to reconciliation with it is gradually paved by both Europe and America.

ORTHODOX COMMUNISM AND THE WEST

As in the case of the revisionist Communism, the response to the orthodox Communism also must be based on the distinction between the immediate threat and the long-range problem. Communist China is our most immediate concern, while the conditions of underdevelopment and socio-economic crisis in Asia, Africa, and Latin America which nourish revolutionary Communism pose the more enduring challenge. Basically, we must combine a policy of repulsing and isolating Communist China with a policy of regionally inspired and not only U.S.-managed economic development.

China is now on the way to establishing itself as the number-one power in Asia. It has successfully humiliated India, and anyone who has recently traveled in Asia comes to be very impressed with India's political isolation, achieved in large measure by China's skillful combination of diplomacy (e.g., toward Nepal and Burma) and military power. In effect, Burma has already become China's Finland, and Cambodia, Ceylon, and Nepal are not far behind. The success of the Chinese policy was well demonstrated by the Colombo powers' negotiations to achieve a settlement of the border war: Of the six powers present, only the non-Asian U.A.R. squarely backed the Indian cause. The view that the United States is not willing to engage itself actively in a conflict with China is widespread in Southeast Asia; one highly placed neutralist spokesman remarked to the writer that Laos (as contrasted with Cuba) made it clear that Asian countries have little choice but to seek their accommodation with China. Whether or not Laos is a fair barometer, the foregoing view is less widespread among Indians, but unfortunately there is still uncertainty as to the degree of American willingness to aid threatened nations.

Therefore, the first and most urgent response should involve the building up of Indian power, especially in the military sphere. The coming generation of Indian political leaders seems to be quite realistic in its assessment of international politics; it has been deeply impressed by the fact that China has not dared to attack a single SEATO power, and it is prepared to seek large-scale Western economic and military aid to challenge China's regional primacy. This leadership will soon dominate India's political scene, especially as Nehru's power to impose his own successor has been weakened by recent events.

It would be illusory, however, to expect India to join a

collective security pact such as SEATO. Too much of an emotional investment has been made in "non-alignment" for even the post-Nehru leadership to reverse it. What is important, however, is not the form of the new Indian-American relationship but its substance. It is more than likely that, in the long run, India will show greater understanding of American interests elsewhere, as, for example, in Berlin and Cuba, and may be in a position to use its influence to restrain more extreme Russian action. The West should not hesitate to make clear to India how it defines its own interests, just as the Indian leadership is not hesitant in making its needs known.

In addition, responsible Indian public opinion seems, by and large, far more willing than the present leadership to seek some adjustment on the Kashmir issue. There is the short-run danger that the anti-Western Left (as well as the Soviet government) will use the Kashmir issue to stimulate a new wave of anti-Westernism (and even, perhaps, to justify a temporary acceptance of the Chinese conditions on the grounds that the alternative is submission to Western blackmail on Kashmir), but here again the longer-range perspective, both in terms of Indian domestic politics and of the defense needs of the Indian subcontinent, dictates a more affirmative and bold Western course, which could also reduce Pakistan's embitterment.

Until such time as India's military power is adequate to neutralize the present Chinese capacity to intimidate India's neighbors, the primary responsibility for preserving the security of Southeast Asia will rest with the United States. Sooner or later, this may require carrying counter-insurgency actions into North Vietnam, in order to force

Ho Chi Minh either to desist in the South or to obtain more direct Chinese assistance, thereby exposing Vietnam to Chinese control, a prospect which few Communist Vietnamese would relish. Such measures would also reassure Thailand, badly shaken by events in Laos, fearful of present trends in Cambodia and Burma, and increasingly subject to Communist insurgency in its own northeast. Hopefully, India will adopt a more understanding attitude in these matters, while its diplomacy could be helpful in obtaining Soviet "neutrality" in the West's purely defensive operations against revolutionary Communism.

Offensive operations against the China mainland would not be opportune. They might precipitate Soviet aid and diminish the schism. But by the same token, it would also be unwise to rush into a political-diplomatic or economic courtship of China. For the time being, the continued isolation and repulsion of China is the policy best calculated to keep internal dissension within the Communist world and to prolong the fundamental economic weakness of China.*

In the meantime, it is to be hoped that efforts to accelerate the development of the new nations will gradually begin to bear fruit. In this connection, it is desirable to encourage more regional leadership of economic and political development by countries other than the United States, thus depriving the Communists of their anti-American appeal. For example, Japan can do much more in

* However, by 1966, conditions had so changed that, in this author's view, an adjustment in American policy toward China had become timely. See the author's "New Guidelines for the West," *New Leader*, March 28, 1966.

Asia, apart from furnishing actual aid and trade, by providing a model for economic development under conditions of raw-materials scarcity and overpopulation. Till now, the Japanese have been reluctant to project themselves as a model for economic development in Asia, but perhaps the growing power of China, including its eventual acquisition of nuclear weapons, will force Japan to assume a more active role in Asia, not only economically but in a broader sense providing some of the inspiration and direction. This would also have the effect of deflecting Japan from its present preoccupation with trade with China. While eventually such trade might become desirable as a means of providing China with an opening to the West and as an inducement to follow more moderate policies, at present it would merely serve to strengthen China's capacity for pursuing revolutionary policies. Japanese resentment against the United States for impeding trade with China may be overcome, if gradually there emerges in Japan a greater consciousness of its regional responsibility for guiding and inspiring the development of Asia.

There are those few moments in history that can rightfully be described as turning points. The Communist schism is one of them. International Communism has lost its momentum, and the rhythm of Communist policy has been disrupted. Gloating over it is not enough, and to pursue policies which were developed during the time of a unified Communist threat could be self-defeating. Our task is to perceive the implications of the schism and to readjust accordingly both our perspectives and policies.

236

8. *Russia and Europe*

The Soviet attitude toward the development of European unity has been ambivalent in both politics and economics. The Kremlin, unable to interpret the European movement accurately, has oscillated from one reaction to another. Meanwhile, the processes of change within the Communist world, intensified by the Sino-Soviet schism, were creating the preconditions for a new historical relationship between the Western and the Eastern parts of the old Continent.

MOSCOW AND THE COMMON MARKET

The Treaty of Rome, establishing Euratom and the Common Market, was signed on March 25, 1957. It was not a sudden move. Coming after many years of discussion and prolonged negotiations, it climaxed the efforts initiated by the Marshall Plan in the late 1940's. Yet despite this lengthy prelude, the Communist leaders at first seemed unable to perceive the Common Market's full implications, and, as a result, their responses to it have been characterized by a high degree of confusion and inconsistency.

In the seven years that have since elapsed, Soviet analyses

237

of European developments, of the Common Market, of the role of the United States, of the re-emergence of France, and of the new Franco-German relationship have undergone several radical revisions. In part, these revisions were necessitated by the rapid flow of events. It would be wrong to imply that flexibility of analysis is in itself proof of the inadequacy of the original analysis. But Soviet statements also reveal that Soviet policy-makers were struggling hard to perceive the implications of a new reality which somehow did not fit their ideologically influenced categories.

An examination of the major Soviet pronouncements and, even more important, of discussions in the serious Soviet academic journals on foreign affairs, suggests that the evolution and revision of Soviet thinking may be seen in terms of four successive major themes, one of course overlapping the next. The latter qualification is important, because it would be misleading to suggest that at any given point the Soviet mood was fixed and absolutely rigid; within a certain spectrum, there was a continuous debate.

Thus, broadly speaking, immediately prior to the Treaty of Rome and for a while afterward, Soviet spokesmen stressed the proposition that politically the Common Market was an American plot to subordinate Europe and that economically it was unimportant. In the late 1950's, the emphasis shifted to the political threat represented by Germany (or, as a variant, to the danger of a joint American-German hegemony), while economically the Common Market was seen in an ambivalent light—no longer simply dismissed as an insignificant irrelevance, but not yet taken quite seriously. In the early 1960's, uncertainty pervaded the political analysis, especially in defining the Soviet stand toward British participation in the Common Market; but economically, the ambivalence gave way to at best a thinly veiled fear of the Common Market's impact on the Communist world. Finally, after mid-1962, the political analysis began to lay primary emphasis on the Franco-German threat, while the economic analysis welcomed any open manifestations of "imperialist contradictions."

In June, 1957, the authoritative Moscow Institute of World Economy and International Relations published its basic theses "On the Creation of the Common Market and Euratom," in which it dismissed categorically, as an illusory hope, the proposition advanced by some supporters of the Common Market that eventually it would make Europe independent of America. Moreover, Soviet observers, writing in the authoritative *International Affairs*, saw it as expressing an inherent capitalist tendency toward domination "by one leading imperialist power over others" and leading toward "American tutelage over France and the whole of Western Europe." As a result, the West European countries would be "robbed" of any possibility of pursuing an independent economic policy. The treaty was defined as "one of the most important links in the chain of Europe's economic and political subordination to the aggressive plans of U.S. monopoly capitalism." However, the writers (introducing a theme which subsequently was to become dominant) warned that the long-range beneficiary of the treaty would be West Germany.

Remarkably little attention was paid to the economic aspects. For example, a joint meeting of the editorial board of *International Affairs* and of the Department of Political Economy of the Academy of Social Sciences of the Central

Committee of the CPSU in April, 1958, which was devoted to the subject of "The Present Economic Situation in the Capitalist World," barely deigned to mention the Common Market, and then only in passing, but instead concentrated on the more ideologically satisfactory matter of "the sharpening of contradictions" in Western Europe. The view tended to be that these contradictions were fundamentally insoluble and that the Common Market would founder on them.

Partly for tactical reasons, and perhaps in part because of genuine fears, the Soviet Union by 1958 had also stepped up the theme of German domination of Western Europe. Not surprisingly, the warnings were most frequently addressed to France, in keeping with the broad thrust of Soviet propaganda since the West began, in the early 1950's, to promote West German rearmament. The Common Market was increasingly represented as a joint American-German conspiracy, designed particularly to subordinate France. Numerous articles appeared in Soviet journals "proving" that West German monopolies were extending their sway over all of Western Europe and underpinning the American effort to secure political supremacy. French interests were depicted as either sacrificed by disloyal French ruling classes or incapable of resisting this overwhelming onslaught. The constant leitmotiv was that French and German national interests were irreconcilable. Even after General de Gaulle had come to power, this view continued to dominate. Some Soviet commentators did gradually concede that the German and French "bourgeoisies" had certain common interests, that outside the French Communist Party "there is no political group of any importance in France which demands an end to the policy of alliance with German militarism," and that there might even be some temporary benefits accruing to French big business from such a *rapprochement*. But the argument usually turned on the basic proposition that France was becoming West Germany's junior partner and that this was inevitable, given the constellation of economic power.

Earlier contemptuous dismissals of the economic importance of the Common Market gradually gave way to a greater, if rather ambivalent, interest in it. Internal economic difficulties were gleefully discussed, and much attention was devoted to the clash of interests between the EEC and EFTA. This was held to validate the original proposition that, from an economic standpoint, the enterprise was doomed to fail. Somewhat inconsistently, however, and certainly in conflict with the analysis made in 1957 by the Institute of World Economy and International Relations, there began to appear, by late 1959, the theme of European-American economic competition. Although France and Germany were still said to be in basic economic conflict, they were seen as already jointly challenging American hegemony, and Secretary Dillon's mission to Europe was described by *Pravda* (December 12, 1959) as an effort to overcome Western Europe's attempts "to weaken somewhat the course of American economic 'guidance'." Thus, Western European economic unity, said to be an impossibility, was paradoxically portrayed as a challenge to American economic domination, which was held to have been enhanced by American efforts to enforce that same European unity.

Within a year, the original thesis of American domination was officially buried. In September, 1960, a contributor to *International Affairs* declared that "in contemporary conditions the former U.S. approach to West European economic problems, as only a means of reinforcing the NATO military bloc, is clearly outdated. The United States has lost control over the process of West Europe's economic integration." This was made authoritative a year later with Khrushchev's statement to the Twenty-second CPSU Congress, which noted that the United States had lost its "absolute superiority" in the capitalist world economy and that this decline, shared also by England and France, was paralleled by the growing power of West Germany and Japan. However, the political implications seem to have been quite hazy to the Soviet leaders. Khrushchev, abandoning hope of interimperialist wars, still stressed intensifying contradictions, while speaking of the decline of the United States, Britain, and France.

The crux of the political uncertainty was the problem of British participation in the Common Market. Since the whole venture was described as an imperialist plot—first purely American and then increasingly taken over by the Franco-German bourgeoisie—the Soviet leaders found difficulty in favoring the adherence of other nations to it. Furthermore, the Kremlin instinctively welcomed the conflict between the EEC and EFTA and feared that the United Kingdom's entry into the Common Market would automatically spell the end of that particular "imperialist contradiction." At the same time, however, the Soviet leaders were probably sincerely concerned lest the decline in relative American power be balanced by a consequent increase in German influence, or possibly by a Franco-

German constellation, thereby giving the Common Market a more anti-Soviet complexion. They doubtless felt that German aspirations were likely to conflict more directly with their own than the more defensive American and British desire to forge an Atlantic community, with the Elbe its eastern limit.

Thus, the Soviet leaders were torn by conflicting considerations. From an economic point of view, Britain's membership in the Common Market would be a further denial of the underlying premises of their ideological perspective; it would round out an even more powerful economic "capitalist" world; and it would be certain to have a further negative impact on the trade of the Soviets and of Communist Eastern Europe. More broadly still, it would intensify the historical appeal of European unity; and this was a consideration which Moscow could not entirely neglect, in view of the revisionist mood among the youth of Eastern Europe and even Russia. By the middle of 1962, the Soviet leaders seem to have awakened to the realization that the Common Market was a reality, and, perhaps overcompensating for their past belief in its "insoluble internal contradictions," they now began to speak of it as a powerful and dangerous instrument of imperialist aggression. In this light, any further expansion of it was unwelcome. At the same time, something would be gained if Britain joined. Germany would be balanced; a restraining voice, perhaps eventually even a pacifist one, would be introduced (so the Soviets reasoned) into the political councils of the Common Market; and the entire political structure would become more complex, which seemed advantageous. As Moscow belatedly began to perceive that

243

a Franco-German axis was being formed, Britain looked like a good counterweight.[1]

This ambivalence about Britain's political role in the Common Market was matched by a growing concern over the organization's economic implications, and the two together made for a very uncertain general line. In May, 1962, Khrushchev delivered a major attack on the Common Market and urged that an international conference be convened to produce in its stead a world-wide trade organization, of which the Communist bloc would be a part. This left little doubt that the Common Market was now being taken seriously and was being interpreted not only as a direct threat to the Communist world but also as an effective mechanism for establishing closer bonds between the Western world and the developing nations. New theses of the Institute of World Economy and International Relations, published shortly afterward, while still speaking of the "knot of imperialist contradictions" as well as noting the French and German claims to leadership in Europe, grudgingly acknowledged that the Common Market could "provide an impetus to increasing the volume of production and of domestic and foreign trade." This was coupled with a strong plea for the most-favored-nation principle.[2] Such proposals were clearly not being made from a position of economic strength.

Soviet optimism was given a new lease on life by General de Gaulle's press conference of January 14, 1963. It was triumphantly proclaimed that "this confirms what Marxists have said all along: Underneath the thin crust of 'Atlantic Unity' there boils the hot lava of imperialist contradictions." For the time being, fears of Franco-German imperialism were laid aside, and the event was seen as renewed proof of the West's inevitable decline. The whole Western Alliance was represented as being at stake, and, while Soviet reporting on the whole took a sympathetic tone toward Britain's plight, the dominant note was clearly one of jubilation. But more somber voices were also heard, and it did not take long for Moscow to perceive that fundamentally not much had really been changed, that the economic threat still persisted, and that in some ways the political picture had become more ominous. V. Nekrasov, writing in *Izvestia*, warned that Britain's exclusion facilitated the transformation of the Common Market into a political-military bloc (the theme of contradictions being quietly ignored), and, by the middle of the year, Moscow was addressing urgent pleas to Paris (Soviet note of May 17, 1963) not to further the nuclear rearmament of West Germany, and unashamedly appealing to the pride of the French (only a short time before portrayed as German vassals): "It will be no exaggeration to say that if the Soviet Union and France, the two greatest powers of the European continent, were to act in concert on the basic issues on which the future of Europe depends, then no forces could rise up and attempt to redraw the map of Europe." The change from contempt to flattery was caused both by the impact of the Common Market on the East and by the reappearance of a French foreign policy.

The foregoing discussion suggests that the Soviets were impeded in gaining any clear perception of the Common Market by: (1) ideological rigidity, with strong emphasis on "inherent" economic contradictions in capitalism; (2) an assumption that old national animosities in Europe would endure, particularly those between France and Germany; (3) a fixation on the American position in Europe and the resulting tendency to judge everything in terms of it; (4) an overestimation of the importance of the failure of the EDC and hence the belief that the EEC would also fail; and (5) a general ignorance of developments in the West, caused by lack of personal contacts and lack of understanding of dominant trends of Western thought, the outcome of many years of self-imposed isolation.

ECONOMIC ASPECTS

If a sense of Soviet weakness and concern was discernible in the realm of politics and ideology, it was even more clear, and also more warranted, in the economic field. The simple fact was that trade with Western Europe was more important to the Communist states than to Western Europe, and the development of the Common Market, with its internal tariff arrangements and new internal trade patterns, was thus a formidable threat. The Communists chose to counteract it by strengthening the long-dormant CEMA. The situation faced by CEMA was that its trade with the EEC represented a percentage of its total trade 2.3 times higher than the corresponding percentage of the EEC's trade with CEMA, relative to the EEC's total trade. Further, while the trade of some of the Communist states with the Common Market did not represent a very significant portion of their total trade, it did represent a major part of their total trade with the "capitalist" world and was a prime source of hard currency.

Because of these considerations, Communist leaders

feared the consequences of lowered customs among the Common Market countries, combined with the introduction of uniform duties in respect to non-member countries. They also feared that the endeavor to establish a common agricultural policy, aiming at self-sufficiency, might affect adversely the exports of some of the Eastern European countries. Finally, they were uneasy that the effort to establish a general commercial policy regarding non-members might give the business community in Common Market countries a new lever in dealings with the East. This was stated frankly by a Polish journal in August, 1963: "A common commercial policy of the Common Market countries creates the possibility of a simultaneous stopping of imports or exports by all six member countries. Let us simply recall the embargo in the recent period of the cold war to realize the full danger contained in this intention of the Common Market countries."[3]

In public, the Soviet reaction to the economic impact of the Common Market was to thunder against it as a political and economic plot. The substantive reaction, beginning in 1960, was to accelerate efforts to develop CEMA. Under its auspices, economic specialization has been introduced into several branches of the heavy industry of member nations; preliminary steps have been taken to establish broad guidelines for national economic planning over a twenty-year period; and, after a long delay, multilateral economic institutions have begun to make their appearance. The operations of CEMA, hitherto largely an *ad hoc* body, were also regularized and institutionalized, and a formal charter was promulgated, outlining in some detail its scope and *modus operandi*. In

October, 1963, a CEMA agreement was signed, providing for a common clearing bank based on a gold ruble (a scheme obviously copied from Western European experience). Energetic efforts were also made to create the necessary statistical basis for effective common planning (a matter of particular importance, given the absence of the market mechanism), and several multilateral economic projects were undertaken involving common pipelines, rail stock, communication cables, etc.

The quest for economically "rational" specialization, however, soon proved incompatible with specific national interests in the Soviet bloc, given the wide disparities in levels of industrial development and proficiency. Applied strictly, it was bound to favor the more industrially developed nations, i.e., the Soviet Union, East Germany, and Czechoslovakia. As a result, the move was opposed by the less developed states, and especially by Rumania, which saw favorable opportunities for its own industrial development. As a Rumanian spokesman said: "Just as on the domestic scene an absolutist criterion of efficiency cannot be countenanced, so in the field of specialization and co-operation between the socialist countries, economic efficiency and profitability cannot be accepted as the one and only criterion with which to evaluate new economic steps." And he asserted: "Building Communism on a world-wide scale is incompatible with the notion of dividing countries into industrial states and agrarian states, into developed countries and underdeveloped countries."[4]

Two factors made it difficult to refute the point made by the Rumanians. One was the development of the Common Market, which, on the one hand, involved the rapid industrial development of a relatively backward country such as Italy (thereby creating an embarrassing example) and, on the other, could present the Rumanians with tempting trade arrangements (e.g., the French have already shown an interest in developing the Rumanian oil industry). The other factor was the development of internal complications within the Communist world. The Chinese, in their attacks on Moscow, have pointedly raised the matter of discriminatory economic development, and this item the Rumanians have demonstratively republished in their own press. Here again, the relative ability of the Common Market to solve similar problems was bound to intrude into the Communist discussions. Indeed, one may suspect that the resentment of the Chinese leaders at the Soviet failure to help their economic development adequately was fed by the sight of the extensive and effective American aid to Europe. The resulting spectacular European recovery contrasted sharply with the continued Chinese failures and with the lack of interest shown by the Soviets, and in that way contributed to internal Communist dissension.

The economic and ideological impact of the Common Market thus challenged the basic proposition of the Communists that they have the key to the future. There were political factors, too, which made them pay more attention to the new strength of Western Europe, among them their failure to resolve the Berlin issue in their favor and the gradual re-emergence of France as an independent European force.

POLITICAL CONSIDERATIONS

The political challenge was personified by de Gaulle and expressed through his assertively independent French policy for Europe. In its short-range aspect, this policy raised the immediate problem of the organization and distribution of power in the West; in its longer-range aspect, it called for the definition of a new relationship with the East. By 1963, the outlines of the former were clear and the latter, although still tentative, was beginning to take shape.

De Gaulle's policy in the West rested on his confidence in the durability of Western Europe's new economic structure and in the capacity of the United States to deter any Soviet military action against Western Europe. If the basic European motivation in the late 1940's can be said to have been fear of Soviet aggression, in the early 1960's, it was self-confidence. Taking this as his point of departure, de Gaulle pressed steadily to diminish American political influence on the Continent and to replace it with Franco-German concord. Given the limits imposed on German rearmament and, more important, the moral and political factors involved, he could reasonably assume that the political (and perhaps also military) leadership in that relationship would inevitably be exercised by France. To assure that end, and also to increase Europe's influence on American military policy (at least to the point of achieving the capacity to involve the United States, even against its desire), de Gaulle undertook to transform France into a nuclear power. The long-range importance of this more than compensated, in his view, for the temporary isolation and even unpopularity of France. Only so could he defeat the Anglo-Saxon conception of an Atlantic community in which, as he saw it, the political and military power would be controlled almost entirely from Washington and London. A tightly integrated Western Europe subject to such "external" control would be, as he put it on September 28, 1963, a Europe "without soul, without backbone, and without roots," subject "to one or the other of the two foreign hegemonies."

Consequently, in his view, such a Europe would become the tool of the two superpowers, the U.S.A. and the U.S.S.R., which in fact had no incompatible interests in Europe at the time. Moscow, it would seem, no longer expected to be able to swallow up (in the near future, at least) the rest of Europe, and was content to remain on the Elbe, busy consolidating its rear. America, despite what its leaders said, accepted that division. De Gaulle stated his belief in this quite openly on July 29, 1963: "The United States, which since Yalta and Potsdam has had nothing to demand from the Soviets, now sees prospects of understanding opening before it. The result is the separate negotiations between the Anglo-Saxons and the Soviets, which, starting from the restricted nuclear test agreement, appear about to be extended to other questions, notably European questions, and so far in the absence of any Europeans. This obviously runs counter to the views of France." Having held America responsible for the division of Europe, de Gaulle then asserted that in time "a complete change in the relations between East and West in Europe" would become possible and that "when this day comes, and I have said this before, France expects to make constructive proposals concerning the peace, equilibrium, and destiny of Europe."

De Gaulle has given several hints as to what these "constructive proposals" might be. In brief, they involve the absorption of Eastern Europe and Russia into a larger European community, based on a common cultural and historical heritage and defined geographically as the area between the Atlantic and the Urals. In a speech on March 25, 1959, de Gaulle launched the slogan "Europe to the Urals," linking it to an eloquent plea for a common sense of European enterprise:

> We, who live between the Atlantic and the Urals, we, who are Europe, possessing with Europe's daughter, America, the principal sources and resources of civilization . . . why do we not pool a percentage of our raw materials, our manufactured goods, our food products, some of our scientists, technologists, economists, some of our trucks, ships, and aircraft in order to vanquish misery, develop the resources, and the trust in work, of less developed peoples? Let us do this not that they should be the pawns of our policies, but to improve the chances of life and peace. How much more worthwhile that would be than the territorial demands, ideological claims, imperialist ambitions which are leading the world to its death!

Since then, de Gaulle has frequently alluded to this concept. Clearly, he sees its realization culminating in a lengthy process of transformation within the Communist states, perhaps accelerated by the Sino-Soviet conflict and by the growing attraction of Europe and the Common Market. Accordingly, de Gaulle has cultivated China, hoping that Russia's new encirclement might even make her anxious to become part of Europe.

In spite of de Gaulle's close ties with Germany, which he sees as the backbone for independent European action, he has hoped gradually to accelerate the process of amalgamating Russia into Europe by lessening the fear of the Eastern Europeans of a renewed German *Drang nach Osten*. In this connection, he has gone farther than Washington. He has seen that acceptance of the present Polish-German frontier on the Oder-Neisse rivers as a permanent one is the *sine qua non* for drawing Poland back into the European orbit.[5] And obviously, given the geographic location of Poland and its present links with Russia, it would be the vital link in any eventual return of Russia to a European orientation.

De Gaulle's preoccupation with Eastern Europe reveals the strong element of French *sacro egoismo* and deception in his policy. Since his concept of Europe is one led by France, it follows that the two best alternatives for France are (1) Europe divided on the Elbe, in which a divided Germany depends on France for eventual reunification, or (2) a united Europe including not only a 70-million-strong Germany but also Eastern Europe (and even Russia), for the latter combined with France would more than balance Germany. He therefore could not welcome a reunification of Germany while Eastern Europe remained in the hands of a hostile, and perhaps fearful, Russia. For this reason, he welcomes and yet abuses the present American policy, which implicitly accepts the division of Germany at the Elbe, while explicitly preaching reunification, but with the eastern frontiers of Germany undefined (thus leaving the Poles no alternative but to support Moscow and Pankow wholeheartedly). This policy further makes it possible for France to gain German support simply by adopting verbally a more militant stand than the United States or Britain on such issues as Berlin. For the time being, German *immobilisme* on the subject of frontiers, together with the Hallstein Doctrine and American tolerance of the division of Europe, are all in keeping with de Gaulle's wishes: Since it is too early to move in the East, Franco-German political unity in the West should be forged meanwhile at the expense of "passive" America. If the United States and Germany should move now to recognize the Oder-Neisse line and attempt a political-economic penetration of Eastern Europe, France would be found unprepared and unable to exercise leadership. But in time, de Gaulle reasons, Germany will realize the futility of the present American approach to its problems; then the moment will be ripe for France to seek actively a "Europe to the Urals." (Could the Soviet realm beyond the Urals be an inducement to the Chinese?)

The Soviet reaction as de Gaulle's design unfolded has been guarded, but there have been signs of mounting concern. Initially, the Soviet leaders seemed to welcome French restiveness, simply because it represented a new complication for the arch rival, the United States.[6] They repeatedly stressed their desire to see France play a greater and more independent (i.e., anti-American) role in international affairs, and de Gaulle's leadership evidently provided further impetus in that direction. *Pravda* made a point of recalling that the Soviet Union, unlike the United States, had given strong backing to de Gaulle's wartime

Committee of National Liberation; and Khrushchev, both before and after his March, 1960, visit to Paris, stressed his respect for the General and his "friendly" relations with him. Parallel efforts were made to invigorate Franco-Soviet trade, which had grown steadily in the late 1950's, and which in 1958 for the first time passed the 1913 level. The growth of France was clearly linked in the Soviet mind with the decline of American power in Europe.

Although the Soviets for a time were hopeful that the resurgence of France might weaken the West, they were quite sensitive to any signs of French interest in Eastern Europe. Thus, after Adenauer's visit to Paris in the early fall of 1958, Khrushchev, in a special "interview," singled out for criticism a phrase in the de Gaulle-Adenauer communiqué about an eventual inclusion of "the maximum possible number of European states" in a European federation. In Khrushchev's words, this meant that de Gaulle and Adenauer "must have lost all sense of reality to count seriously on success in any venture in Eastern Europe." He reiterated the point two days later to a German journalist.[7]

These fears mounted as the Franco-German alliance took shape. By 1960, it was clear from the tone of denunciations used by the Soviet spokesmen that they had reappraised the French role and were beginning to see in it a long-range political danger. France was represented as not only seeking to dominate Western Europe but also encouraging the proliferation of nuclear weapons and led by an Olympian figure who had lost all sense of reality. By 1962, France was frequently represented as the chief obstacle to the relaxation of international tensions, and

de Gaulle's trip to Germany was officially attacked as part
of a plot to establish a "Europe to the Urals" (this phrase
was quoted), which would involve the liquidation of the
Communist regimes of Eastern Europe; this was to be
achieved by joint Franco-German cooperation, including
the sharing of nuclear weapons. The denunciations
reached their peak in 1963, after France's refusal to sign
the test-ban agreement.

Since de Gaulle's plans appear vague even to his own
followers, they probably also appear vague to the Soviets.
Yet this very vagueness, combined with the strong overtones of assertiveness toward Russia and Eastern Europe,
might seem to the Soviets more dangerous than the known
and basically static Anglo-American "interest" in the areas
east of the Elbe. As a result, the Soviet attitude toward the
American position in Europe became more ambivalent.
From a political point of view, a possible Franco-German
challenge based on continental Europe represented a
greater threat than the American-sponsored Atlantic community. Yet, from an economic viewpoint, and even more
militarily, it was certainly the United States and NATO
that posed by far the greater threat. How to reconcile these
alternatives became increasingly a dominant dilemma for
the Soviets, and by 1963 they seemed to be somewhat less
anxious than, for instance, the Chinese to see the United
States excluded politically from the Continent.[8] Instead,
they were more inclined to try to maneuver the United
States into a position of joint sponsorship of the division
of Europe, in the hope of stabilizing the present partition
and, perhaps, eventually creating new political opportunities for Soviet diplomacy.

In this regard, the Soviet confrontation with the United States in Cuba in late 1962 can be viewed as a particularly important watershed. It convinced the Soviets that, for the time being, their means were inadequate to their ends and that their policy of pressing both politically and militarily for a breakthrough in Europe by means of the squeeze on Berlin was doomed to failure and in fact had already become counterproductive. The United States would not yield, and the effect of the Soviet pressure in Cuba was to strengthen the "aggressive" forces in France and Germany. However, by striving for a Soviet-American *rapprochement,* based on an acceptance by Washington of the division of Europe, the Franco-German challenge might be converted into a destructive feud inside the Western Alliance and possibly might even lead ultimately to a new Rapallo. Apparently resigning itself for the time being to French and German hostility, the Kremlin decided to try to make certain that the Franco-German alignment would not receive American political and military backing. Thus, Moscow has vigorously opposed the American scheme for establishing a European Multilateral Nuclear Force (MLF) on the grounds that it would strengthen the German political and military posture.[9] Yet failure to set up the MLF would make General de Gaulle's policies more attractive to Bonn, and might even result in the creation of an independent German nuclear force, or at least a joint Franco-German force. Such a force would serve French and German political ambitions, which are less compatible with the maintenance of Soviet control over Central Europe than American objectives are. The Soviet opposition to MLF thus played into the hands of Paris and increased

Soviet uncertainty about how to handle the increasingly complex problem of relations with Europe.*

IMPLICATIONS FOR THE WEST

Russian and American cooperation could maintain the division of Europe, but there would be no guarantee that at some moment Russia might not choose to exploit European frustrations over current policies of the United States, Russia's real global competitor. For the United States to join Russia in supporting the division of Europe would, therefore, be dangerous. European collaboration with Russia against America could come about only as a consequence of European resentment of American leadership, due to what was felt to be some American betrayal of European interests. A precedent condition would, therefore, have to be an American-Soviet entente, based on joint acceptance of the *status quo* in Europe. This is the goal now being sought by the Soviet Union. Without that preliminary, European-Russian collaboration appears most unlikely, given the Soviet desire to perpetuate its hegemony over half of Europe and the increasing West European determination to challenge it. American collaboration with Europe to reunite Europe and to reintegrate Russia into the Western civilization, a process now being favored by

* The collapse of a Franco-German axis, and the consequent decision of General de Gaulle to seek on his own a new relationship with the East while at the same time weakening NATO in the West, caused a shift in the Soviet outlook. No longer fearful that de Gaulle was creating a powerful anti-Soviet phalanx—and because of Vietnam less inclined to seek an American-Soviet detente—the Kremlin rulers decided in 1965 to exploit tactically the de Gaulle gambit for the purpose of weakening American-European ties. Author's note, 1966.

the Sino-Soviet schism, appears to be the strongest and most enduring combination, one which is in harmony with both American and European long-range interests.

More than ever, Russia is now becoming susceptible to the attraction of Europe. In the past, the Russian attitude toward Europe had fluctuated. On the one hand, there was arrogant talk of Moscow being the Third Rome, then of its being the source of a new and universal ideology. On the other hand, there was a deep-seated sense of inferiority to the West and a desire to imitate it. The Russian Communists combined the sense of superiority with a drive to erase the inferiority (through imitation, i.e., industrialization). By narrowing the technical, economic, and cultural gap between Europe and Russia, the Soviet leaders have created for the first time the possibility of a relationship that is equal and honorable to both. Meanwhile, the Sino-Soviet schism marred the universalist aspect of the ideology, while Soviet control of Eastern Europe not only has diminished Russian fears of the West but also has created a transmission belt for Western values. Without knowing it, the Soviet leaders have performed the historical function of preparing the ground for a larger Europe, but— alas for them—not a Communist one.

The challenge posed by France is a sign that Europe is now looking ahead, is no longer fearful for its survival. This reawakening has necessarily involved a realignment of power in the West, with consequent tensions in the Western Alliance. But the real challenge points eastward. Ideologically, the concept of European unity, with the Common Market as the initial symbol, is proving itself more captivating as an image of the future than a Europe split into conflicting groups as the Marxist-Leninists hoped. Economically, Western Europe has shown a far more impressive development in trade, in the pooling of common resources, and in the general improvement of the standard of living than have the Communist countries. In politics, the public debates and disagreements among Western powers have been far less intense and bitter than the parallel conflicts and reciprocal excommunications within the Communist world. All this provides the West with an advantageous platform from which to invite the East to abandon its futile and old-fashioned ideological positions and to join in an undertaking that is also in its interest.

This could be done jointly by the United States and Western Europe in a variety of ways, ranging initially from long-term, bilateral trade arrangements (now being undertaken) to, eventually, a multilateral economic development plan, based on the principle of European unity. Step by step, the Eastern European states should be encouraged to become associated, remotely and indirectly at first, and then more and more closely and directly, with the Common Market.[10] Western Europe could also take the initiative in opening its frontiers to the youth of the East— and leave it to the Communist regimes, if they wish, to prevent their young people from sharing in growing European unity. It is doubtful that pressures for close ties, which would be so clearly in the interest of the peoples concerned, could long be resisted by their Communist governments. Resist they surely will, and the present efforts to develop rapidly the institutions and operations of CEMA reflect the realization of the Communist leaders that without a strengthened economic framework the Soviet bloc will be unable to match the West and contain the forces of national self-assertion within each member state. These efforts should not be underrated. But for the time being, the concept of a united Europe is still ideologically more appealing and economically more promising. Unless the Soviet Union succeeds in enlisting American support on behalf of the *status quo,* or unless America and Western Europe fail to exploit the present opportunity and look on passively as the Soviet bloc is reconsolidated, Europe is not likely long to remain "without soul, without backbone, and without roots."

NOTES

Notes

Chapter 1: PATTERNS OF AUTOCRACY

1. Vladimir N. Kokovtsov, *Out of My Past* (Stanford, Calif.: Stanford University Press, 1935).

2. For excellent descriptions of some of the leading figures in the court life of late nineteenth-century Russia, see the diaries of such dignitaries as A. A. Polovtsev, E. A. Peretz, K. Golovin, and P. A. Valuiev.

3. See, for instance, the texts of the Czarina's letters to the Czar while he was at the front, in F. R. Golder, *Documents of Russian History* (New York and London: The Century Co., 1927).

4. Konstantin Petrovich Pobedonostsev, *Memoires politiques, correspondance officielle et documents inedits relatifs a l'histoire du regne de l'empereur Alexandre III de Russie* (Paris: Payot, 1927).

5. A good source is I. Blinov, *Gubernatory: istoriko-iuridicheskii ocherk* (St. Petersburg, 1905).

6. Marc Raeff, "The Russian Autocracy and Its Officials," in McLean, Malia, and Fischer (eds.), *Russian Thought and Politics* (Cambridge, Mass.: Harvard University Press, 1957), p. 80, mentions the example of a somewhat earlier provincial governor whose routine included signing 270 papers daily, or about 100,000 a year. Recent Soviet discussions of bureaucratic difficulties suggest a striking continuity in this reliance on written and signed instructions: One regional agricultural administration reported that during 1953 it received from the Ministry of Agriculture no less than 7,569 letters; in 1954, 8,459, and an average of about 30 instructions per day (*Partiinaia zhizn*, no. 3 [1956], pp. 60–61). Czarist literature, and more recently even some Soviet, gives us brilliant descriptions of crushed bureaucrats, fearful of inspections, giving their all to the daily dose of instructions, requests, statistics, and so on. See also *Krokodil* for cartoon treatment, and Khrushchev's 1957 speeches on decentralization. For an interesting and informative account of bureaucratic vicissitudes under the Czarist regime, see Flerovsky, *op. cit.*, especially pp. 19–136. He describes his initial career as a civil servant of the Ministry of Justice in St. Petersburg, the internal intrigues and nepotism, the lack of expertise of some of the higher

functionaries, and the rather widespread disregard for established laws and rights on the part of higher and also lower officials.

7. According to the 1879 census, the Gendarme Corps numbered 800 officers and 50,000 men, the police force 104,500 men, and there was an unknown number of Okhrana functionaries and collaborators —this compared to the 435,000 public officials in the same period. (G. Alexinsky, *Modern Russia* [New York: Charles Scribner's Sons, 1913], pp. 178, 182, and 186.)

8. Samuel Kucherov, *Courts, Lawyers, and Trials Under the Last Three Tsars* (New York: Frederick A. Praeger, 1953), pp. 201–3.

9. The Russian criminal code was quite liberal in defining anti-state activities and was even more generous in assigning the death penalty for them. The death penalty was provided for any actions or conspiracies that would endanger the "life, liberty, or health" of the Czar, or would "limit" the powers of the throne (Articles 99 and 101). Furthermore, the death penalty was provided for anyone plotting to change the Russian government, or to change it in any part of Russia, or for anyone plotting to separate any part of Russia from the Russian state (Article 100). The death penalty also was provided for anyone who made an attempt on the life of a member of the Imperial household (Article 105). In addition, "armed resistance to authority or attacks on army or police officials and on all official functionaries in the execution of their assigned duties" were to be punished by the death penalty "if these crimes are accompanied by murder, or attempted murder, infliction of wounds, grievous assault, or arson." See M. I. Gernet, *Smertnaia kazn'* (Moscow, 1913), p. 54. Other offenses, punishable by death, are also enumerated. For various statistics on the frequency of the death penalty, see Kucherov, *op. cit.;* Alexinsky, *op. cit.;* and S. Usherovich, *Smertnie kazi v tsarskoi Rossii* (Kharkov, 1933). These sources also include accounts of mistreatment and flogging of political prisoners.

10. The judges were administratively subordinate to the Minister of Justice. Flerovsky, a civil servant in the ministry, cites cases of the overbearing treatment of the judges by the minister (*op. cit.,* p. 65).

11. A. T. Vassilyev, *The Ochrana* (Philadelphia: J. B. Lippincott Co., 1930), p. 39. See also N. N. Beliavsky, *Politseiskoe pravo* (Petrograd, 1915); and A. I. Elistratov, *Uchebnik russkago administrativnago prava* (Moscow, 1910). Vassilyev, quoted above, was not entirely correct, for, in emergencies, captured revolutionaries were

frequently executed on orders of the provincial governors who based themselves on Articles 17 and 18 of the Special Law for the Preservation of Order.

12. P. L. Lavrov observed in 1870: "Law in Russian eyes never stood on the level of 'written reason,' never became sacred just because it was law. Law was regulation convenient to the momentary whim of the government." ("Philosophy of the History of the Slavs," quoted in J. Kucharzewski, *Od Bialego Caratu do Czerwonego* [Warsaw, 1931], V, 53.) See P. Milyoukov, *Russia and Its Crisis* (Chicago: University of Chicago Press, 1905), especially pp. 165-85, for a general analysis of the weakness of the legal tradition. The failure of the Senate, which was meant to be the watchdog of laws, is illustrative. Filled with retired administrators and even former police functionaries, it never fulfilled its role and became a mouthpiece for the executive. See Flerovsky, *op. cit.*, p. 62, for some specific instances.

13. Merle Fainsod, *Smolensk Under Soviet Rule* (Cambridge, Mass.: Harvard University Press, 1958).

14. Andrei Vishinsky, *Teoriia sudebnykh dokuzatel'stv po sovetskomu pravu* (Moscow, 1941), p. 31.

15. For comparative treatments of the censorship systems, see M. Karpovich, "Historical Background of Soviet Thought Control," in W. Gurian (ed.), *The Soviet Union: A Symposium* (Notre Dame, Ind.: University of Notre Dame Press, 1951); Merle Fainsod, "Censorship in the U.S.S.R.: A Documented Record," *Problems of Communism*, V (March-April, 1956), 12-19; and Alex Inkeles, *Public Opinion in Soviet Russia* (rev. ed.; Cambridge, Mass.: Harvard University Press, 1958).

16. For a detailed treatment of the conspiratorial activity, see A. P. Men'shchikov, *Okhrana i revoliutsiia* (Moscow, 1925–32); and A. Kornilov, *Obshchestvennoe dvizhenie pri Aleksandre II* (Paris, 1905). Count Pahlen reported to Alexander II that the chief reason for the success of revolutionary propaganda was the sympathy that existed for it among large sections of the population (Kornilov, *Obshchestvennoe* . . . , p. 160).

17. *Pis'ma Pobedonostseva k Aleksandra III* (Moscow, 1925–26), I, 318–19.

18. Cf. Isaiah Berlin, "The Silence in Russian Culture," *Foreign Affairs*, October, 1957, with the following account of a meeting of

young Russian revolutionaries on New Year's Eve, 1880, when arrests were already auguring a not-too-happy future for them:

The preparation of the punch left a particularly plastic image in my memory. On a round table in the middle of the room a vase was placed, filled with pieces of sugar, lemon, roots, sprinkled with arrack and wine. It was a magic sight when the arrack was fired and the candles extinguished. The flickering flame, mounting and waning, lit the severe faces of the men surrounding it; Kolodkevich and Zheliabov stood closest. Morozov took out his stiletto, then another, then another, placed them, crossed, on the vase, and, without preparation, with a sudden impetus, the powerful, solemn melody of the well-known *haidamak* song was heard: *"Hai, ne dyvuites, dobryie ludi, shcho na Ukrainie povstaniie."* The sounds of the song spread and mounted, they were joined by fresh voices, and the shimmering flame flickered, bursting out with a red glow, as if steeling the weapons for struggle and death. [Ólga Lubatovich, in *Byloe,* June, 1906, pp. 123–24; quoted in Kucharzewski, *op. cit.,* V, 304–5.]

19. For an interesting recent analysis, see George Fischer, *Russian Liberalism* (Cambridge, Mass.: Harvard University Press, 1957).

20. See Kucherov, *op. cit.;* and Alexinsky, *op. cit.* The latter comments: "To be elected a juror, a man must be a landowner. The composition of the jury was subject to the control of the bureaucracy. . . . Preliminary examinations fell almost exclusively to the charge of the police." (pp. 193 ff.)

21. See S. L. Levitsky, "Legislative Initiative in the Russian Duma," *American Slavic and East European Review,* XV (October, 1956), 315–24; see also S. A. Piontkovskii, *Ocherki istorii SSSR XIX i XX veka* (Moscow, 1935), for a discussion of the electoral system.

Chapter 2: TOTALITARIANISM AND RATIONALITY

1. Much is made of this in J. L. Talmon, *The Origins of Totalitarian Democracy* (New York: Frederick A. Praeger, 1961).

2. *Totalitarianism* (Cambridge, Mass.: Harvard University Press, 1954), p. 53. The author acknowledges his debt to Carl Friedrich, with whom he has collaborated in teaching a graduate seminar on dictatorship. A product of that collaboration is their book, *Totalitarian Dictatorship and Autocracy* (Cambridge, Mass.: Harvard University Press, 1956; New York: Frederick A. Praeger, paperback edition, 1961).

3. For a fuller discussion, see Brzezinski, *The Permanent Purge— Politics in Soviet Totalitarianism* (Cambridge, Mass.: Harvard University Press, 1956), especially pp. 1-8, 168-75.

4. *Ibid.*, particularly chaps. 4 and 5.

5. Isaac Deutscher, *Russia: What Next?* (New York: Oxford University Press, 1953), p. 227. Deutscher's argument should not be confused with the reasoned analysis of Barrington Moore, Jr., in *Terror and Progress USSR* (Cambridge, Mass.: Harvard University Press, 1954). This weighs alternative patterns of development in terms of the possibility of continued totalitarian development, or a technical-rational pattern, or the emergence of a traditionalist form.

6. For another example, consider the political implications of Kafka's *Trial*.

Chapter 3: THE NATURE OF THE SOVIET SYSTEM

1. See Barrington Moore, Jr., *Political Power and Social Theory* (Cambridge, Mass.: Harvard University Press, 1958), chap. 2.

2. For a theoretical analysis of this relationship, see William Kornhauser, *The Politics of the Mass Society* (Chicago: The Free Press, 1959).

3. For a discussion of these studies, see A. Etzioni, "Authority Structure and Organizational Effectiveness," *Administrative Science Quarterly*, IV, no. 1 (1959); and the following sources cited therein: Robert Dubin, *Human Relations in Administration* (New York: Prentice-Hall, 1951); M. Dalton, "Conflicts Between Staff and Line Managerial Officers," *American Sociological Review*, L, no. 15; A. W. Gouldner, "Cosmopolitans and Locals: Toward an Analysis of Latent Social Roles," *Administrative Science Quarterly*, no. 2 (1957).

Chapter 4: TRANSFORMATION OR DEGENERATION

1. Angelica Balabanoff, *Impressions of Lenin* (Ann Arbor, Mich.: University of Michigan Press, 1964); Louis Fischer, *Life of Lenin* (New York: Harper and Row, Publishers, 1964); Stefan Possony, *Lenin, the Compulsive Revolutionary* (Chicago: Henry Regnery, 1964); and Bertram D. Wolfe, *Three Who Made a Revolution* (New York: The Dial Press, 1948).

2. For a discussion of "routinized charisma," see Amitai Etzioni, *A Comparative Analysis of Complex Organizations* (Glencoe, Ill.: Free Press of Glencoe, 1961), pp. 26 ff.

3. Compare the types discussed by J. L. Talmon in his *Political Messianism: The Romantic Phase* (New York: Frederick A. Praeger, 1960), with Barrington Moore, Jr., *Political Power and Social Theory* (Cambridge, Mass.: Harvard University Press, 1958), especially chap. 2 on "Totalitarian Elements in Pre-Industrial Societies," or Karl Wittfogel, *Oriental Despotism* (New Haven: Yale University Press, 1957).

4. It seems that these considerations are as important to the understanding of the Stalinist system as the psychopathological traits of Stalin that Robert C. Tucker rightly emphasizes in his "The Dictator and Totalitarianism," *World Politics,* July, 1965.

5. For a good treatment of Soviet military debates, see Thomas Wolfe, *Soviet Strategy at the Crossroads* (Cambridge, Mass.: Harvard University Press, 1964).

6. See S. Bialer, "An Unstable Leadership," *Problems of Communism,* July-August, 1965.

7. Writing about modern bureaucracy, V. A. Thompson, *Modern Organization* (New York: Alfred A. Knopf, 1961), p. 91, observed: "In the formally structured group, the idea man is doubly dangerous. He endangers the established distribution of power and status, and he is a competitive threat to his peers. Consequently, he has to be suppressed." For a breezy treatment of some analogous experience, see also E. J. Hegarty, *How to Succeed in Company Politics* (New York: McGraw-Hill Book Co., 1964).

8. Margaret Mead, *Continuities in Cultural Evolution* (New Haven: Yale University Press, 1964), p. 181. See also the introduction, especially p. xx.

9. J. V. Stalin, *Problems of Leninism* (Moscow, 1940), p. 338.

10. Roger Pethybridge, *A Key to Soviet Politics* (New York: Frederick A. Praeger, 1962). See also Myron Rush, *The Rise of Khrushchev* (Washington, D.C.: Public Affairs Press, 1958).

11. Samuel P. Huntington, "Political Development and Political Decay," *World Politics,* April, 1965.

12. *Ibid.,* p. 414.

13. M. Lakatos, "On Some Problems of the Structure of Our Political System," *Pravny obzor* (Bratislava), no. 1, 1965, as quoted in Gordon Skilling's illuminating paper, "Interest Groups and Communist Politics," read to the Canadian Political Science Association in June, 1965.

14. See the report delivered by A. Kosygin to the Central Committee Plenum on September 27, 1965, proposing the reorganization of the Soviet economy. See also his speech at a meeting of the U.S.S.R. State Planning Committee in *Planovoe khoziaistvo* (Moscow), April, 1965; and the frank discussion by A. E. Lunev, "Democratic Centralism in Soviet State Administration," *Sovetskoe gosudarstvo i pravo* (Moscow), no. 4, 1965.

15. "Ideological Hardening of Communists" (editorial), *Pravda,* June 28, 1965. There has been a whole series of articles in this vein, stressing the inseparability of ideological and organizational work. For details of a proposed large-scale indoctrination campaign, see V. Stepakov, head of the Department of Propaganda and Agitation of the Central Committee of the CPSU, "Master the Great Teaching of Marxism-Leninism," *Pravda,* August 4, 1965.

16. Stepakov, *op. cit.,* explicitly states that in recent years "many comrades" who have assumed leading posts in the "directive aktivs" of the Party have inadequate ideological knowledge, even though they have excellent technical backgrounds; and he urges steps against the "replacement" of Party training "by professional-technical education."

17. For a general discussion and a somewhat different formulation, see Huntington, *op. cit.,* pp. 415—17.

18. G. Lefebvre, *The French Revolution* (New York: Columbia University Press, 1965), II, 205.

Chapter 5: COMMUNIST IDEOLOGY AND INTERNATIONAL AFFAIRS

1. See Barrington Moore, Jr., *Soviet Politics: The Dilemma of Power* (Cambridge, Mass.: Harvard University Press, 1950), p. 415:

> Students of language have pointed out how the structure of a language may make it difficult to understand, that is, to make the desired responses to concepts that have originated in another language and culture. On these grounds it is at least a reasonable hypothesis that a set of ideas, or a system of political notation, such as Marxism-Leninism, would make certain types of political responses difficult, or perhaps even impossible, whereas it would make others relatively easy. Although the limits of assistance of political notation are probably not as definite as those in the linguistic and mathematical symbol systems, it seems a very probable inference that such limits do exist.

A variant of this problem is raised in Kazimierz Krauz, *Materializm ekonomiczny* (Krakow, 1908). Krauz discusses the inherent proclivity of various social classes to accept or reject certain new social insights without being conscious of the fact that they are, in effect, exercising a selectivity that reflects their interests. He labels this phenomenon "apperception." The emphasis on interest may be misleading, but there can be little doubt that the social conditioning of various groups disposes them to be sympathetic or unsympathetic toward new social insights, or to interpret them in their own manner (but not always in their interest, as Krauz implies), distorting them in the process. A similar phenomenon is discussed in Lucien Goldmann, *Sciences humaines et philosophie* (Paris: Presses universitaires de France, 1952); he calls it *"conscience possible."* For a discussion of both from the Marxist point of view, see Oskar Lange, *Ekonomia Polityczna* (Warsaw: Ksiazka i Wiedza, 1959), pp. 279–82.

2. They also run like a thread through his speeches, recently published in this country: Nikita Khrushchev, *For a Victory in Peaceful Competition with Capitalism* (New York: E. P. Dutton & Co., 1960).

3. It can readily be seen how the combination of Marxism,

Western European reformist experience and economic development, and the successes of labor movements within the democratic framework resulted in an altogether different conception of organic and interrelated world change, often spontaneous but still discernible. For the latest Soviet effort to define its world viewpoint, see O. V. Kuusinen, *Osnovy Marksizma-Leninizma* (Moscow: Gospolitizdat, 1959).

4. See the following books for more specific treatment of Communist ideology in Soviet foreign-policy conduct and for evidence of how it has affected that conduct in particular historical situations: Alexander Dallin (ed.), *Soviet Conduct in World Affairs* (New York: Columbia University Press, 1960); R. A. Goldwin (ed.), *Readings in Russian Foreign Policy* (New York: Oxford University Press, 1959); and A. Z. Rubenstein (ed.), *The Foreign Policy of the Soviet Union* (New York: Random House, 1958).

5. For example, Khrushchev's discussion of the reasons why, according to him, Rockefeller's drive for the Presidential nomination met with failure (*Izvestiya*, January 15, 1960).

6. While reading the following citation, the reader might well wonder whether it is not Khrushchev's image of the world:

What is fundamental and new, deciding and permeating all events for this period in the sphere of foreign relations, is that a certain temporary equilibrium of forces has been established between our country, which is building socialism, and the countries of the capitalist world, an equilibrium which has determined the present phase of *"peaceful coexistence"* [italics added] between the land of Soviets and the capitalist lands. That which we at one time thought of as a brief breathing space after the war changed into an entire period of respite. Hence a certain equilibrium of forces and a certain period of "peaceful coexistence" between the world of the bourgeoisie and the world of the proletariat.

At the bottom of all this lies the internal weakness, the weakness and powerlessness of world capitalism on the one hand, and the growth of the revolutionary movement of the workers in general, particularly the growth of forces here, in the land of the Soviets, on the other.

What lies at the basis of this weakness of the capitalist world?

At the basis of this weakness lie those antagonisms which capitalism cannot overcome, within which the entire international situation takes shape—antagonisms which the capitalist countries cannot surmount and which can be overcome only in the course of development of the proletarian revolution.

The statement is not Khrushchev's but is an extract from a ·1925 speech by Stalin at the Fourteenth Congress of the CPSU; quoted in Jane Degras (ed.), *Soviet Documents on Foreign Policy*, Vol. II: 1925–32 (London: Oxford University Press, 1952), pp. 69–72.

7. This view is implicit in Professor E. A. Korovin, *Osnovnie Printsipy Vneshnei Politiki SSSR* (Moscow: Pravda, 1951), chapter on "Various Forms of the Struggle of Peace in the Different Stages of Development of the Soviet State," pp. 21–30. For instance, he asserts (on p. 28): "We are for peace also because, armed with the scientific Marxist-Leninist insight and building Communism, we know that time is working for us, that the fall of capitalism as a system is inescapable, and that all roads lead to Communism."

8. M. A. Kaplan and N. de B. Katzenbach, "The Patterns of International Politics and of International Law," *The American Political Science Review*, LIII (1959), 693–712.

9. This leads even some otherwise astute observers to conclude that the Soviet leaders are merely motivated by "the familiar objectives of a great power, to realize its interests and ambitions as one state in a world of rival states." (Louis Halle, in *The New York Times Magazine*, June 28, 1959.)

10. Even today, when the Soviet Union claims to be the world's mightiest power, it justifies the continued need for vigilance and state power by reference to the existence of systems based on private property. See M. Karpovich in Dallin, *op. cit.*; also Brzezinski, *The Soviet Bloc* (Cambridge, Mass.: Harvard University Press, 1960; New York: Frederick A. Praeger, 1961 [rev. ed., paperback], chaps. 1 and 16, for the application of this Soviet concept of security to practice within the bloc.

11. This view is also implicit in Khrushchev's statement to Adlai Stevenson: "You must understand, Mr. Stevenson, that we live in an epoch when one system is giving way to another. When you established your republican system in the eighteenth century, the English did not like it. Now, too, a process is taking place in which

the peoples want to live under a new system of society; and it is necessary that one agree and reconcile oneself with this fact. The process should take place without interference." (Quoted in *The New York Times*, August 28, 1959.)

12. A perceptive treatment of "neutrality of alignment" is to be found in Kaplan and Katzenbach, *op. cit.*, pp. 707-8.

13. Leopold Labedz, "Ideology: The Fourth Stage," *Problems of Communism*, VIII, no. 6 (1959), 1–10.

14. See Moore, *Soviet Politics*.

15. Warnings against this trend have been voiced in the bloc. See, for instance, Romana Granas, "Where is the School of Communism?" *Polityka*, September 26, 1959. This veteran Polish Communist expressed the feeling of many dedicated Communists when she warned that it was easier to maintain a sense of ideological commitment when the Party was out of power. She rejected the excuse that "social consciousness lags behind changes in material reality" as not applicable to Communists who ought to be in the forefront of the struggle and not wait for material plenty to make them into good Communists. An example of the kind of ideological erosion that may take place is provided by *Sovetskaia Latviia*, December 16, 1959, which violently attacks suggestions that were apparently published in Soviet Latvia in 1956 to the effect that the CPSU ought to open its ranks to all able people—i.e., abandon its most elite character.

16. See Brzezinski, *The Soviet Bloc*.

17. It is interesting to note in this connection (regardless of the actual correctness of the assertion) that the importance of purely Chinese factors in the victory of the Communist Party in China is clearly asserted by the Chinese: "The victory of China's revolution and construction is the result of integrating the universal truth of Marxism-Leninism with the reality of China by the Chinese Communist Party and Comrade Mao Tse-tung." (Teng Hsiao-Ping, in *Jen Min Jih Pao*, October 2, 1959.)

18. L. H. Haimson, *The Russian Marxists and the Origins of Bolshevism* (Cambridge, Mass.: Harvard University Press, 1955).

19. Numerous examples of such apparently varied perspectives can be adduced, not to mention altogether different approaches to India and to Southeast Asian nationalism in general. The following paragraphs from the major statement by Khrushchev in his speech to the

Supreme Soviet on October 31, 1959, might well have been addressed to Peking: "We have no reason to fear that the peoples of the socialist countries will be seduced by the capitalist devil and give up socialism. To think differently means not to believe wholly in the strength of socialism, the strength of the working class and its creative abilities." Khrushchev then went on to cite Trotsky as an example of a Communist unable to distinguish between concessions of principle and expediency. On another occasion, Khrushchev warned: "We must make a sensible use of the great advantages of the socialist system and strengthen. the world socialist camp in every way. We must not fall behind or go too far ahead. We must, figuratively speaking, synchronize our watches. If the leadership of this or that country becomes conceited, this can only play into the hands of the enemy." (Speech to the Hungarian Party Congress, quoted in *The New York Times,* December 2, 1959.) The foregoing remarks become more meaningful if one considers the remarks that Khrushchev allegedly made to President Sukarno with respect to China, to the effect that the Chinese were pushing their industrialization at "too heavy a cost."

For an official Chinese justification of their domestic methods, refuting all criticisms and incidentally revealing intraparty opposition to such policies, see Liu Shao-chi, "The Victory of Marxism-Leninism in China," in *Jen Min Jih Pao,* October 1, 1959. At one point, Liu Shao-chi states: "To find fault with our big leap and people's communes means to find fault with our Party's general line for building socialism. Who are these people finding fault with the Party's general line? In our own ranks, they are the right opportunists, they represent bourgeois ideology within the Party." He does not reveal who the people outside the Chinese Party are. However, he goes on to assert: "The fact that Marxism-Leninism has lately been disseminated in such a large Eastern country as ours with a population of 650 million and that it has resulted in victory in the mutual practice of the revolution and construction must by all accounts be considered a big event in the history of the development of Marxism-Leninism. Of course, revolution and construction in China have features peculiar to this country. But it is also possible that some of these important special features may reappear in some other country. In this sense, Chinese experience is to a certain extent of international significance." With respect to international affairs, the Chinese seem determined to convince the other Communist parties that the major threat to international peace lies in the warlike intentions of the United States. On the occasion of President Eisenhower's 1960 "State of the Union" message, a *Jen Min Jih Pao* editorial, entitled "What Do the U.S. Presidential Messages Show?" stressed the fact that the purpose of U.S. policy was the promotion of aggression throughout the world. After producing a series of proofs for this proposition and warning against the Western policy of encouraging "evolution" within the Soviet orbit (attacking, incidentally, the report of the Center for International Affairs at Harvard University, prepared by this author, for suggesting such policies), the editorial concluded as follows: "The task of the peace-loving people of the world is to maintain vigilance against all U.S. schemes in the disguise of peace, and expose them, unite and keep up the struggle, defeat the forces of war with U.S. imperialism at their head, and extend the successes of the peace forces of the world." This theme was energetically asserted at the Warsaw Treaty Conference in Moscow by the Chinese observer Kang Sheng, candidate-member of the Politburo. His speech, much more vigorous than the official Conference communiqué, ignored by the Soviet and East European press, was broadcast by the Peking radio on February 5, 1960.

20. A translation of this draft is contained in *Yugoslavia's Way* (Yugoslav Communist Party; New York: All Nations Press, 1958).

21. These views are also concerned with broader international issues, and they frequently deviate from the Soviet version. For instance, recently Erik Molnar, a Hungarian Communist historian, has challenged the standard Soviet position that capitalism is doomed because of the operation of its internal contradictions. The substance of Mr. Molnar's views is contained in a book entitled *Some Economic Problems of Contemporary Capitalism* (Budapest: Szikra, 1959). The theoretical monthly journal of the Hungarian Communist Party, *Tarsadalmi Szemle,* contains a summary of Molnar's views and of the Party's criticisms. According to *The New York Times,* January 10, 1960, the substance of Molnar's views is as follows:

First, certain social laws that govern the growth and decline of the capitalist system (as defined by the Marxists) can be nullified by the conscious actions and cooperation of the people or the various classes within the framework of a capitalist society.

Second, the laws formulated by Karl Marx about the class struggle and the inevitable pauperization of the people, according to which the exploitation of the working class is inexorably increased, are no longer valid.

Third, the so-called law of general crisis of the capitalist system, as defined by Stalin, cannot be considered valid since World War II.

The role of defense expenditures in a capitalist society does not have the economic and social importance attributed to it by dogmatic Communists. Mr. Molnar advanced as evidence for his position on this point the fact that, though defense expenditures were radically reduced after World War II, unemployment did not increase substantially.

No wonder the new history of the CPSU is designed in large part to provide guidance to the other ruling Communist parties.

22. Speech on December 1, 1959, in Budapest. It is noteworthy that the reactions of the other elites in Eastern Europe, particularly the Poles, but even the Bulgarians, were relatively restrained as far as this particular point is concerned.

23. This led Radek to state: "The attempt to represent the foreign policy of the Soviet Union as a continuation of Czarist policy is ridiculous. Bourgeois writers who do so have not grasped even the purely external manifestations of this policy. . . . Czarism, or any other bourgeois regime in Russia, would necessarily resume the struggle for the conquest of Poland and of the Baltic states, as is doubtless clear to any thoughtful bourgeois politician in those countries. The Soviet Union, on the contrary, is most anxious to establish friendly relations with these countries, considering their achievement of independence as positive and progressive historical factors." (Karl Radek, "The Basis of Soviet Foreign Policy," *Foreign Affairs*, XII [1934], p. 194.) These words have an ironic meaning today.

24. See Isaac Deutscher, *The Prophet Unarmed* (London and New York: Oxford University Press, 1959). He shows what a gross oversimplification it is to suggest that this was merely a tactical move

on the part of Stalin. In reality, this was part of the continuing and often dialectical process of ideology and reality interacting.

25. Moore, *Soviet Politics*, p. 383.

26. Their feeling appears to be based on the following kind of analysis:

The testing of the capitalist system is now historically settled. It is doomed to extinction, to make way for a higher social system—Communism. It is difficult to forecast when this process will be completed on the world scale or the forms it will take. There are weighty grounds for assuming that the Soviet Union's peaceful policy, the growing economic and political power of the socialist camp, and the increasing activity of ever broader masses in the capitalist countries will combine to prevent a third world war. The transition to socialism in some countries may possibly assume comparatively peaceful forms. Marx's idea that the bourgeoisie may be "bought off" in individual countries may become a reality.

The forecast for a briefer period is the following.

In the next ten to fifteen years the U.S.S.R. will draw ahead of the U.S.A. economically and become the country with the world's most powerful economy.

The disintegration of the colonial system will be completed. The former colonies will undergo rapid economic development with help from the Soviet Union and other countries in the socialist camp.

The concentration of capital and rapid technical progress in the advanced capitalist countries will lead to growing unemployment and the exacerbation of the class struggle. The desire to prolong the capitalist system's existence will to some extent compel capital to make certain concessions in its contest with the working class.

Cycles will show a tendency to shorten, for with today's technology the renewal and expansion of basic capital takes place more rapidly than before.

The struggle among the imperialist countries and the antagonistic groupings in the capitalist camp is sure to continue. Apprehension over the fate of capitalism, however, will stand in the way of world wars between these groupings.

279

The exceptional complexity of the situation involving the historical transition from capitalism to socialism precludes any more specific predictions. [E. Varga, "The Capitalism of the Twentieth Century," *Kommunist,* no. 17, November, 1959.]

27. The November, 1957, declaration of the ruling Communist parties.

28. That the Soviets are already facing this dilemma was illustrated by the following exchange between an Indian newsman and Frol R. Kozlov during the latter's trip to India in February, 1960, as reported by *Pravda* on February 6, 1960:

Question: You have seen our work, our economy and our democracy. Are you convinced in spite of Communist ideology that socialism can be built by peaceful means? Answer [Kozlov]: There is no use in your challenging me to an ideological debate here at the press conference. You know our point of view on this question. We formulated it clearly at the Twentieth Party Congress in full conformity with the Leninist principle of peaceful coexistence of states with different social and political systems. This point of view is that decision in matters of internal development and the methods of the political and economic organization of a society is the internal affair of each nation. The kind of system you have is your affair. We ourselves in the Soviet Union have built socialism and are building Communism, we believe *that under our conditions* [italics added] that is a good way, the only way of development that ensures genuine progress in all spheres of the people's life and an increase in the Soviet people's well being.

While the first part of Kozlov's remarks adds nothing new, the implication of the second part seems to be an acceptance of the proposition that India is building socialism.

29. See H. S. Dinerstein, *War and the Soviet Union: The Revolution in Soviet Military and Political Thinking* (New York: Frederick A. Praeger, 1958); and Raymond L. Garthoff, *The Soviet Image of Future War* (Washington, D.C.: Public Affairs Press, 1959).

30. While formally still asserting the proposition that a nuclear war would spell the doom of capitalism, Khrushchev's remarks concerning the price the U.S.S.R. would have to pay for such a victory

are bound to have the effect of discouraging anyone from wishing to pay it: "In various speeches, Khrushchev has said that war would bring tremendous disaster to all mankind, great devastation to the U.S.S.R., big losses to the U.S.S.R., and has stated that it would be a prodigious catastrophe if the United States and the U.S.S.R. were to fight." (Louis Marengo, "Peaceful Coexistence" [unpublished study; Cambridge, Mass.: Center for International Affairs, Harvard University, 1960].) This awareness is accompanied by a much more sophisticated insight into problems of "deterrence," as shown by Khrushchev's discussion on January 15, 1960, of the importance of a "second-strike" capability to guarantee effective retribution for a surprise attack.

One may also assume that the Soviet desire to promote an atom-free zone in Asia in 1958 and 1959 was related to the above considerations and had as its purpose the perpetuation of Soviet nuclear monopoly within the Soviet camp. These suggestions were studiously ignored by the Chinese, a consideration not irrelevant to our earlier discussion. (See Robert W. Barnett, "Quemoy—The Use and Consequence of Nuclear Deterrence" [unpublished study; Cambridge, Mass.: Center for International Affairs, Harvard University, 1960].)

The Soviet interest in disarmament has also led Khrushchev to argue in the following somewhat unorthodox way:

> Some people in the West assert that disarmament threatens grave consequences for the economy of the capitalist countries. They say that if the production of bombs, guns, submarines, and other means of destruction were stopped, ruin would result and hundreds of thousands of people would be deprived of work and a means of livelihood. However, only people who see no other way of developing the economy than by subordinating it to the interests of preparing for war can reason in this way.
>
> The least that can be said about such assertions is that they are completely unsubstantiated. I have had occasion to talk with many representatives of American business circles, and the most reasonable of them have nowhere near so gloomy a viewpoint and are confident that U.S. industry is fully able to cope with the task of shifting the entire economy to production of goods for peaceful uses. [*Pravda*, January 15, 1960.]

281

Chapter 6: DEVIATION CONTROL

1. Among the growing literature on the Sino-Soviet relationship, the following books may be suggested: A. Doak Barnett, *Communist China and Asia* (New York: Harper & Brothers, 1960), especially chap. 12; G. F. Hudson, R. Lowenthal, and R. MacFarquhar, *The Sino-Soviet Dispute* (London: The China Quarterly, 1961; New York: Frederick A. Praeger, 1961); K. London, ed., *Unity and Contradiction: Major Aspects of Sino-Soviet Relations* (New York: Frederick A. Praeger, 1962); D. Zagoria, *The Sino-Soviet Conflict, 1956–1961* (Princeton, N.J.: Princeton University Press, 1962). On Eastern European affairs, see P. Zinner, ed., *National Communism and Popular Revolt in Eastern Europe* (New York: Columbia University Press, 1957); J. H. Hallowell, ed., *Soviet Satellite Nations* (Gainesville, Fla.: Kallman, 1958); R. Bass and E. Marbury, eds., *The Soviet-Yugoslav Controversy, 1948–1958* (New York: Prospect Books, 1959); F. Vali, *Rift and Revolt in Hungary* (Cambridge, Mass.: Harvard University Press, 1961). On the general problem of Communist bloc relations, see Z. Brzezinski, *The Soviet Bloc: Unity and Conflict* (rev. ed.; New York: Frederick A. Praeger, 1961).

2. It could be argued that the failure of the West to appraise Communism in terms other than those traditional to the West helped Communism in the phase of its weakness. Cf. George Kennan, *Russia and the West under Lenin and Stalin* (Boston: Little, Brown and Co., 1961).

3. I have relied largely on L. Pastor, *History of the Popes* (32 vols.; London: B. Herder Book Co., 1928-40).

4. For this reason, both organizations have established exclusive standards for membership. Cf. Lenin's "Twenty-one Conditions" and, for example, the difficulties faced by the Chaldean monks in the seventeenth century.

5. Relatively, as compared to some others, less doctrinal, less disciplined, etc. Another way of looking at them would be to see them as international systems, but this tends to underestimate the internally binding factor of ideological commitment. See G. Modelski, *The International Communist System* (mimeo.; Princeton, 1960), for a definition of "international system."

6. For instance, the French king and the French Church always stressed the traditions of Gallicanism as a justified restraint on Papal power. See the lengthy treatment in L. Pastor, *op. cit.*, XXXII, 246–325.

7. For different definitions of its special position of primacy, see the November, 1957, Twelve-Party Declaration and the December, 1960, Eighty-One–Party Declaration.

8. See Brzezinski, *The Soviet Bloc* and "The Challenge of Change in the Soviet Bloc," *Foreign Affairs,* April, 1961.

9. Opposition to the Papacy was based on the argument that the earlier organization of the Church involved equality of all bishops: "Without prejudice to its agreement with the Church Universal in all essential points, every church manages its own affairs with perfect freedom and independence, and maintains its own traditional usages and discipline, all questions not concerning the whole Church, or of primary importance, being settled on the spot. . . . Laws and Articles of faith, of universal obligation, are issued only by the full church, concentrated and represented at an Oecumenical Council." Janus, *The Pope and the Council* (London, 1869), pp. 85–86. (Janus, a nineteenth-century writer, was bitterly opposed to the doctrine of Papal infallibility.) A less one-sided source is the *Cambridge Medieval History* (Cambridge: Cambridge University Press, 1957), Vols. IV, V; see also P. Sigmund, Jr., *Hierarchy and Consent: The Political Theory of Nicholas of Cusa* (Ph.D. thesis; Harvard University, 1959). I am much indebted to Dr. Sigmund for his critical but constructive comments.

10. Although both institutions also contributed to the development of the intellectual underpinnings of Averroism and Gallicanism, respectively. See Janus, *op. cit.*, pp. 151–81; also Pastor, *op. cit.*, and Sigmund, *op. cit.*, for fuller and less hostile accounts.

11. For example, "Savonarola's crime was disobedience to the Pope —and that Pope was Alexander VI. He was not a rebel against the apostolic See; but he was torn between the claims of obedience to God and submission to the orders of an unworthy Pope." W. Nigg, *Warriors of God* (New York: Alfred A. Knopf, 1959), p. 278.

12. Bishop Wazo of Liège, Bishop Hildebart of Le Mans, Rupert of Deutz, and Saint Bernard (see Janus, *op. cit.*, p. 238).

13. Cf. L. Schapiro, *The Origin of the Communist Autocracy*

(Cambridge, Mass.: Harvard University Press, 1955; New York: Frederick A. Praeger, paperback edition, 1965).

14. Cf. Brzezinski, *The Permanent Purge—Politics of Soviet Totalitarianism* (Cambridge, Mass.: Harvard University Press, 1956).

15. In the case of Luther, see the report of the official Roman *Censor Librorum*, "In praesumptuosas M. Lutheri Conclusiones Dialogus," and Luther's "Responsio ad Silv. Prierietatis Dialogum," in which he, however, still accepted Papal authority; in Tito's case, see the Stalin-Tito correspondence, in Bass and Marbury, *op. cit.*

16. My principal sources have been Pastor, *op. cit.*, Vols. XXIX–XXXII; M. Tollemache, *French Jansenists* (London, 1893); and N. Abercrombie, *The Origins of Jansenism* (Oxford: Oxford University Press, 1936). Specialists in Church history will perhaps forgive me for this very sketchy treatment. In my analysis, I will not attempt a detailed historical summary nor deal with the theological content of Jansenism but only focus on those aspects which are relevant to the purposes of this study. Basically, the Jansenists, not unlike the Calvinists, took a rather dim view of man's capacity to resist sin; they urged such intense and demanding standards before partaking of Holy Communion that many of them abstained from the sacrament for years at a time.

17. The full title was *Augustinus, seu doctrina Sancti Augustini de Humanae Naturae Sanitate, Aegritudine, Medicina, Adversus Pelagianos et Massilienses* (3 vols.; Louvain, 1640).

18. Pastor, *op. cit.*, XXIX, 109. The Jansenist principles were: "(1) some of God's commandments are impossible to just men who wish and strive to keep them considering the powers they actually have; the grace by which these precepts may become possible is also wanting; (2) in the state of fallen nature no one ever resists interior grace; (3) to merit, or to demerit in the state of fallen nature we must be free from all external constraint, but not from interior necessity; (4) the Semipelagians admitted the necessity of interior preventing grace for all acts, even for the beginning of faith; but they fell into heresy in pretending this grace is such that man may either follow it or reject it; (5) to say that Christ died or shed his blood for all men is Semipelagianism." *Catholic Encyclopedia* (New York: Universal Knowledge Foundation, 1913), VIII, 288.

19. Pastor, *op. cit.*, XXIX, 114 ff.

20. After Arnauld published in 1643 his *De La Frequente Communion*, the French government was prepared to apply sanctions against him, but he was protected by the leading Paris circles and by some of the French bishops. Gallicanism resembles domesticism more than national Communism; for the distinction, see Brzezinski, *The Soviet Bloc*, pp. 52–53. See Pastor, *op. cit.*, Vol. XXXII, chap. 4.

21. The Jesuits were among the most active proponents of frequent communion. See Pastor, *op. cit.*, XXIX, 136.

22. *Ibid.*, p. 150.

23. *Ibid.*, p. 145.

24. *Ibid.*, p. 155.

25. "Dogmatism and sectarianism . . . lead the isolation of Communists from the masses. . . ." N. Khrushchev, speech of January 6, 1961.

26. Pastor, *op. cit.*, XXXI, 198.

27. *Ibid.*, XXIX, 146.

28. ". . . the severity of the Jansenist principles, excessive though it was, operated in favor of the party." *Ibid.* XXXI, 261.

29. *Ibid.*, pp. 225–27. In this, too, there are contemporary parallels. For instance, the Albanians like to cite the Chinese on the subject of revisionism.

30. But even here he equivocated somewhat. He thus made a distinction between infallibility of dogma and fact. *Ibid.*, pp. 174–75.

31. *Ibid.*, p. 216.

32. *Ibid.*, pp. 199–200.

33. Compare to the Soviet effort to restrict the discussion of Chinese dogmatism only to the bloc, and the Chinese insistence on the participation of eighty-one parties. See Brzezinski, *The Soviet Bloc*, Epilogue.

34. Pastor, *op. cit.*, XXXI, 385–92. This arrangement bears great resemblance to the Tito-Khrushchev compromise, in which the Yugoslavs acted as if the Soviets had repudiated all the Cominform declarations, while the Soviets knew that this was not the case but remained silent. Similarly, when Rome placed on the Index a prayer book written by one of the pro-Jansenist French bishops, the Papal nuncio did not publish the decree in France. *Ibid.*, p. 359.

35. *Ibid.*, p. 385.

36. The above decision did not come easily. A vigorous debate

took place within the top councils of the organization's center, and sharply conflicting points of view were presented. Some cardinals advised acceptance of the compromise, since "the sincerity of the subscription was vouched for by a public document, whereas the opposite rested solely on rumors and unreliable writings" (*ibid.*, p. 395). The opposite point of view warned against accepting the alleged submission, when it was well known that it was not genuine. Cardinal Albizzi, who handled much of this matter, pleaded: "I cannot suffer that an attempt should be made to persuade the world that this heresy had been destroyed, seeing that in spite of its seeming destruction it appears more vigorous than ever" (*ibid.*, p. 396). It may be assumed that Moscow has also faced similar dilemmas. There is evidence that on the Yugoslav issue Molotov pleaded with Khrushchev not to create the impression that Yugoslavia is again orthodox, since it would undermine international Communism. Brzezinski, *The Soviet Bloc*, pp. 175–77.

37. Pastor, *op. cit.*, XXXI, 485.

38. *Ibid.* XXXII, 424, 656 ff., for efforts to kill with kindness.

39. *Ibid.*, pp. 310–12.

40. Tollemache, *op. cit.*, p. 250.

41. For a fascinating account of Jesuit efforts in China, see *China in the Sixteenth Century: The Journals of Matthew Ricci, 1583–1610* (New York: Random House, 1953). An interesting statement of the tactical problems faced by the Jesuits is in P. Duignan, "Early Jesuit Missionaries: A Suggestion for Further Study," *The American Anthropologist*, August, 1958. This account was prompted by Mr. Duignan's analysis.

42. Ricci, *op. cit.*, pp. 142, 147.

43. Quoted by Nigg, *op. cit.*, p. 335.

44. Ricci, *op. cit.*, pp. 93, 96. See also Duignan, *op cit.*

45. Ricci, *op. cit.*, pp. 137–39.

46. Pastor, *op. cit.*, XXV, 355.

47. Ricci, *op. cit.*, p. 325. Elsewhere he says, "The Fathers have made an effort to merit a reputation for learning, not as a matter of vain glory but with a view to the end for which they came here, namely to further the cause of Christianity, which on all occasions they purposely weave into their conversations," p. 201. Similar techniques were employed by the Jesuits, under Roberto de Nobili, in their approach to Indian Brahmins. Pastor, *op. cit.*, XXV, 359–61.

48. Compare "Present-day leftism in the Communist movement is also manifested in both concealed and overt resistance to the Communist parties' policy of establishing collaboration with working people in the ranks of social-democratic, Catholic, and various other bourgeois-radical parties and organizations" (*Sovietskaya Rossiya,* June 10, 1960); and the warning contained in *Kommunist,* no. 13, 1960, against those who exaggerate revolutionary feelings and "call for direct revolutionary overthrow," with the following Chinese statements: "History teaches us that people's revolutions in all countries stem from the needs of the people and are the result of the development of class struggle" (*Hungch'i,* no. 20–21, 1960), and "The modern revisionists and certain representatives of the bourgeoisie try to make people believe that it is possible to achieve socialism without a revolutionary party. . . . This is sheer nonsense and deception" (*Hungch'i,* no. 8, 1960). See Hudson et al., *op. cit.,* for detailed treatment.

49. Pastor, *op. cit.,* XXV, 150.

50. Nigg, *op. cit.,* p. 351.

51. Pastor, *op. cit.,* XXIX, 250.

52. The Communist Kirkuk rising took place in July, 1959. *The World Marxist Review,* April, 1960, contains a self-criticism by the Iraqi Communist Party, which reveals that an allegedly dissident group of Communists was responsible for this highly premature action.

53. See Pastor, *op. cit.,* XXXI, 165–69, concerning the disputed practices.

54. This tactic was used by the University of Louvain, when confronted by instructions from Rome. *Ibid.,* p. 263.

55. T. Schelling, *The Strategy of Conflict* (Cambridge, Mass.: Harvard University Press, 1960), p. 161.

56. Khrushchev had to face this difficulty in 1960, when criticized by the Chinese. He responded: "If we act like children who, studying the alphabet, compile words from letters, we shall not go very far. Marx, Engels, and Lenin created their immortal works which will not fade away in centuries. . . . On the basis of the teaching of Marxism-Leninism we must think ourselves, profoundly study life, analyze the present situation and draw the conclusions which benefit the common cause of Communism." (Speech of June 21, 1960.) The more "revisionist" the position, the more difficult it is to resist "literalist"

criticism. The Chinese warned that "as pupils of Lenin and as Leninists, we must utterly smash all attempts of the modern revisionists to distort and carve up the teachings of Lenin." (*Hungch'i*, no. 8, 1960.)

57. The center must watch against the danger that a precipitous condemnation of the deviant can actually force distantly potential deviants into deviation. For instance, the Dominicans feared that condemnation of Jansenism would reflect on them (Pastor, *op. cit.*, XXIX, 118). Might not some Communist parties object to an explicit condemnation of the dogmatists for fear that this would reflect on them as well?

58. For this reason, posthumous personalization of deviation has some merit, since it allows room for hope that unity ultimately will be restored. However, premature personalization runs the risk that emotion may obscure reason. We might thus distinguish between spontaneous, personal conflict—one involving the role of personal antipathy or of personality which tends to become emotional, direct, and all-out; and protracted, institutional conflict, which leaves greater room for skilled management and more tacit bargaining (cf. Schelling, *op. cit.*, p. 21).

59. See Modelski, *op. cit.*, p. 67, for in-system conflict resolution. It is revealing to observe that after the Suez crisis, the British Conservative and Labour parties were also much more lenient with their respective "fundamentalist" deviants than with their "moderates." See L. D. Epstein, "British M.P.s and their Local Parties: the Suez Cases," *The American Political Science Review*, June, 1960, esp. pp. 381–85.

60. See Schelling, *op. cit.*, p. 115, for a discussion of the role of "inherently unknowable factors."

61. This has resulted in a paradoxical situation whereby Tito, who is outside the Communist orbit, is closer to Khrushchev than Hoxha, who is within it. See the excellent discussion in W. E. Griffith, "Peiping, Tirana and Moscow," *East Europe*, July, 1961.

62. The fullest and most systematic treatment of the nature of praxeology (principles of correct, rational decisions) is in T. Kotarbinski, *Traktat o dobrej robocie* (Warsaw, 1955).

63. See Modelski, *op. cit.*, p. 23, for a discussion of system-orientation toward expansion. The analogy here is between the attitude of a

given Communist state, even a deviant one, toward a general Communist expansion, and the attitude of a Christian state toward the Crusades.

64. See Brzezinski, "The Challenge of Change in the Soviet Bloc," for a discussion.

65. R. S. Tarn, "Continuity in Russian Foreign Policy," *International Journal*, Autumn, 1950; and the symposium on ideology in A. Dallin, ed., *Soviet Conduct in World Affairs* (New York: Columbia University Press, 1960). See also chap. 5, above, "Communist Ideology and International Affairs."

66. A good discussion is in R. Lowenthal, "Diplomacy and Revolution: The Dialectics of a Dispute," in Hudson, Lowenthal, and MacFarquhar, *op. cit.*, pp. 9–34.

67. See A. Halpern, "The Chinese Communist Line on Neutralism," RAND Mimeograph Study 2026, July, 1960; D. Zagoria, "Sino-Soviet Friction in Underdeveloped Areas," *Problems of Communism*, March-April, 1961; T. Thornton, "Peking, Moscow, and the Underdeveloped Areas," *World Politics*, July, 1961; and A. Whiting, "Moscow and Peking: Suspended Dialogue?", *Current Scene*, June 21, 1961.

68. An obvious rule of thumb runs as follows: The death of friendly leaders always makes relations worse; the death of unfriendly leaders can improve them if the conflict has not become institutionalized by organizational clashes. For some recent discussions of the problem of succession, see R. Conquest, *Power and Policy—USSR* (New York: St. Martin's Press, 1960); H. Hinton, "The Succession Problem in Communist China," *Current Scene,* July 19, 1961; and M. Rush, *The Khrushchev Succession Problem*, RAND Mimeograph Study 2283, 1961.

Chapter 8: RUSSIA AND EUROPE

1. Some Soviet observers went so far as to negate their previous warnings about "German hegemony" and talked about "French hegemony in Western Europe." For example, see I. Lemin, "European Integration: Some Results and Perspectives," *Mirovaia Ekonomika i Mezhdunarodnie Otnosheniia,* Part II, May, 1962, pp. 42–55; and V. Cherpakov, "The Common Market—An Instrument for the Intensification of Monopolistic Oppression and Aggression," *Kommunist,* May, 1962, pp. 22–35.

2. *Pravda,* August 26, 1962. For a more ideological and also over-simplified restatement of these themes, see V. Gantman, "Imperialist Integration and International Relations," *Kommunist,* November, 1962, pp. 96–107. See also the proceedings of the Moscow Conference on Contemporary Capitalism, Summer, 1962, published in *Mirovaia Ekonomika i Mezhdunarodnie Otnosheniia,* November and December, 1962, pp. 54–71 and 59–79, respectively, which cast an interesting light on the role of non-Russian Marxists in enlightening their Russian colleagues about affairs in Europe.

3. Presumably because of this fear, some Communist spokesmen have shown interest in a trial balloon launched in the late summer of 1963 by Austrian Foreign Minister Kreisky, proposing an EFTA-CEMA trade agreement (cf. *Rynki Zagraniczne,* September 14, 1963).

In September, 1963, the EEC made its first joint tariff move with respect to the U.S.S.R., demanding Soviet acceptance of the EEC tariff while offering the benefits of the lower internal EEC tariff on four Soviet export items (*Le Monde,* weekly ed., October 17–23, 1963).

4. I. Rachmuth, "The Importance of Establishing a Rate of Development Which Will Level Off the Economic Progress of All Socialist Countries," *Probleme Economice* (Bucharest), July, 1963.

5. De Gaulle said in his press conference, March 25, 1959: "The reunification of the two parts into a single Germany which would be entirely free seems to us the normal destiny of the German people, *provided they do not reopen the question of their present frontiers to the west, the east, the north, and the south,* and that they move toward integrating themselves one day in a contractual organization of all Europe for cooperation, liberty and peace." (Italics added.)

6. This was in line with the thesis of inherent Franco-American economic contradictions. See V. Liubimova, "The Problems of France's Participation in the 'Common Market,'" *Mirovaia Ekonomika i Mezhdunarodnie Otnosheniia,* March, 1957.

7. *Pravda* commented on September 24, 1958: "Chancellor Adenauer and Premier de Gaulle were concerned even at their first meeting not only with reaching agreement on their actions within their own countries but, it seems, also with how to draw the countries of Eastern Europe into the so-called European federation, which is nothing but a branch of the aggressive North Atlantic bloc."

8. For a Chinese view, see "The Imperialist Bloc Is Fast Disintegrating," *Jen Min Jih Pao* (Peking), February 24, 1963.

9. This ambivalence is well reflected in V. Nekrasov, "The Vicious Circle of 'Atlantic Policy,'" *Pravda,* December 27, 1963.

10. For a fully elaborated statement of this author's views on Western policy toward the Soviet Union and Eastern Europe, see *Alternative to Partition* (New York: McGraw-Hill Book Co., 1965).